1998 SUPPLEMENT

to

CASES AND MATERIALS

ON

PLEADING AND PROCEDURE

STATE AND FEDERAL

By

GEOFFREY C. HAZARD, JR.
Trustee Professor of Law, University of Pennsylvania

COLIN C. TAIT
Professor of Law, University of Connecticut

and

WILLIAM A. FLETCHER
Professor of Law, University of California, Berkeley (Boalt Hall)

SEVENTH EDITION

New York, New York
FOUNDATION PRESS
1998

COPYRIGHT © 1995, 1996, 1997 FOUNDATION PRESS

COPYRIGHT © 1998

By

FOUNDATION PRESS
All rights reserved

ISBN 1–56662–696–X

TEXT IS PRINTED ON 10% POST CONSUMER RECYCLED PAPER

TABLE OF CONTENTS

TABLE OF CASES	ix
Chapter 1. Introduction	1
A. An Overview of the System	1
Historical Note on Procedure	1
B. The Adversary System	3
Note on Professional Courtesy	3
Chapter 2. Remedies	4
A. Plenary Judicial Remedies	4
1. Damages	4
BMW of North America, Inc. v. Gore	4
Note on Punitive Damages	16
D. Costs of Litigation	17
1. Court Costs	17
Note on Court Costs	17
2. Attorneys' Fees	18
Introductory Note on Attorneys' Fees	18
Further Note on Attorneys' Fees	19
Chapter 3. Choosing the Proper Court	21
A. Territorial Jurisdiction	21
1. Historical Formulae: The Relevance of State Boundaries	21
2. Twentieth Century Syntheses	21
a. Minimum Contacts	21
Notes and Questions	21
Notes and Questions	21
b. Reformulation of Minimum Contacts?	22
Notes and Questions on Asahi and the Possible Reformulation of "Minimum Contacts"	22
c. Notice	25
Note on Service of Process	25
d. Long–Arm Statutes	26
1. State Long–Arm Statutes	26
Notes and Questions	26
2. Federal Long–Arm Statutes	29
Notes and Questions	29
f. Consent to Jurisdiction	30
2. Consent by Contract	31
Notes and Questions	31
B. Subject Matter Jurisdiction	32
2. Federal Courts	32

TABLE OF CONTENTS

B.	Subject Matter Jurisdiction—Continued		
	a. Federal Question Jurisdiction		32
	Further Note on 28 U.S.C. § 1331		32
	b. Diversity Jurisdiction		33
	Note on *Mas v. Perry* and Assorted Problems of Diversity Jurisdiction		33
	c. Supplemental Jurisdiction		34
	Note on Supplemental Jurisdiction		34
	Free v. Abbott Laboratories		35
	Notes and Questions		40
	d. Removal		41
	Note on Removal		41
	e. Challenging Federal Subject Matter Jurisdiction		43
	Note on Direct Challenge to Federal Subject Matter Jurisdiction		43
C.	Venue		44
	1. State Courts		44
	Note on Venue in State Courts		44
	2. Federal Courts		44
	a. Venue		44
	Note on Venue in Federal Courts		44
	b. Change of Venue and Related Topics		45
	Note on *Ferens v. John Deere*, Change of Venue Under § 1404, Dismissal or Transfer for Lack of Venue Under § 1406(a), and Other Transfers		45
D.	Forum Non Conveniens		46
	Note on *Forum Non Conveniens*		46

Chapter 4. The *Erie* Problem 48

A. The Law Applied in Federal Court: The Problem of *Erie Railroad v. Tompkins* 48
Notes and Questions 48
Note on Statutes of Limitations, Relation Back Under Rule 15(c), and *Erie* 49
B. "Reverse *Erie*": Federal Law in State Courts 50
Note on Federal Law in State Courts 50
C. Ascertaining State Law 51
Note on Ascertaining State Law 51
D. Federal Common Law 52
Notes and Questions 52

Chapter 5. Claims and Defenses 53
B. Pleadings 53
1. The Elements of a Sufficient Complaint 53
Note on Sufficiency of Pleadings; Burden of Pleading, Persuasion, and Proof; and Presumptions 53
2. The Problem of Specificity 54
Note on Requiring a More Specific Statement of Claim 54

TABLE OF CONTENTS

B.	Pleadings—Continued	
	Note on Pleading Under the Federal Private Securities Reform Act of 1995	56
C.	Amended and Supplemental Pleadings	58
	1. Amended Pleadings	58
	Note on Rule 15(c) and Relation Back	58
D.	Substantiality of Claims and Defenses	58
	Note on Rule 11	58

Chapter 6. The Size of the Litigation — 60

A. Collateral Regulation of the Size of the Litigation — 60
   1. Res Judicata and Collateral Estoppel — 60
      a. Preclusion as Between the Same Parties — 60
         Note on Res Judicata Between the Same Parties — 60
      b. Preclusion as Against Other Parties — 62
         Further Note on Preclusion — 62
         Note on *Martin v. Wilks* and the Problem of Precluding Non–parties — 63
   2. Recognition of Judgments From Other Jurisdictions — 64
      a. Interstate Recognition of Judgments — 64
         Note on Full Faith and Credit — 64
      b. Federal–State Recognition of Judgments — 65
         Note on Federal–State and International Recognition of Judgments — 65

C. Joinder of Parties — 67
   2. Basic Concepts of Party Joinder — 67
      a. Permissive Joinder — 67
         Note on Permissive Joinder of Parties — 67
      b. Compulsory Joinder — 68
         Note on Compulsory Joinder of Parties — 68
   3. Devices for Adding Parties — 68
      b. Intervention — 68
         Further Note on Intervention — 68
   4. Nominal Parties — 69
      Note on the Real Party in Interest Rule — 69
   6. Class Suits — 69
      b. Uses and Administration of Class Suits — 69
         Note on Class Suits in Product Liability and Mass Tort Litigation — 69
         In re Rhone–Poulenc Rorer, Inc. — 70
         Note on Class Certification — 82
         Further Note on the Uses and Administration of Class Suits — 84
      c. Settlement of Class Suits — 87
         Amchem Products, Inc. v. Windsor — 87
         Note on Settlement Classes — 102

TABLE OF CONTENTS

Chapter 7. The Pretrial Stage — 109
B. Disclosure of the Evidence — 109
Introductory Note on Discovery — 109
  2. Trial Preparation Privileges — 111
    a. The Attorney–Client and Work Product Privileges — 111
        Note on the Work–Product Privilege — 111
        Swidler & Berlin v. United States — 112
        Further Note on the Attorney–Client Privilege — 121
    b. Examinations and Experts — 125
        Note on Discovery of Expert Witnesses — 125
  3. Other Privileges — 125
    Further Note on Privileged Matter — 125
  4. Discovery Abuses — 125
    Note on Abuse of Discovery: Sanctions and Controls — 125
C. The Pretrial Conference — 126
Note on the Pretrial Conference — 126
Note on the Pretrial Conference in Federal Court: Who Can Be Compelled to Attend? — 126

Chapter 8. Trial — 128
A. Judgment Without Trial — 128
  1. Devices to Avoid Plenary Trial — 128
    Note on Devices to Avoid Plenary Trial — 128
  2. Default Judgments — 128
    Note on Defaults and Default Judgments — 128
  3. Settlement — 129
    Note on Settlement Agreements — 129
  4. Summary Judgment — 130
    Note on Summary Judgment — 130
B. The Right to Jury Trial — 131
  2. The Seventh Amendment — 131
    Note on the Right to Jury Trial Under the United States Constitution — 131
    Notes and Questions — 131
    Note on the Seventh Amendment, Administrative Courts, and Other Non–Article III Courts — 131
    Note on Demanding and Waiving Jury Trial — 134
C. Selection of the Trier of Fact — 134
  1. The Jury — 134
    a. The Jury Panel — 134
        Note on the Jury Panel — 134
    b. Voir Dire — 134
        Note on Voir Dire — 134
        Further Note on Voir Dire — 135
        Note on Jury Size and Unanimity — 138
  2. The Judge — 138
    Note on the Recusal of the Judge — 138

TABLE OF CONTENTS

E.	The Province of the Jury	140
	2. Putting the Case to the Jury	140
	Note on Instructions to the Jury	140
	4. Motions After Verdict	140
	Note on Setting Aside a Verdict	140
	Note on Excessive or Inadequate Verdicts	140

Chapter 9. Special Problems of Modern Litigation 141
C. Arbitration 141
    Note on Arbitration 141

Chapter 10. Review of the Disposition 142
B. Federal Appellate Review 142
    1. Reviewability of Decisions 142
       Digital Equipment Corp. v. Desktop Direct, Inc. 142
       Note on Appealability of Non–final Orders in Federal Courts 149
E. Extraordinary Relief From Judgments 150
    Note on Procedures for Relief From a Judgment 150

*

TABLE OF CASES

Principal cases are in italic type. Non-principal cases are in roman type. References are to Pages.

Acri v. Varian Associates, Inc., 34
Adams v. Robertson, 520 U.S. 83, p. 85
Adams v. Robertson, 676 So.2d 1265, p. 85
Adams, United States v., 150
Administaff, Inc. v. Kaster, 42
Ahearn v. Fibreboard Corp., 104
Allbritton v. Commissioner, 63
Amchem Products, Inc. v. Windsor, 87, 103, 104, 108
American Council of the Blind of Colorado, Inc. v. Romer, 20
American Dredging Co. v. Miller, 46, 47
American Eutectic Welding Alloys Sales Co. v. Dytron Alloys Corp., 26
American Medical Systems, Inc., In re, 84
Arenson v. Southern University Law Center, 140
Arnold v. United Artists Theatre Circuit, Inc., 85
Arnstein v. Porter, 3
Asahi Metal Industry Co., Ltd. v. Superior Court of California, Solano County, 22
Associated Dry Goods Corp. v. Towers Financial Corp., 68
Atherton v. F.D.I.C., 52

Baker by Thomas v. General Motors Corp., 66
Bartley v. Isuzu Motors Ltd., 111
Batson v. Kentucky, 135, 136, 137, 138
Batts v. Tow–Motor Forklift Co., 51
Baumgartner v. Harrisburg Housing Authority, 20
Beggerly, United States v., 150
Bensusan Restaurant Corp. v. King, 23
Berg v. Leason, 32, 33
Berman v. American Nat. Red Cross, 133
Bhatnagar v. Surrendra Overseas Ltd., 46
Birmingham Reverse Discrimination Employment Litigation, In re, 63
BMW of North America, Inc. v. Gore, 701 So.2d 507, p. 16
BMW of North America, Inc. v. Gore, 517 U.S. 559, pp. **4,** *16*
Boddie v. Connecticut, 18

Boll v. Department of Revenue, State of Neb., 18
Borough of (see name of borough)
Bradshaw v. Golden Road Motor Inn, 62
Branch v. Tunnell, 55
Brown v. Ticor Title Ins. Co., 85
Bullard v. Chrysler Corp., 58
Burger King Corp. v. Rudzewicz, 22
Byrd v. Blue Ridge Rural Elec. Co-op., Inc., 48

Cady v. City of Chicago, 20
California Teachers Assn. v. California, 18
Campbell v. Lousiana, 135
Carnival Cruise Lines, Inc. v. Shute, 31, 32
Castano v. American Tobacco Co., 82
Caterpillar Inc. v. Lewis, 43
Chicago, City of v. International College of Surgeons, 42
Chick Kam Choo v. Exxon Corp., 66
Chilcutt v. United States, 110
Chirac v. Reinicker, 121
Chiropractic Alliance of New Jersey v. Parisi, 126
Cirami, United States v., 128
Circle Chevrolet Co. v. Giordano, Halleran & Ciesla, 60
City of (see name of city)
Clement v. American Honda Finance Corp., 108
Compagno v. Commodore Cruise Line, Ltd., 31
CompuServe, Inc. v. Patterson, 24
Continental Trend Resources, Inc. v. OXY USA Inc., 16
Coopers & Lybrand v. Livesay, 82, 142
Copley Pharmaceutical, Inc., In re, 161 F.R.D. 456, p. 84
Copley Pharmaceutical, Inc., In re, 158 F.R.D. 485, p. 84
Crawford–El v. Britton, 55, 57
Creative Technology, Ltd. v. Aztech System Pte., Ltd., 46
Cybersell, Inc. v. Cybersell, Inc., 23

ix

TABLE OF CASES

Daubert v. Merrell Dow Pharmaceuticals, Inc., 125
Davis, State v., 137
Dawson v. United States, 126
DDI Seamless Cylinder Intern., Inc. v. General Fire Extinguisher Corp., 141
DES Cases, In re, 27, 28
Development Finance Corp. v. Alpha Housing & Health Care, Inc., 69
DeWeerth v. Baldinger, 51, 52
Diamond v. Charles, 69
Digital Equipment Corp. v. Desktop Direct, Inc., 142
Director, Office of Workers' Compensation Programs, Dept. of Labor v. Greenwich Collieries, 54
DiTrolio v. Antiles, 61
Doe v. American Nat. Red Cross, 133
Dresser Industries, Inc. v. Underwriters at Lloyd's of London, 33

Eckstein v. Balcor Film Investors, 45
Effron v. Sun Line Cruises, Inc., 32
Elem v. Purkett, 136
El Fenix de Puerto Rico v. The M/Y Johanny, 138
Elliott v. Perez, 54
Emerson Electric Co. v. Superior Court, 109
Epstein v. MCA, Inc., 65, 86
Erie R. Co. v. Tompkins, 48, 49, 50
ESAB Group, Inc. v. Centricut, Inc., 30
Espinoza v. United States, 26
Executive Software North America, Inc. v. United States Dist. Court for Cent. Dist. of California, 34

Farrar v. Hobby, 19, 20
F.D.I.C. v. Conner, 110
Federated Dept. Stores, Inc. v. Moitie, 41, 42
Felder v. Casey, 51
Feltner v. Columbia Pictures Television, Inc., 131
Ferens v. John Deere Co., 45
Flanagan v. Ahearn, 104
Free v. Abbott Laboratories, 35, 40, 41, 43, 87
Frye v. United States, 125

Garza v. National American Ins. Co., 68
Gasperini v. Center for Humanities, Inc., 48, 49, 51
General Elec. Co. v. Joiner, 125
General Motors Corp. Pick-up Truck Fuel Tank Products Liability Litigation, In re, 134 F.3d 133, p. 65
General Motors Corp. Pick-Up Truck Fuel Tank Products Liability Litigation, In re, 55 F.3d 768, p. 102

G. Heileman Brewing Co., Inc. v. Joseph Oat Corp., 126
GlenFed, Inc. Securities Litigation, In re, 57
Gomez v. Toledo, 55
Grand Jury Subpoena Duces Tecum, In re, 124
Gray v. American Radiator & Standard Sanitary Corp., 22
Griffin v. Dana Point Condominium Ass'n, 68
Grover by Grover v. Eli Lilly and Co., 128
Guaranty Trust Co. of N.Y. v. York, 48, 50

Hamm v. Nasatka Barriers Inc., 133
Hanna v. Plumer, 48
Haworth, Inc. v. Herman Miller, Inc., 112
Hetzel v. Prince William County, Va., 140
Honda Motor Co., Ltd. v. Oberg, 17
Hymowitz v. Eli Lilly and Co., 26

Ingraham v. Carroll, 28
In re (see name of party)
Inset Systems, Inc. v. Instruction Set, Inc., 24
International Shoe Co. v. State of Wash., Office of Unemployment Compensation and Placement, 21
IUE AFL–CIO Pension Fund v. Herrmann, 30

Jaffee v. Redmond, 125
Janmark, Inc. v. Reidy, 26
Johnson v. Fankell, 50

Kabealo v. Davis, 42
Karn v. Rand, 112
Kelly, People v., 125
Kirk v. Raymark Industries, Inc., 135
Kokkonen v. Guardian Life Ins. Co. of America, 41
Korean Air Lines Disaster of Sept. 1, 1983, In re, 45
Kras, United States v., 18
Kulko v. Superior Court of California In and For City and County of San Francisco, 21

Landgraf v. United StatesI Film Products, 61, 131
Launey v. Carnival Corp., 31
Leahy, People v., 125
Leatherman v. Tarrant County Narcotics Intelligence and Coordination Unit, 54, 55
Lebow v. American Trans Air, Inc., 131
Lesnick v. Hollingsworth & Vose Co., 22

TABLE OF CASES

Lexecon Inc. v. Milberg Weiss Bershad Hynes & Lerach, 46
Liberty Mut. Ins. Co. v. Ward Trucking Corp., 42
Lim v. Central DuPage Hosp., 61
Little Rock School Dist. v. Pulaski County Special School Dist., No. 1, 20
Lords Landing Village Condominium Council of Unit Owners v. Continental Ins. Co., 52
Lundwall, United States v., 110
Lundy v. Adamar of New Jersey, Inc., 58

Macumber, State v., 124
Marcella v. Brandywine Hosp., 133
Markman v. Westview Instruments, Inc., 517 U.S. 370, p. 132
Markman v. Westview Instruments, Inc., 52 F.3d 967, p. 133
Marrese v. American Academy of Orthopaedic Surgeons, 65
Martin v. Wilks, 63, 64
Mas v. Perry, 33
Matsushita Elec. Indus. Co., Ltd. v. Epstein, 65, 86
Matter of (see name of party)
Matusevitch v. Telnikoff, 67
Mausolf v. Babbitt, 69
Maywalt v. Parker & Parsley Petroleum Co., 85
McKnight v. General Motors Corp., 61
Mendoza, United States v., 63
Menowitz v. Brown, 45
Merrell Dow Pharmaceuticals Inc. v. Thompson, 33
Merrill Lynch, Pierce, Fenner & Smith, Inc. v. Lauer, 141
Metropolitan Federal Bank of Iowa, F.S.B. v. W.R. Grace & Co., 128
Metropolitan Life Ins. Co. v. Robertson–Ceco Corp., 22
Mitchell v. Forsyth, 149
M.L.B. v. S.L.J., 17
Moore v. DeBiase, 42
Mortgagelinq Corp. v. Commonwealth Land Title Ins. Co., 60
Myers v. County of Lake, Ind., 34
Mystic Isle Development Corp. v. Perskie & Nehmad, 60

New York County DES Litigation, In re, 28
Nowak v. Tak How Investments, Ltd., 29

O'Brien v. National Property Analysts Partners, 56
Oetiker v. Jurid Werke, G. m. b. H., 30
O'Gilvie v. United States, 17
O'Melveny & Myers v. F.D.I.C., 52

Omni Capital Intern. v. Rudolf Wolff & Co., Ltd., 30
Owen Equipment & Erection Co. v. Kroger, 35

Pacific Mut. Life Ins. Co. v. Haslip, 4
Panavision Intern., L.P. v. Toeppen, 23
Parker v. Anderson, 86
Parsons Steel, Inc. v. First Alabama Bank, 66
Patterson Enterprises v. Bridgestone/Firestone, Inc., 68
People v. _____ (see opposing party)
Petrucelli v. Bohringer and Ratzinger, 26
Phillips Petroleum Co. v. Shutts, 85
Postow v. OBA Federal Sav. and Loan Ass'n, 86
Presbyterian University Hosp. v. Wilson, 29
Pretzel & Stouffer, Chartered v. Imperial Adjusters, Inc., 128
Purkett v. Elem, 135, 136, 137

Rambersed, People v., 138
Rhone–Poulenc Rorer Inc., Matter of, 70, 82, 84
Richards v. Jefferson County, Ala., 64
Riley v. Murdock, 109
Rivers v. Roadway Exp., Inc., 61
Rivet v. Regions Bank of Louisiana, 41, 42, 66
Rodriguez v. Doral Mortg. Corp., 53
Ross v. A. H. Robins Co., Inc., 56
Ross v. Oklahoma, 134, 135
Ruggiero v. Compania Peruana de Vapores, 133
Russaw v. Voyager Life Ins. Co., 42

Sacramona v. Bridgestone/Firestone, Inc., 109
S.A. Healy Co. v. Milwaukee Metropolitan Sewerage Dist., 49
Schultea v. Wood, 55
Schwarzschild v. Tse, 86
S.E.C. v. Monarch Funding Corp., 63
Shepherd v. American Broadcasting Companies, Inc., 110
Silicon Graphics, Inc. Securities Litigation, In re, 1997 WL 337580, p. 57
Silicon Graphics, Inc. Securities Litigation, In re, 970 F.Supp. 746, p. 57
Silicon Graphics, Inc. Securities Litigation, In re, 1996 WL 664639, p. 57
Smith v. Diamond Offshore Drilling, Inc., 109
Smith v. Doe, 31
Somerstein, United States v., 138
S–1 and S–2 v. State Bd. of Educ. of North Carolina, 20
State v. _____ (see opposing party)
State of (see name of state)

TABLE OF CASES

Steel Co. v. Citizens for a Better Environment, 44
St. Mary's Honor Center v. Hicks, 54
Stromberg Metal Works, Inc. v. Press Mechanical, Inc., 40, 41, 68
Swidler & Berlin v. United States, 112, 124
Swint v. Chambers County Com'n, 149

Ted Lapidus, S.A. v. Vann, 58
Thomas v. American Home Products, Inc., 52
Ticor Title Ins. Co. v. Brown, 85
Tull v. United States, 132

United Mine Workers of America v. Gibbs, 34
United States v. _____ (see opposing party)
United States Bancorp Mortg. Co. v. Bonner Mall Partnership, 62
United States Postal Service v. Brennan, 69

Universal Consol. Companies, Inc. v. Bank of China, 133
University of Tennessee v. Elliott, 62
Upjohn Co. v. United States, 123

Veney v. Hogan, 55

Waldridge v. American Hoechst Corp., 130
Walker v. Armco Steel Corp., 25, 49
Ward v. CSX Transp., Inc., 109
Washington, State of, United States v., 139
Watts, United States v., 63
Weiss v. Glemp, 903 P.2d 455, p. 25
Weiss v. Glemp, 792 F.Supp. 215, p. 25
West v. Conrail, 25
West Mifflin, Borough of v. Lancaster, 42

Zahn v. International Paper Co., 40, 86, 87
Zinn by Blankenship v. Shalala, 20

1998 SUPPLEMENT

to

CASES AND MATERIALS

ON

PLEADING AND PROCEDURE

STATE AND FEDERAL

*

Chapter 1

INTRODUCTION

A. AN OVERVIEW OF THE SYSTEM

p. 30

HISTORICAL NOTE ON PROCEDURE

6. Legislative Reform

In 1990 Congress passed the Civil Justice Reform Act (CJRA) which required each of the 94 federal districts to devise and implement plans to reduce expense and delay in civil litigation. The plans focus on case management issues such as discovery, issue formulation and settlement. Further, the CJRA required ten districts to establish "pilot" programs to incorporate specified case management principles into their plans. Many federal judges were initially hostile to the CJRA, and most academics were similarly unenthusiastic. See, e.g., Mullenix, "The Counter-Reformation in Procedural Justice," 77 Minn.L.Rev. 375 (1992); Robel, "Fractured Procedure: The Civil Justice Reform Act of 1990," 46 Stan.L.Rev. 1447 (1994); Tobias, "Civil Justice Reform and the Balkanization of Federal Civil Procedure," 24 Ariz.St.L.J. 1393 (1992).

In 1996 the RAND Institute for Civil Justice published an extensive study of the results of the CJRA. It concluded that the pilot programs overall "had little effect on time to disposition, litigation costs, and attorneys' satisfaction and views of the fairness of case management." Kakalik, et al., Just, Speedy, and Inexpensive? An Evaluation of Judicial Case Management Under the Civil Justice Reform Act 1 (1996). More specifically, the study concluded that some judicial case management techniques, such as setting early trial dates and requiring that litigants be available for settlement conferences, significantly reduced time for disposing of a case; but that they also significantly increased attorney work hours, and, hence, costs to litigants. But the study concluded that other techniques, such as early cutoff times for discovery, significantly reduced attorney work hours. Id., at 1–2. A useful discussion of the CJRA is "Symposium: Evaluation of the Civil Justice Reform Act," 49 Ala.L.Rev. 1 (1997). See also Burbank and Silberman, "Civil Procedure Reform in Comparative Context: The United States of America," 45 Am.J. of Comp.Law 675 (1997)(describing the CJRA in the context of other procedural reforms).

7a. Threatened "Balkanization" of Federal Procedure

A principal aim of the Federal Rules in 1938 was to produce a uniform system of procedure in civil cases in the federal courts. On the whole, the federal rules have been successful achieving that uniformity, but in recent years a combination of several factors has led to an increasing disuniformity.

First, federal District Courts all have local rules that supplement the Federal Rules of Civil Procedure. 28 U.S.C. § 2071 authorizes individual federal District Courts to adopt local rules: "(a) Such [local] rules shall be consistent with ... [the Federal Rules of Civil Procedure]. (b) Any [local rule] shall be prescribed only after giving appropriate public notice and opportunity for comment." § 2071(a) and (b). Fed.R.Civ.P. 83 essentially implements § 2071: "Each district court by action of a majority of the judges thereof may from time to time, after giving appropriate public notice and an opportunity to comment, make and amend rules governing its practice not inconsistent with these rules." Recognizing the increasing importance of local rules, the requirement for public notice and comment was added to Rule 83 in 1985 and to § 2071 in 1988. A proposed revision to Fed.R.Civ.P. 83 states, "A local rule must be consistent with—but not duplicative of—Acts of congress and rules adopted under 28 U.S.C. §§ 2072 and 2075, and must conform to any uniform numbering system prescribed by the Judicial Conference of the United States." 161 F.R.D. 161 (1995).

Local rules have proliferated to a remarkable degree. A 1989 study concluded that some local rules "modify or contradict the Federal Rules," despite the requirement of § 2071 that they be "consistent" with the Rules. Further,

> There are nearly 5,000 local rules in the 94 federal districts, and the number is growing. There are thousands of additional standing orders. To give one example, the Central District of California, based in Los Angeles, has 31 local rules with 434 subrules, supplemented by 275 standing orders. These are published in three volumes that are hard even to lift, let alone read. At the other extreme, the Middle District of Georgia, based in Macon, has only one local rule and just 11 standing orders.

Coquillete, Squiers and Subrin, "The Role of Local Rules," 75 A.B.A.J. (4) 62 (1989). See also Subrin, "Federal Rules, Local Rules, and State Rules: Uniformity, Divergence, and Emerging Procedural Patterns," 137 U.Pa. L.Rev. 1999 (1989).

Second, the Civil Justice Reform Act of 1990 (note 6 supra) perpetuated, indeed increased, variation in procedural rules in federal district courts. Professor Wright has lamented the proliferation of local rules—the " 'soft underbelly' of federal procedure." Any hopes of making local rules more uniform were "dashed by the unnecessary and unwise Civil Justice Reform Act of 1990, with its encouragement to each district to invent its own plan for reducing expense and delay in litigation." Wright, "Foreword: The Malaise of Federal Rulemaking," 14 Rev. of Litig. 1, 10 (1994).

Third and most recently, Rule 26(a)(1), as amended in 1993, explicitly permits local district courts and individual judges to "opt out" of the rule. Rule 26(a)(1) requires parties to disclose certain information at an early stage in the lawsuit without being specifically asked to do so. See discussion in casebook, pp. 932–935. Partly due to controversy surrounding the adoption of this amendment, Rule 26(a)(1) applies "[e]xcept to the extent otherwise stipulated or directed by order or local rule." For the bewildering variety of District Court responses to Rule 26(a)(1), see Chemerinsky and Friedman, "The Fragmentation of Federal Rules," 46 Mercer L.Rev. 757, 775–778 (1995).

Judge Charles Clark, sometimes known as the father of the federal rules, frequently emphasized the goal of having "simple rules which shall be uniform throughout the country." See, e.g., Arnstein v. Porter, 154 F.2d 464, 479 (2d Cir.1946)(Clark, J., dissenting). Professor Mullenix has recently noted, "Judge Clark must be rolling over in his grave." Mullenix, supra, at 376.

The balkanization of procedural rules has not been confined to the District Courts. See Sisk, "The Balkanization of Appellate Justice: The Proliferation of Local Rules in the Federal Circuits," 68 Colo.L.Rev. 1 (1997).

8. Modern Litigation

Professor Yeazell summarizes the trend in modern litigation:

[T]he past century, particularly the last fifty years, has seen a significant change in the location of final authority in civil lawsuits. ... At the start of the period trials lay at the center of litigation, and appellate courts could control the outcome of trials. Neither proposition holds true today. "Litigation" usually meaning discovery, summary judgment, settlement negotiations, alternatives to judicial process, sanctions for lawyer misbehavior, and similar pretrial matters, lies at the center of judges' and lawyers' attention. Trials are an endangered species. Appellate courts, while now more active than ever, no longer control the outcome of a high proportion of cases.

Yeazell, "The Misunderstood Consequences of Modern Civil Process," 1994 Wisc.L.Rev. 631, 666–67. See also Resnik, "From 'Cases' to 'Litigation'," 54 (3) Law & Contemp.Probs. 5 (1991); Resnik, "Failing Faith: Adjudicatory Procedure in Decline," 53 U.Chi.L.Rev. 494 (1986).

For a useful summary of procedural developments in the last decade, particularly in large complex cases, see Tidmarsh, "Civil Procedure: The Last Ten Years," 46 J.of Leg.Ed. 503 (1996).

B. THE ADVERSARY SYSTEM

p. 44

NOTE ON PROFESSIONAL COURTESY

See Cary, "Rambo Depositions: Controlling an Ethical Cancer in Civil Litigation," 25 Hofstra L.Rev. 561 (1996); McGuire, "Reflections of a Recovering Litigator: Adversarial Excess in Civil Proceedings," 164 F.R.D. 283 (1996); Symposium, "Professionalism in the Practice of Law: A Symposium on Civility and Judicial Ethics in the 1990s," 28 Valpar.U.L.Rev. 513 (1994).

Chapter 2

REMEDIES

A. PLENARY JUDICIAL REMEDIES

1. DAMAGES

p. 62.   Replace PACIFIC MUT. LIFE INS. CO. v. HASLIP with the following case.

BMW OF NORTH AMERICA, INC. v. GORE
United States Supreme Court, 1996.
517 U.S. 559, 116 S.Ct. 1589, 134 L.Ed.2d 809.

STEVENS, J., delivered the opinion of the Court, in which O'CONNOR, KENNEDY, SOUTER, and BREYER, JJ., joined. BREYER, J., filed a concurring opinion, in which O'CONNOR and SOUTER, JJ., joined. SCALIA, J., filed a dissenting opinion, in which THOMAS, J., joined. GINSBURG, J., filed a dissenting opinion, in which REHNQUIST, C.J., joined.

JUSTICE STEVENS delivered the opinion of the Court.

The Due Process Clause of the Fourteenth Amendment prohibits a State from imposing a " 'grossly excessive' " punishment on a tortfeasor. TXO Production Corp. v. Alliance Resources Corp., 509 U.S. 443, 454, 113 S.Ct. 2711, 2718, 125 L.Ed.2d 366 (1993) (and cases cited). The wrongdoing involved in this case was the decision by a national distributor of automobiles not to advise its dealers, and hence their customers, of predelivery damage to new cars when the cost of repair amounted to less than 3 percent of the car's suggested retail price. The question presented is whether a $2 million punitive damages award to the purchaser of one of these cars exceeds the constitutional limit.

I.

In January 1990, Dr. Ira Gore, Jr. (respondent), purchased a black BMW sports sedan for $40,750.88 from an authorized BMW dealer in Birmingham, Alabama. After driving the car for approximately nine months, and without noticing any flaws in its appearance, Dr. Gore took the car to "Slick Finish," an independent detailer, to make it look " 'snazzier than it normally would appear.' " 646 So.2d 619, 621 (Ala. 1994). Mr. Slick, the proprietor, detected evidence that the car had been repainted.[1] Convinced that he had been cheated, Dr. Gore brought suit against petitioner BMW of North America (BMW), the American distributor of BMW automobiles. Dr. Gore alleged, inter alia, that the failure to disclose that the car had been repainted constituted suppression of a material fact. The complaint prayed for $500,000 in compensatory and punitive damages, and costs.

At trial, BMW acknowledged that it had adopted a nationwide policy in 1983 concerning cars that were damaged in the course of manufacture or transportation. If the cost of repairing the damage exceeded 3 percent of the car's suggested retail price, the car was placed in company service for a period of time and then sold as used. If the repair cost did not exceed 3 percent of the suggested retail price, however, the car was sold as new without advising the dealer that any repairs had been made. Because the $601.37 cost of repainting Dr. Gore's car was only about 1.5 percent of its suggested retail price, BMW did not disclose the damage or repair to the Birmingham dealer.

Dr. Gore asserted that his repainted car was worth less than a car that had not been refinished. To prove his actual damages of $4,000, he relied on the testimony of a former BMW dealer, who estimated that the value of a repainted BMW was approximately 10 percent less than the value of a new car that had not been damaged and repaired. To support his claim for punitive damages, Dr. Gore introduced evidence that since 1983 BMW had sold 983 refinished cars as new, including 14 in Alabama, without disclosing that the cars had been repainted before sale at a cost of more than $300 per vehicle. Using the actual damage estimate of $4,000 per vehicle, Dr. Gore argued that a punitive award of $4 million would provide an appropriate penalty for selling approximately 1,000 cars for more than they were worth.

In defense of its disclosure policy, BMW argued that it was under no obligation to disclose repairs of minor damage to new cars and that Dr. Gore's car was as good as a car with the original factory finish. It disputed Dr. Gore's assertion that the value of the car was impaired by the repainting and argued that this good-faith belief made a punitive award inappropriate. BMW also maintained that transactions in jurisdictions other than Alabama had no relevance to Dr. Gore's claim.

The jury returned a verdict finding BMW liable for compensatory damages of $4,000. In addition, the jury assessed $4 million in punitive damages, based on a determination that the nondisclosure policy constituted "gross, oppressive or malicious" fraud.

BMW filed a post-trial motion to set aside the punitive damages award. The company introduced evidence to establish that its nondisclo-

---

1. The top, hood, trunk, and quarter panels of Dr. Gore's car were repainted at BMW's vehicle preparation center in Brunswick, Georgia. The parties presumed that the damage was caused by exposure to acid rain during transit between the manufacturing plant in Germany and the preparation center.

sure policy was consistent with the laws of roughly 25 States defining the disclosure obligations of automobile manufacturers, distributors, and dealers. The most stringent of these statutes required disclosure of repairs costing more than 3 percent of the suggested retail price; none mandated disclosure of less costly repairs. Relying on these statutes, BMW contended that its conduct was lawful in these States and therefore could not provide the basis for an award of punitive damages.

BMW also drew the court's attention to the fact that its nondisclosure policy had never been adjudged unlawful before this action was filed. Just months before Dr. Gore's case went to trial, the jury in a similar lawsuit filed by another Alabama BMW purchaser found that BMW's failure to disclose paint repair constituted fraud. Yates v. BMW of North America, Inc., 642 So.2d 937 (Ala.Civ.App.1993). Before the judgment in this case, BMW changed its policy by taking steps to avoid the sale of any refinished vehicles in Alabama and two other States. When the $4 million verdict was returned in this case, BMW promptly instituted a nationwide policy of full disclosure of all repairs, no matter how minor.

In response to BMW's arguments, Dr. Gore asserted that the policy change demonstrated the efficacy of the punitive damages award. He noted that while no jury had held the policy unlawful, BMW had received a number of customer complaints relating to undisclosed repairs and had settled some lawsuits. Finally, he maintained that the disclosure statutes of other States were irrelevant because BMW had failed to offer any evidence that the disclosure statutes supplanted, rather than supplemented, existing causes of action for common-law fraud.

The trial judge denied BMW's post-trial motion, holding, inter alia, that the award was not excessive. On appeal, the Alabama Supreme Court also rejected BMW's claim that the award exceeded the constitutionally permissible amount. 646 So.2d 619 (1994). The court's excessiveness inquiry applied the factors articulated in Green Oil Co. v. Hornsby, 539 So.2d 218, 223–224 (Ala.1989), and approved in Pacific Mut. Life Ins. Co. v. Haslip, 499 U.S. 1, 21–22, 113 L.Ed.2d 1, 111 S.Ct. 1032 (1991). 646 So.2d at 624–625. Based on its analysis, the court concluded that BMW's conduct was "reprehensible"; the nondisclosure was profitable for the company; the judgment "would not have a substantial impact upon [BMW's] financial position"; the litigation had been expensive; no criminal sanctions had been imposed on BMW for the same conduct; the award of no punitive damages in Yates reflected "the inherent uncertainty of the trial process"; and the punitive award bore a "reasonable relationship" to "the harm that was likely to occur from [BMW's] conduct as well as ... the harm that actually occurred." Id., at 625–627.

The Alabama Supreme Court did, however, rule in BMW's favor on one critical point: The court found that the jury improperly computed the amount of punitive damages by multiplying Dr. Gore's compensatory damages by the number of similar sales in other jurisdictions. Id., at 627. Having found the verdict tainted, the court held that "a constitutionally reasonable punitive damages award in this case is $2,000,000," id., at 629, and therefore ordered a remittitur in that amount. The court's discussion of the amount of its remitted award expressly disclaimed any reliance on "acts that occurred in other jurisdictions"; instead, the court explained that it had used a "comparative analysis" that considered Alabama cases, "along with cases from other jurisdictions, involving the sale of an automobile where the seller misrepresented the condition of the vehicle and the jury awarded punitive damages to the purchaser." Id., at 628.

Because we believed that a review of this case would help to illuminate "the character of the standard that will identify constitutionally excessive awards" of punitive damages, see Honda Motor Co. v. Oberg, 512 U.S. ___, ___, ___ S.Ct. ___, ___, ___ L.Ed.2d ___ (1994) (slip op., at 4), we granted certiorari, 513 U.S. ___, 115 S.Ct. 932, 130 L.Ed.2d 879 (1995).

II.

Punitive damages may properly be imposed to further a State's legitimate interests in punishing unlawful conduct and deterring its repetition. Gertz v. Robert Welch, Inc., 418 U.S. 323, 350, 94 S.Ct. 2997, 3012, 41 L.Ed.2d 789 (1974); Newport v. Fact Concerts, Inc., 453 U.S. 247, 266–267, 101 S.Ct. 2748, 2759–2760, 69 L.Ed.2d 616 (1981); Haslip, 499 U.S., at 22, 111 S.Ct., at 1045–1046. In our federal system, States necessarily have considerable flexibility in determining the level of punitive damages that they will allow in different classes of cases and in any particular case. Most States that authorize exemplary damages afford the jury similar latitude, requiring only that the damages awarded be reasonably necessary to vindicate the State's legitimate interests in punishment and deterrence. See TXO, 509 U.S., at 456, 113 S.Ct., at 2719–2720; Haslip, 499 U.S., at 21, 22, 111 S.Ct., at 1045, 1045–1046. Only when an award can fairly be categorized as "grossly excessive" in relation to these interests does it enter the zone of arbitrariness that violates the Due Process Clause of the Fourteenth Amendment. Cf. TXO, 509 U.S., at 456, 113 S.Ct., at 2719–2720. For that reason, the federal excessiveness inquiry appropriately begins with an identification of the state interests that a punitive award is designed to serve. We therefore focus our attention first on the scope of Alabama's legitimate interests in punishing BMW and deterring it from future misconduct.

No one doubts that a State may protect its citizens by prohibiting deceptive trade practices and by requiring automobile distributors to disclose presale repairs that affect the value of a new car. But the States need not, and in fact do not, provide such protection in a uniform manner. Some States rely on the judicial process to formulate and enforce an appropriate disclosure requirement by applying principles of contract and tort law. Other States have enacted various forms of legislation that define the disclosure obligations of automobile manufacturers, distributors, and dealers.[13] The result is a patchwork of rules representing the diverse policy judgments of lawmakers in 50 States.

That diversity demonstrates that reasonable people may disagree about the value of a full disclosure requirement. Some legislatures may conclude that affirmative disclosure requirements are unnecessary because the self-interest of those involved in the automobile trade in developing and maintaining the goodwill of their customers will motivate them to make voluntary disclosures or to refrain from selling cars that do not comply with self-imposed standards. Those legislatures that do adopt affirmative disclosure obligations may take into account the cost of government regulation, choosing to draw a line exempting minor repairs from such a requirement. In formulating a disclosure standard, States may also consider other goals, such as providing a "safe harbor" for automobile manufacturers, distributors, and dealers against lawsuits over minor repairs.

13. Four States require disclosure of vehicle repairs costing more than 3 percent of suggested retail price. Ariz.Rev.Stat.Ann. § 28–1304.03 (1989); N.C.Gen.Stat. § 20–305.1(d)(5a) (1995); S.C.Code § 56–32–20 (Supp.1995); Va.Code Ann. § 46.2–1571(D) (Supp.1995). An additional three States mandate disclosure when the cost of repairs exceeds 3 percent or $500, whichever is greater. Ala.Code § 8–19–5(22)(c) (1993); Cal.Veh.Code Ann. §§ 9990–9991 (West Supp.1996); Okla.Stat., Tit. 47, § 1112.1 (1991). Indiana imposes a 4 percent disclosure threshold. Ind.Code §§ 9–23–4–4, 9–23–4–5 (1993). Minnesota requires disclosure of repairs costing more than 4 percent of suggested retail price or $500, whichever is greater. Minn.Stat. § 325F.664 (1994). New York requires disclosure when the cost of repairs exceeds 5 percent of suggested retail price. N.Y.Gen.Bus.Law §§ 396–p(5)(a), (d) (McKinney Supp.1996). Vermont imposes a 5 percent disclosure threshold for the first $10,000 in repair costs and 2 percent thereafter. Vt.Stat.Ann., Tit. 9, § 4087(d) (1993). Eleven States mandate disclosure only of damage costing more than 6 percent of retail value to repair. Ark.Code Ann. § 23–112–705 (1992); Idaho Code § 49–1624 (1994); Ill.Comp.Stat., ch. 815, § 710/5 (1994); Ky.Rev.Stat.Ann. § 190.0491(5) (Baldwin 1988); La.Rev.Stat. Ann. § 32:1260 (Supp.1995); Miss. Motor Vehicle Comm'n, Regulation No. 1 (1992); N.H.Rev.Stat.Ann. § 357–C:5(III)(d) (1995); Ohio Rev.Code Ann. § 4517.61 (1994); R.I.Gen.Laws §§ 31–5.1–18(d), (f) (1995); Wis.Stat. § 218.01(2d)(a) (1994); Wyo.Stat. § 31–16–115 (1994). Two States require disclosure of repairs costing $3,000 or more. See Iowa Code Ann. § 321.69 (Supp.1996); N.D.Admin.Code § 37–09–01–01 (1992). Georgia mandates disclosure of paint damage that costs more than $500 to repair. Ga.Code Ann. §§ 40–1–5(b)–(e) (1994) (enacted after respondent purchased his car). Florida requires dealers to disclose paint repair costing more than $100 of which they have actual knowledge. Fla.Stat. § 320.27(9)(n) (1992). Oregon requires manufacturers to disclose all "post-manufacturing" damage and repairs. It is unclear whether this mandate would apply to repairs such as those at issue here. Ore. Rev.Stat. § 650.155 (1991).

Many, but not all, of the statutes exclude from the computation of repair cost the value of certain components—typically items such as glass, tires, wheels and bumpers—when they are replaced with identical manufacturer's original equipment. E.g., Cal.Veh.Code Ann. §§ 9990–9991 (West Supp.1996); Ga.Code Ann. §§ 40–1–5(b)–(e) (1994); Ill.Comp.Stat., ch. 815, § 710/5 (1994); Ky.Rev.Stat.Ann. § 190.0491(5) (Baldwin 1988); Okla.Stat., Tit. 47, § 1112.1 (1991); Va.Code Ann. § 46.2–1571(D) (Supp.1995); Vt.Stat.Ann., Tit. 9, § 4087(d) (1993).

We may assume, arguendo, that it would be wise for every State to adopt Dr. Gore's preferred rule, requiring full disclosure of every presale repair to a car, no matter how trivial and regardless of its actual impact on the value of the car. But while we do not doubt that Congress has ample authority to enact such a policy for the entire Nation, it is clear that no single State could do so, or even impose its own policy choice on neighboring States. * * *

We think it follows from these principles of state sovereignty and comity that a State may not impose economic sanctions on violators of its laws with the intent of changing the tortfeasors' lawful conduct in other States. Before this Court Dr. Gore argued that the large punitive damages award was necessary to induce BMW to change the nationwide policy that it adopted in 1983. But by attempting to alter BMW's nationwide policy, Alabama would be infringing on the policy choices of other States. To avoid such encroachment, the economic penalties that a State such as Alabama inflicts on those who transgress its laws, whether the penalties take the form of legislatively authorized fines or judicially imposed punitive damages, must be supported by the State's interest in protecting its own consumers and its own economy. Alabama may insist that BMW adhere to a particular disclosure policy in that State. Alabama does not have the power, however, to punish BMW for conduct that was lawful where it occurred and that had no impact on Alabama or its residents. Nor may Alabama impose sanctions on BMW in order to deter conduct that is lawful in other jurisdictions.

In this case, we accept the Alabama Supreme Court's interpretation of the jury verdict as reflecting a computation of the amount of punitive damages "based in large part on conduct that happened in other jurisdictions." 646 So.2d at 627. * * * When the scope of the interest in punishment and deterrence that an Alabama court may appropriately consider is properly limited, it is apparent—for reasons that we shall now address—that this award is grossly excessive.

III.

Elementary notions of fairness enshrined in our constitutional jurisprudence dictate that a person receive fair notice not only of the conduct that will subject him to punishment but also of the severity of the penalty that a State may impose. Three guideposts, each of which indicates that BMW did not receive adequate notice of the magnitude of the sanction that Alabama might impose for adhering to the nondisclosure policy adopted in 1983, lead us to the conclusion that the $2 million award against BMW is grossly excessive: the degree of reprehensibility of the nondisclosure; the disparity between the harm or potential harm suffered by Dr. Gore and his punitive damages award; and the difference between this remedy and the civil penalties authorized or imposed in comparable cases. We discuss these considerations in turn.

Degree of Reprehensibility

Perhaps the most important indicium of the reasonableness of a punitive damages award is the degree of reprehensibility of the defendant's conduct. As the Court stated nearly 150 years ago, exemplary damages imposed on a defendant should reflect "the enormity of his offense." Day v. Woodworth, 13 How. 363, 371, 14 L.Ed. 181 (1852). See also St. Louis, I. M. & S. R. Co. v. Williams, 251 U.S. 63, 66–67, 40 S.Ct. 71, 73, 64 L.Ed. 139 (1919) (punitive award may not be "wholly disproportioned to the offense"); Browning–Ferris Industries of Vt., Inc. v. Kelco Disposal, Inc., 492 U.S. 257, 301, 109 S.Ct. 2909, 2934, 106 L.Ed.2d 219 (1989) (O'CONNOR, J., concurring in part and dissenting in part) (reviewing court "should examine the gravity of the defendant's conduct and the harshness of the award of punitive damages"). * * *

In this case, none of the aggravating factors associated with particularly reprehensible conduct is present. The harm BMW inflicted on Dr. Gore was purely economic in nature. The presale refinishing of the car had no effect on its performance or safety features, or even its appearance for at least nine months after his purchase. BMW's conduct evinced no indifference to or reckless disregard for the health and safety of others. To be sure, infliction of economic injury, especially when done intentionally through affirmative acts of misconduct, id., at 453, or when the target is financially vulnerable, can warrant a substantial penalty. But this observation does not convert all acts that cause economic harm into torts that are sufficiently reprehensible to justify a significant sanction in addition to compensatory damages.

Dr. Gore contends that BMW's conduct was particularly reprehensible because nondisclosure of the repairs to his car formed part of a nationwide pattern of tortious conduct. Certainly, evidence that a defendant has repeatedly engaged in prohibited conduct while knowing or suspecting that it was unlawful would provide relevant support for an argument that strong medicine is required to cure the defendant's disrespect for the law. See id., at 462, n. 28, 113 S.Ct., at 2722, n. 28. Our holdings that a recidivist may be punished more severely than a first offender recognize that repeated misconduct is more reprehensible than an individual instance of malfeasance. See Gryger v. Burke, 334 U.S. 728, 732, 68 S.Ct. 1256, 1258–1259, 92 L.Ed. 1683 (1948).

* * *

That conduct is sufficiently reprehensible to give rise to tort liability, and even a modest award of exemplary damages, does not establish the high degree of culpability that warrants a substantial punitive damages award. Because this case exhibits none of the circumstances ordinarily associated with egregiously improper conduct, we are persuaded that BMW's conduct was not sufficiently reprehensible to warrant imposition of a $2 million exemplary damages award.

Ratio

The second and perhaps most commonly cited indicium of an unreasonable or excessive punitive damages award is its ratio to the actual harm inflicted on the plaintiff. See TXO, 509 U.S., at 459, 113 S.Ct., at 2721; Haslip, 499 U.S., at 23, 111 S.Ct., at 1046. The principle that exemplary damages must bear a "reasonable relationship" to compensatory damages has a long pedigree. Scholars have identified a number of early English statutes authorizing the award of multiple damages for particular wrongs. Some 65 different enactments during the period between 1275 and 1753 provided for double, treble, or quadruple damages. Our decisions in both Haslip and TXO endorsed the proposition that a comparison between the compensatory award and the punitive award is significant.

In Haslip we concluded that even though a punitive damages award of "more than 4 times the amount of compensatory damages," might be "close to the line," it did not "cross the line into the area of constitutional impropriety." Haslip, 499 U.S., at 23–24, 111 S.Ct., at 1046. TXO, following dicta in Haslip, refined this analysis by confirming that the proper inquiry is " 'whether there is a reasonable relationship between the punitive damages award and the harm likely to result from the defendant's conduct as well as the harm that actually has occurred.' " TXO, 509 U.S., at 460, 113 S.Ct., at 2721 (emphasis in original), quoting Haslip, 499 U.S., at 21, 111 S.Ct., at 1045. Thus, in upholding the $10 million award in TXO, we relied on the difference between that figure and the harm to the victim that would have ensued if the tortious plan had succeeded. That difference suggested that the relevant ratio was not more than 10 to 1.

The $2 million in punitive damages awarded to Dr. Gore by the Alabama Supreme Court is 500 times the amount of his actual harm as determined by the jury. Moreover, there is no suggestion that Dr. Gore or any other BMW purchaser was threatened with any additional potential harm by BMW's nondisclosure policy. The disparity in this case is thus dramatically greater than those considered in Haslip and TXO.

Of course, we have consistently rejected the notion that the constitutional line is marked by a simple mathematical formula, even one that compares actual and potential damages to the punitive award. TXO, 509 U.S., at 458, 113 S.Ct., at 2720. Indeed, low awards of compensatory damages may properly support a higher ratio than high compensatory awards, if, for example, a particularly egregious act has resulted in only a small amount of economic damages. A higher ratio may also be justified in cases in which the injury is hard to detect or the monetary value of noneconomic harm might have been difficult to determine. It is appropriate, therefore, to reiterate our rejection of a categorical approach. Once again, "we return to what we said ... in Haslip: 'We need not, and indeed we cannot, draw a mathematical bright line between the constitutionally acceptable and the constitutionally unacceptable that would fit every case. We can say, however, that [a] general concern of reasonableness ... properly enters into the constitutional calculus.'" TXO, 509 U.S., at 458, 113 S.Ct., at 2720 (quoting Haslip, 499 U.S., at 18). In most cases, the ratio will be within a constitutionally acceptable range, and remittitur will not be justified on this basis. When the ratio is a breathtaking 500 to 1, however, the award must surely "raise a suspicious judicial eyebrow." TXO, 509 U.S., at 482, 113 S.Ct., at 2731 (O'CONNOR, J., dissenting).

Sanctions for Comparable Misconduct

Comparing the punitive damages award and the civil or criminal penalties that could be imposed for comparable misconduct provides a third indicium of excessiveness. As JUSTICE O'CONNOR has correctly observed, a reviewing court engaged in determining whether an award of punitive damages is excessive should "accord 'substantial deference' to legislative judgments concerning appropriate sanctions for the conduct at issue." Browning–Ferris Industries of Vt., Inc. v. Kelco Disposal, Inc., 492 U.S., at 301, 109 S.Ct., at 2934 (O'CONNOR, J., concurring in part and dissenting in part). In Haslip, 499 U.S., at 23, 111 S.Ct., at 1046, the Court noted that although the exemplary award was "much in excess of the fine that could be imposed," imprisonment was also authorized in the criminal context. In this case the $2 million economic sanction imposed on BMW is substantially greater than the statutory fines available in Alabama and elsewhere for similar malfeasance.

The maximum civil penalty authorized by the Alabama Legislature for a violation of its Deceptive Trade Practices Act is $2,000; other States authorize more severe sanctions, with the maxima ranging from $5,000 to $10,000. Significantly, some statutes draw a distinction between first offenders and recidivists; thus, in New York the penalty is $50 for a first offense and $250 for subsequent offenses. None of these statutes would provide an out-of-state distributor with fair notice that the first violation—or, indeed the first 14 violations—of its provisions might subject an offender to a multimillion dollar penalty. Moreover, at the time BMW's policy was first challenged, there does not appear to have been any judicial decision in Alabama or elsewhere indicating that application of that policy might give rise to such severe punishment.

The sanction imposed in this case cannot be justified on the ground that it was necessary to deter future misconduct without considering whether less drastic remedies could be expected to achieve that goal. The fact that a multimillion dollar penalty prompted a change in policy sheds no light on the question whether a lesser deterrent would have adequately protected the interests of Alabama consumers. In the absence of a history of noncompliance with known statutory requirements, there is no basis for assuming that a more modest sanction would not have been sufficient to motivate full compliance with the disclosure requirement imposed by the Alabama Supreme Court in this case.

IV.

* * *

As in Haslip, we are not prepared to draw a bright line marking the limits of a constitutionally acceptable punitive damages award. Unlike that case, however, we are fully convinced that the grossly excessive award imposed in this case transcends the constitutional limit. Whether the appropriate remedy requires a new trial or merely an independent determination by the Alabama Supreme Court of the award necessary to vindicate the economic interests of Alabama consumers is a matter that should be addressed by the state court in the first instance.

The judgment is reversed, and the case is remanded for further proceedings not inconsistent with this opinion.

It is so ordered.

JUSTICE BREYER, with whom JUSTICE O'CONNOR and JUSTICE SOUTER join, concurring.

* * *

[T]he rules that purport to channel discretion in this kind of case, here did not do so in fact. That means that the award in this case was both (a) the product of a system of standards that did not significantly constrain a court's, and hence a jury's, discretion in making that award; and (b) was grossly excessive in light of the State's legitimate punitive damages objectives.

The first of these reasons has special importance where courts review a jury-determined punitive damages award. That is because one cannot expect to direct jurors like legislators through the ballot box; nor can one expect those jurors to interpret law like judges, who work within a discipline and hierarchical organization that normally promotes roughly uniform interpretation and application of the law. Yet here Alabama expects jurors to act, at least a little, like legislators or judges, for it permits them, to a certain extent, to create public policy and to apply that policy, not to compensate a victim, but to achieve a policy-related objective outside the confines of the particular case.

To the extent that neither clear legal principles, nor fairly obvious historical or community-based standards (defining, say, especially egregious behavior) significantly constrain punitive damages awards, is there not a substantial risk of outcomes so arbitrary that they become difficult to square with the Constitution's assurance, to every citizen, of the law's protection? The standards here, as authoritatively interpreted, in my view, make this threat real and not theoretical. And, in these unusual circumstances, where legal standards offer virtually no constraint, I believe that this lack of constraining standards warrants this Court's detailed examination of the award.

The second reason—the severe disproportionality between the award and the legitimate punitive damages objectives—reflects a judgment about a matter of degree. I recognize that it is often difficult to determine just when a punitive award exceeds an amount reasonably related to a State's legitimate interests, or when that excess is so great as to amount to a matter of constitutional concern. Yet whatever the difficulties of drawing a precise line, once we examine the award in this case, it is not difficult to say that this award lies on the line's far side. The severe lack of proportionality between the size of the award and the underlying punitive damages objectives shows that the award falls into the category of "gross excessiveness" set forth in this Court's prior cases.

These two reasons taken together overcome what would otherwise amount to a "strong presumption of validity." TXO, 509 U.S., at 457, 113 S.Ct., at 2720. And, for those two reasons, I conclude that the award in this unusual case violates the basic guarantee of nonarbitrary governmental behavior that the Due Process Clause provides.

JUSTICE SCALIA, with whom JUSTICE THOMAS joins, dissenting.

Today we see the latest manifestation of this Court's recent and increasingly insistent "concern about punitive damages that 'run wild.'" Pacific Mut. Life Ins. Co. v. Haslip, 499 U.S. 1, 18, 111 S.Ct. 1032, 1043, 113 L.Ed.2d 1 (1991). Since the Constitution does not make that concern any of our business, the Court's activities in this area are an unjustified incursion into the province of state governments.

* * *

I.

The most significant aspects of today's decision—the identification of a "substantive due process" right against a "grossly excessive" award, and the concomitant assumption of ultimate authority to decide anew a matter of "reasonableness" resolved in lower court proceedings—are of course not new. Haslip and TXO revived the notion, moribund since its appearance in the first years of this century, that the measure of civil punishment poses a question of constitutional dimension to be answered by this Court. Neither of those cases, however, nor any of the precedents upon which they relied, actually took the step of declaring a punitive award unconstitutional simply because it was "too big." At the time of adoption of the Fourteenth Amendment, it was well understood that punitive damages represent the assessment by the jury, as the voice of the community, of the measure of punishment the defendant deserved. * * * Today's decision, though dressed up as a legal opinion, is really no more than a disagreement with the community's sense of indignation or outrage expressed in the punitive award of the Alabama jury, as reduced by the State Supreme Court. It reflects not merely, as the concurrence candidly acknowledges, "a judgment about a matter of degree"; but a judgment about the appropriate degree of indignation or outrage, which is hardly an analytical determination.

* * *

II.

One might understand the Court's eagerness to enter this field, rather than leave it with the state legislatures, if it had something useful to say. In fact, however, its opinion provides virtually no guidance to legislatures, and to state and federal courts, as to what a "constitutionally proper" level of punitive damages might be.

* * *

III.

In Part III of its opinion, the Court identifies "three guideposts" that lead it to the conclusion that the award in this case is excessive: degree of reprehensibility, ratio between punitive award and plaintiff's actual harm, and legislative sanctions provided for comparable misconduct. The legal significance of these "guideposts" is nowhere explored, but their necessary effect is to establish federal standards governing the hitherto exclusively state law of damages. Apparently (though it is by no means clear) all three federal "guideposts" can be overridden if "necessary to deter future misconduct"—a loophole that will encourage state reviewing courts to uphold awards as necessary for the "adequate protection" of state consumers. By effectively requiring state reviewing courts to concoct rationalizations—whether within the "guideposts" or through the loophole—to justify the intuitive punitive reactions of state juries, the Court accords neither category of institution the respect it deserves.

Of course it will not be easy for the States to comply with this new federal law of damages, no matter how willing they are to do so. In truth, the "guideposts" mark a road to nowhere; they provide no real guidance at all. * * *

These criss-crossing platitudes yield no real answers in no real cases. And it must be noted that the Court nowhere says that these three "guideposts" are the only guideposts; indeed, it makes very clear that they are not—explaining away the earlier opinions that do not really follow these "guideposts" on the basis of additional factors, thereby "reiterating our rejection of a categorical approach." In other words, even these utter platitudes, if they should ever happen to produce an answer, may be overridden by other unnamed considerations. The Court has constructed a framework that does not genuinely constrain, that does not inform state legislatures and lower courts—that does nothing at all except confer an artificial air of doctrinal analysis upon its essentially ad hoc determination that this particular award of punitive damages was not "fair."

* * *

For the foregoing reasons, I respectfully dissent.

JUSTICE GINSBURG, with whom THE CHIEF JUSTICE joins, dissenting.

The Court, I am convinced, unnecessarily and unwisely ventures into territory traditionally within the States' domain, and does so in the face of reform measures recently adopted or currently under consideration in legislative arenas. The Alabama Supreme Court, in this case, endeavored to follow this Court's prior instructions; and, more recently, Alabama's highest court has installed further controls on awards of punitive damages. I would therefore leave the state court's judgment undisturbed, and resist unnecessary intrusion into an area dominantly of state concern.

* * *

p. 79, 81

NOTE ON PUNITIVE DAMAGES

1a. *Gore* on remand. On remand, the Alabama Supreme Court reduced Dr. Gore's punitive damages from $2,000,000 to $50,000, based on a comparison with punitive damage awards in two other Alabama cases in which repaired automobiles had been sold as new. BMW of North America, Inc. v. Gore, 701 So.2d 507 (Ala.1997).

1b. Effect of *Gore*. In a case where plaintiff recovered compensatory damages of $269,000, the Court of Appeals for the Tenth Circuit reduced a punitive damage award from $30,000,000 to $6,000,000:

> With the guidance of the BMW opinion, ... we conclude that $30,000,000 exceeds the constitutional limit. The harm in this case, though egregious, was entirely economic, and thus less worthy of punishment than harm to health and safety. Further, the ratio between the award and the harm to these plaintiffs ... is too large. [Defendant's] wealth is not irrelevant, but $30,000,000 is far more than necessary to secure its attention and modify its behavior in Oklahoma.

Continental Trend Resources, Inc., v. OXY USA, Inc., 101 F.3d 634, 642 (10th Cir.1996).

2. Constitutionalizing punitive damages. The unusual split among the Justices in *Gore* shows that attitudes toward constitutionalizing punitive damages do not break cleanly along liberal and conservative lines. Has the majority opinion responded sufficiently to Justice Scalia's charge that the Court's "guideposts ... provide no real guidance at all"? Has it sufficiently responded to Justice Ginsburg's charge that it "unnecessarily and unwisely ventures into territory traditionally within the States' domain"?

In Honda Motor Co., Ltd. v. Oberg, 512 U.S. 415, 114 S.Ct. 2331, 2340–41, 129 L.Ed.2d 336 (1994), Oregon law allowed appellate review of an award of punitive damages, but did not allow any review of the *amount* awarded. The United States Supreme Court held that the lack of review violated the due process clause of the Fourteenth Amendment:

> Punitive damages pose an acute danger of arbitrary deprivation of property. ... Judicial review of the amount awarded was one of the few procedural safeguards which the common law provided against this danger. Oregon has removed that safeguard without providing any substitute procedure and without any indication that the danger of arbitrary awards has in any way subsided over time.

6. Taxability of Punitive Damage Awards. The Supreme Court has recently held that punitive damage awards in personal injury cases are taxable as income under the Internal Revenue Code. O'Gilvie v. United States, 519 U.S. 79, 117 S.Ct. 452, 136 L.Ed.2d 454 (1996). (Compensatory damage awards in personal injury cases are not taxable. 26 U.S.C. § 104(a)(2). Punitive damages in non-personal injury cases were taxable even before the Court's decision in *O'Gilvie. Id.*)

7. Additional Reading. See Polinsky and Shavell, "Punitive Damages: An Economic Analysis," 111 Harv.L.Rev. 870 (1998) (economic analysis of how "rational parties will respond to punitive damages"); Sunstein, Kahneman, and Schkade, "Assessing Punitive Damages (with notes on Cognition and Valuation in Law)," 107 Yale L.J. 2071 (1998) (analysis of "what might be missing, impractical, or wrong in standard economic approaches to punitive damage awards").

D. COSTS OF LITIGATION

1. COURT COSTS

p. 148

NOTE ON COURT COSTS

In M.L.B. v. S.L.J., 519 U.S. 102, 117 S.Ct. 555, 136 L.Ed.2d 473 (1996), a divorced biological mother's parental rights to her two minor children were terminated in a trial court proceeding in which the stepmother—now married to the father—was permitted to adopt the children. The biological mother was unable to pay the estimated $2,352.36 cost of preparing the record for appeal of the decision. Because of her inability to pay, her appeal was dismissed by the Mississippi appellate court. In a 5–4 decision, the United States Supreme Court held that the state was required to pay the cost of preparing "a 'record of sufficient completeness' to permit proper [appellate] consideration of [her] claims.'" at 570. The Court distinguished *Kras* as entailing no "fundamental interest." at 562. Here, by contrast, the right to maintain parental rights was at stake: "Choices about marriage, family life, and the upbringing of children are among associational rights this Court has ranked as 'of basic importance in our society.'" at 564.

In Boll v. Nebraska Department of Revenue, 247 Neb. 473, 528 N.W.2d 300 (1995), a Nebraska statute taxed the acquisition or possession of controlled substances. Appellants were assessed a tax of $18,800, plus a penalty in the same amount, plus interest, under the statute. Under Nebraska law no challenge was allowed unless plaintiffs first posted security of $18,800. The Nebraska Supreme Court held that the security requirement violated the due process clause of the Fourteenth Amendment because it was "so harsh as to effectively deny them access to the courts." The court distinguished *United States v. Kras* on the ground that *Kras* "involve[d] the claimant's affirmative actions for a benefit, the benefit being release from his debts."

In California Teachers Association v. California, 59 Cal.App.4th 516, 69 Cal.Rptr.2d 261 (1997), pet. for review granted, 72 Cal.Rptr.2d 215 (1998), a California public school teacher was discharged after an administrative hearing before a Commission on Professional Competence. The teacher was charged $7,747.97 under a California law providing that a losing teacher must pay half the expense of the hearing. The Court of Appeal held that the assessment of the charge violated federal due process. According to the court, the hearing before the Commission was "'the only effective means of resolving the dispute at hand and denial of a defendant's full access to that process raises grave problems for its legitimacy'" [quoting *Boddie v. Connecticut*]. 59 Cal.App.4th at 525. Review of the decision is pending in the California Supreme Court.

2. ATTORNEYS' FEES

p. 150

INTRODUCTORY NOTE ON ATTORNEYS' FEES

Alone among the American states, Alaska has a version of the "English rule" for attorneys' fees, requiring the loser to pay a portion of the winner's attorney's fees in most civil cases. A recent study of the rule found its effects "complex and often contradictory," and "playing only a minor role in most cases." Among the findings of the study:

> Rule 82 [the Alaska rule governing attorneys' fees] awards are ordered or collected in only a small percentage of civil cases. Awards occurred in only 10 percent of the state court sample and 6 percent of the federal cases. Even cases likely to contain fee awards—those resolved at trial or on dispositive motion—contained relatively few awards. These cases lacked fee awards for several reasons: either they settled after trial but before the fee award was made, neither party prevailed, both parties prevailed in some respect, or a contract provision or statute rather than Rule 82 governed the fee award.

* * *

> [E]ven when fee awards were made, they often were not paid. In only 40 percent of the 57 reported cases that had a fee award did the

prevailing party collect the award. Parties did not collect because the person against whom the award was made had no assets or declared bankruptcy, or because the prevailing party waived fees as part of a post-judgment settlement. Attorneys who represented insurance companies in tort lawsuits observed that their clients always satisfied fee awards against them but seldom were able to collect fee awards in their favor from non-prevailing tort claimants.

* * *

[T]he rule tended to discourage potential litigants with moderate financial assets in all types of cases from initial filing, unless the litigants believed their case to be strong. The weaker the case, the more likely the possibility of an adverse award and therefore the greate[r] discouragement from filing, at least for those who had assets to lose. This chilling effect did not occur as often among wealthier parties, and it occurred hardly at all among "judgment-proof" parties with few financial resources.

* * *

The rule may occasionally encourage a litigant to pursue more aggressively a case perceived to be especially strong. This effect was most often observed in contract and debt, as opposed to tort, cases.

* * *

Finally, the rule may have encouraged the filing of some public-interest lawsuits. . . . In Alaska, the supreme court interprets Rule 82 to encourage public interest lawsuits by holding that successful public interest plaintiffs are entitled to full, reasonable fees, and that public interest plaintiffs are protected from adverse fee awards when they lose.

Di Pietro, "The English Rule at Work in Alaska," 80 Judicature 88, 89–90 (1996); see also Di Pietro and Carns, "Alaska's English Rule: Attorney's Fee Shifting in Civil Cases," 13 Alask.L.Rev. 333 (1996).

p. 176

FURTHER NOTE ON ATTORNEYS' FEES

1. The Contingent Fee

See "Symposium: Contingency Fee Financing of Litigation in America," 47 DePaul L.Rev. 227 (1998).

3. Civil Rights Attorney's Fees Awards Act

As noted in the casebook, *Farrar v. Hobby* held that a plaintiff must obtain an enforceable judgment, or comparable relief through a consent decree or settlement, in order to be a "prevailing party" entitled to attorneys' fees. Whether *Farrar* left intact the "catalyst theory" for awarding fees is not fully settled. Under this theory, plaintiff's suit is a "catalyst" if it induces defendant to change its behavior without waiting for a court order. In such a case, plaintiff is a prevailing party for purposes of attorneys' fees even though there is no judgment, decree, or formal settlement. Four Courts of Appeals have held that the catalyst theory survives *Farrar*; one has held that it does not. *Catalyst theory survives*: Zinn by Blankenship v. Shalala, 35 F.3d 273 (7th Cir.1994); Baumgartner v. Harrisburg Housing Authority, 21 F.3d 541 (3d Cir.1994); Little Rock School Dist. v. Pulaski County Special School Dist., No. 1, 17 F.3d 260 (8th Cir.1994); American Council for the Blind of Colorado, Inc. v. Romer, 992 F.2d 249 (10th Cir.), cert. denied 510 U.S. 864, 114 S.Ct. 184, 126 L.Ed.2d 143 (1993). *Catalyst theory does not survive*: S–1 and S–2 v. State Board of Education, 21 F.3d 49 (4th Cir.1994)(en banc).

Under the "catalyst theory," a defendant must not only change its behavior; the change must also redress a plaintiff's grievance. In Cady v. City of Chicago, 43 F.3d 326 (7th Cir.1994), plaintiff sought an injunction requiring the Chicago airport to place his religious literature on a rack located outside the airport chapel. Prior to the suit, the airport allowed some religious literature on the rack, but refused to allow that belonging to plaintiff. After plaintiff filed suit, the airport removed the rack altogether, thereby curing any constitutional violation and mooting the suit. The Court of Appeals denied attorneys' fees on the ground that plaintiff had not achieved his objective. Would plaintiff have been entitled to attorneys' fees if he had sought an injunction that asked, in the alternative, for an order either to place his literature in the rack or to remove the rack altogether?

Chapter 3
CHOOSING THE PROPER COURT

A. TERRITORIAL JURISDICTION

1. HISTORICAL FORMULAE: THE RELEVANCE OF STATE BOUNDARIES

p. 191

For further historical analysis see Oakley, "The Pitfalls of 'Hint and Run' History: A Critique of Professor Borcher's 'Limited View' of *Pennoyer v. Neff*," 28 U.C.Davis L.Rev. 591 (1995).

2. TWENTIETH CENTURY SYNTHESES

a. MINIMUM CONTACTS

p. 211

NOTES AND QUESTIONS

6. For an interesting historical narrative of the litigation in *International Shoe*, see Cameron and Johnson, "Death of a Salesman? Forum Shopping and Outcome Determination under *International Shoe*," 28 U.C.Davis L.Rev. 769 (1995).

p. 232

NOTES AND QUESTIONS

1a. *Kulko* represents a class of "property" family law cases in which child support, alimony, or marital property is sought and in which the defendant must have minimum contacts with the forum state. By contrast, cases in which divorce or child custody is sought are "status" cases in which *in personam* jurisdiction is generally proper where the divorcing spouse or the custody-seeking parent resides, irrespective of any minimum contacts between the defendant and the forum state. For an analysis and criticism of the distinction between "property" and "status" cases, see Wasserman, "Parents, Partners, and Personal Jurisdiction," 1995 U.Ill.L.Rev. 813.

b. REFORMULATION OF MINIMUM CONTACTS?

p. 269

NOTES AND QUESTIONS ON ASAHI AND THE POSSIBLE REFORMULATION OF "MINIMUM CONTACTS"

7. In Lesnick v. Hollingsworth & Vose Co., 35 F.3d 939 (4th Cir.1994), the estate of a cigarette smoker who died of cancer brought suit in federal court in Maryland against the cigarette manufacturer and the manufacturer of the filter attached to the cigarette. The filter manufacturer, Hollingsworth and Vose, contested *in personam* jurisdiction. The decedent had consistently smoked Kent brand cigarettes from the early 1950s to the early 1970s. He lived in Maryland and purchased and smoked most of his cigarettes in Maryland. The filter in question was the "Micronite Filter," which had formed an important part of the advertising campaign and brand identity of Kent cigarettes. According to the complaint, the filter contained asbestos between 1952 and 1956.

Defendant Hollingsworth and Vose manufactured the filters in Massachusetts and shipped them to cigarette factories owned by the cigarette manufacturer in New Jersey and Kentucky. Finished cigarettes from these two factories were shipped all over the United States, including to Maryland. Hollingsworth and Vose cooperated in various ways with the cigarette manufacturer in the development of the filter, and the manufacturer agreed to indemnify Hollingsworth and Vose for any liability arising out of harmful effects of the filter. The Maryland long-arm statute asserted *in personam* jurisdiction to the maximum extent permitted under the due process clause.

The Court of Appeals held that mere placing of the filter in the stream of commerce was not enough to satisfy due process, and that the cooperation between Hollingsworth and Vose was not enough " 'additional conduct.' " The totality of Hollingsworth and Vose's conduct did not "rise to the level of establishing jurisdiction because none of the conduct is in any way directed *toward the state of Maryland*." at 946–47 (emph. in orig.). Is this holding consistent with *Gray v. American Radiator* (p. 268, n. 2 in the casebook)?

8. The *Asahi* "reasonableness" factors were applied to deny jurisdiction in a general jurisdiction case in Metropolitan Life Ins. Co. v. Robertson–Ceco Corp., 84 F.3d 560 (2d Cir.1996). (Recall that both *Asahi* and *Burger King* were specific jurisdiction cases.) Metropolitan Life Insurance (Met Life) sued Robertson–Ceco based on alleged misrepresentations and faulty "curtain walls" supplied for a building constructed for Met Life in Miami, Florida. Met Life is a New York corporation with its principal place of business in New York. Robinson–Ceco is a Delaware corporation with its principal place of business in Pennsylvania. Met Life filed suit in federal District Court in Vermont because the Vermont statute of limitations was longer than other states'. The Court of Appeals held that Robinson–Ceco had sufficient minimum contacts with Vermont, based on $4 million in Vermont sales over a 6–year period, on relationships with a network of dealers in Vermont, on advertising, and on other factors. Based on *Asahi*, the court nevertheless held that it was unreasonable to assert jurisdiction:

Plaintiff, a non-resident suing on a cause of action that arose in Florida, has no interest in the lawsuit proceeding in Vermont. No witness or other evidence is located in Vermont, and defendant is a non-resident.... Florida, the locus of the alleged tort, and New York, plaintiff's domicile, have far more significant interests in resolving the dispute.

at 573.

9. Personal jurisdiction over companies doing business on the Internet has been a fruitful source of recent litigation. Recent cases include:

(1) In Panavision International v. Toeppen, 141 F.3d 1316 (9th Cir. 1998), defendant Toeppen, an Illinois domiciliary, registered "domain names" of over 100 well-known companies such as Delta Airlines, Neiman Marcus, Eddie Bauer, Lufthansa and Panavision with the central Internet registry maintained by Network Solutions, Inc. When plaintiff Panavision attempted to register on the Internet as Panavision.com it was informed that Toeppen had already registered that name. Panavision's counsel wrote a letter from California to Toeppen informing him that Panavision was a registered trademark and requesting that he cease using it as a domain name. Toeppen responded in a letter to California, offering to "settle" the matter if Panavision would pay him $13,000. When Panavision refused, Toeppen registered another Panavision trademark, "Panaflex" as a domain name. Panavision then brought suit in federal district court in California under federal trademark law and California "anti-dilution" law. The Court of Appeals upheld personal jurisdiction over Toeppen, finding that he had "purposefully availed himself of the privilege of conducting activities" in California and that the claims arose out of those activities.

(2) In Cybersell, Inc. v. Cybersell, Inc., 130 F.3d 414 (9th Cir.1997), defendant Cybersell FL operated an "essentially passive" web site in Florida, advertising consulting services for marketing on the web. Plaintiff Cybersell AZ, who operated a website in Arizona offering largely the same services, brought suit for trademark infringement and other wrongs in federal District Court in Arizona. Defendant Cybersell FL had no 800 telephone number; received no telephone calls from Arizona; made no sales in Arizona; and sent no messages to Arizona. The only message it received over the Internet from Arizona was from plaintiff Cybersell AZ. The court held that Cybersell FL's did not have "minimum contacts" because there was no "purposeful availment" of the privilege of conducting activities in Arizona. "Otherwise," wrote the court, "every complaint arising out of alleged trademark infringement on the Internet would automatically result in personal jurisdiction wherever the plaintiff's principal place of business is located." at 420.

(3) In Bensusan Restaurant Corp. v. King, 126 F.3d 25 (2d Cir.1997), defendant owned and operated a jazz club named "The Blue Note" in Columbus, Missouri. Plaintiff owned and operated a jazz club of the same name in New York City. Defendant created a website for its Missouri jazz club containing the following: "The Blue Note's Cyberspot should not be confused with one of the world's finest jazz club[s] Blue Note, located in the heart of New York's Greenwich Village. If you should ever find yourself in the big apple give them a visit." This was followed by a hyperlink allowing a

computer user to connect to a website maintained by plaintiff. After complaint by plaintiff, defendant changed the text to read: "The Blue Note, Columbia, Missouri should not be confused in any way, shape, or form with Blue Note Records or the jazz club, Blue Note, located in New York. The Cyberspot is created to provide information for Columbia, Missouri area individuals only[.]" Plaintiff brought suit in federal District Court in New York alleging trademark violation and unfair competition. The Court of Appeals held that defendant did not have sufficient contacts to satisfy New York's long-arm statute, which asserts jurisdiction over out-of-state defendants who commit wrongful acts having consequences within the state and who, in addition, derive substantial revenue from interstate commerce. NYCPLR § 302(a)(3).

(4) In CompuServe, Inc. v. Patterson, 89 F.3d 1257 (6th Cir.1996), Patterson, a resident of Texas, entered into a "Shareware Registration Agreement" with CompuServe, a computer information service headquartered in Ohio. Patterson transmitted 32 master software files to CompuServe. CompuServe subscribers could then download this software onto their own computers and, if they chose, could pay Patterson. Patterson sold $650 worth of software to subscribers in Ohio through this mechanism, and an undisclosed amount to subscribers in other states. When CompuServe began marketing a software product similar to one provided by Patterson, Patterson objected on grounds of common law trademark violation. CompuServe brought suit in federal District Court in Ohio for a declaratory judgment that it had not violated Patterson's rights. The court held that there was a prima facie case of jurisdiction because "Patterson purposefully availed himself of the privilege of doing business in Ohio. He knowingly reached out to CompuServe's Ohio home, and he benefitted from CompuServe's handling of his software and the fees it generated." at 1266–67.

(5) In Inset Systems, Inc. v. Instruction Set, Inc., 937 F.Supp. 161 (D.Conn.1996), Inset registered its name as a federal trademark. Sometime later, Instruction Set obtained "inset.com" as its Internet address and a toll-free telephone number of 1–800–US–INSET. Inset and Instruction Set are both in the business of providing software and/or computer support. Inset is located in Connecticut, and Instruction Set is located in Massachusetts. Instruction Set has no office and no employees in Connecticut. Customers can contact Instruction Set via the Internet, and there are over 10,000 Internet users in Connecticut. In a trademark infringement suit brought in federal District Court in Connecticut by Inset, the court upheld jurisdiction: Instruction Set "directed its advertising activities via the Internet and its toll-free number not to only the state of Connecticut, but to all states. . . . [Instruction Set] has therefore purposefully availed itself of the privilege of doing business within Connecticut." at 165.

There is a growing academic literature on personal jurisdiction in Internet cases. See, e.g., Perritt, "Jurisdiction in Cyberspace," 41 Vill.L.Rev. 1 (1996); "From the Internet to Court: Exercising Jurisdiction over World Wide Communications," 65 Fordham L.Rev. 2241 (1997); Note, "The Presence of a Web Site as a Constitutionally Permissible Basis for Personal

Jurisdiction," 73 Ind.L.Rev. 297 (1997); Note, "If the International Shoe Fits, Wear It: Applying Traditional Personal Jurisdiction Analysis to Cyberspace in *CompuServe, Inc. v. Patterson*," 42 Vill.L.Rev. 1213 (1997).

10. For a useful long-term perspective on personal jurisdiction, see Symposium, "Fifty Years of *International Shoe:* The Past and Future of Personal Jurisdiction," 28 U.C.Davis L.Rev. 513 (1995).

c. NOTICE

p. 286

NOTE ON SERVICE OF PROCESS

1. Mechanics of service of process. a. Federal District Court. (1) Service on individuals. (a) Personal service. (b) "Dwelling house or usual place of abode".

Rabbi Weiss tried again. (See Weiss v. Glemp, 792 F.Supp. 215 (S.D.N.Y.1992), p. 282 in the casebook.) In Weiss v. Glemp, 127 Wash.2d 726, 903 P.2d 455 (1995), Archbishop Glemp made a three-day visit to Seattle. Rabbi Weiss filed suit in a Washington state court and attempted to serve process. A process server, accompanied by a Polish interpreter, came to the rectory where Glemp was staying. A priest came to the door and said that Glemp was having breakfast and asked them to return later. After waiting about two hours for Glemp to emerge, the process server went to a window through which he could see Glemp about four feet away. He yelled, "Jozef Glemp, Oficjaline dostracham [official documents]! Jozef Glemp, you have been served!" Glemp turned to look at the process server who then placed the documents on the sill outside the window.

The Washington Supreme Court held that such service did not comply with Washington State's service of process rules (which parallel the relevant federal rules). The court held that the process server had not served Glemp "personally." Further, without deciding whether a three-day stay qualified the rectory as a "place of abode," the court held that the process server had not left the documents with "some person of suitable age and discretion."

2a. Statutes of limitations and service of process in suits based on federal law.

Fed.R.Civ.P. 3 provides that a suit is "commenced" in federal court by filing a complaint. Rule 4(m) provides that service of process must be made is made within 120 days of filing the complaint.

a. Federal Rules operate as a tolling rule in federal cases. In suits based on federal law, Rules 3 and 4(m) operate together to provide the tolling rule. If a complaint is filed and service of process is accomplished within the period prescribed by Rule 4(m), the statute of limitations is tolled as of the date of filing the complaint. West v. Conrail, 481 U.S. 35, 107 S.Ct. 1538, 95 L.Ed.2d 32 (1987). (In suits based on state law, by contrast, Rules 3 and 4(m) do not provide the tolling rule. In such suits, state tolling rules are followed. Walker v. Armco Steel Corp., 446 U.S. 740, 100 S.Ct. 1978, 64 L.Ed.2d 659 (1980). See discussion, casebook p. 286 and 532–533.)

b. 120–day period under Rule 4(m). Rule 4(m) provides a 120–day period after filing within which the complaint must be served. If "good cause" is shown for a failure to serve within 120 days, "the court shall extend the time for an appropriate period." Even if good cause is not shown, the court may, in its discretion, extend the period beyond 120 days. Espinoza v. United States, 52 F.3d 838 (10th Cir.1995); Petrucelli v. Bohringer & Ratzinger, GMBH, 46 F.3d 1298 (3d Cir.1995).

d. LONG–ARM STATUTES

1. STATE LONG–ARM STATUTES

p. 296

NOTES AND QUESTIONS

5. Injury under New York's long-arm statute compared to injury under the due process clause. The definition of "injury" used in *American Eutectic* is based on New York's long-arm statute rather than on the due process clause of the Constitution. Compare Janmark, Inc. v. Reidy, 132 F.3d 1200 (7th Cir.1997), a suit in federal District Court in Illinois. The parties were business competitors who both sold mini-shopping carts throughout the United States. Defendant Reidy, a California corporation, made a telephone call to a New Jersey customer of plaintiff Janmark, an Illinois corporation, alleging copyright infringement by Janmark. As a result of the call, the New Jersey customer canceled its order with Janmark. The Illinois long-arm statute asserts jurisdiction as far as the due process clause permits. The Court of Appeals held that the cancellation of the order, with adverse financial consequences in Illinois, was sufficient injury to allow assertion of jurisdiction in Illinois.

6. New York DES cases. In a pair of mass tort product liability cases, a federal District Court and a state appellate court in New York have found *in personam* jurisdiction based on a "market share" theory. Plaintiffs claimed damage resulting from exposure to the drug DES while in utero. DES is synthetic form of estrogen that was routinely given during the 1950s and 1960s to prevent miscarriages. DES was effective for this purpose, but caused a number of disorders in female children born to women who took the drug. Use of DES was approved by the Food and Drug Administration beginning in 1947. Its use was disapproved in 1971 after the side effects had become apparent.

New York allocates liability in mass tort product liability cases based on a market share theory. Hymowitz v. Eli Lilly and Co., 73 N.Y.2d 487, 541 N.Y.S.2d 941, 539 N.E.2d 1069, cert. denied 493 U.S. 944, 110 S.Ct. 350, 107 L.Ed.2d 338 (1989). Assuming there is *in personam* jurisdiction, a defendant manufacturer owes damages to a defendant based on the defendant's national market share. For example, if a defendant manufacturer in a DES case had a 3 percent share of the national market at the time plaintiff's mother ingested the drug, it is liable for 3 percent of plaintiff's damages. It is unnecessary to show that any of the defendant's product was actually sold or ingested in New York.

a. *Federal District Court decision*. In In re DES Cases, 789 F.Supp. 552 (E.D.N.Y.1992), appeal dismissed 7 F.3d 20 (2d Cir.1993), jurisdictional objections were raised by two defendants.

The Boehringer defendant: Defendant Boehringer is a Delaware corporation with its principal place of business in Connecticut. It has been licensed to do business in New York since its inception. It markets its products (which have never included DES) in all 50 states. Boehringer merged with Stayner Corp. in 1979 and because of the merger became responsible for all Stayner's liabilities. Stayner manufactured DES tablets in California and sold them four western states between 1949 and 1971. Stayner was never licensed to do business in New York, never maintained an office in New York, never solicited business in New York, and never shipped DES to New York.

The court held that Boehringer was subject to general jurisdiction in New York. It then applied New York substantive law to liabilities incurred by Stayner and assumed by Boehringer under the merger.

The Boyle defendant: Defendant Boyle is a closely held California corporation. It manufactured DES in California between 1949 and 1960 and sold it only in states west of the Mississippi River. Boyle's national market share in DES sales was less than 0.5% during this period. Boyle has never been licensed to do business in New York, has never maintained an office or agent in New York, has never advertised in New York, and has neither shipped DES to New York nor sold it there.

The court applied the New York long-arm statute, which provides for *in personam* jurisdiction over

> any non-domiciliary ... who in person or through an agent ... commits a tortious act without the state causing injury to person or property within the state ... if he ... (ii) expects or should reasonably expect the act to have consequences in the state and derives substantial revenue from interstate or international commerce.

N.Y.C.P.L.R. § 302(a)(3)(ii). The court held that in a mass tort case, it is unnecessary under the New York statute for a plaintiff to show that she has been injured by the conduct of the particular defendant. It is enough that she has been injured by the product manufactured by the defendant, and that the defendant have some share of the national market in the product.

The court then applied the due process clause of the Fourteenth Amendment. "[I]nquiry into the defendant's territorial contacts with the forum takes the form of an inquiry into the forum state's interest in the litigation and the defendant's relative ability to mount a defense in the forum without undergoing substantial hardship." at 593. The court found that New York had a substantial interest in the litigation and that the burden on defendant Boyle of litigating in New York was not great:

> In presenting its defense, Boyle continues to benefit from economies of scale, a feature of mass tort litigation.... For pre-trial motions including this one, Boyle has properly joined in the motions of other defendants rather than submitting duplicative papers. At trial a central issue

for all of the defendants will be market share. Boyle will in all likelihood not present evidence on any other issue and will rely on counsel for co-defendants to handle other matters. ... Moreover, ... most corporate defendants' litigation costs are paid by national or international insurance companies. There is no indication here that insurance coverage has been exhausted.

at 593. The court concluded that the assertion of *in personam* jurisdiction over Boyle did not violate due process.

b. *New York appellate court decision.* In a separate case, the New York Supreme Court, Appellate Division, upheld *in personam* jurisdiction over Boyle. In re New York County DES Litigation, 202 A.D.2d 6, 615 N.Y.S.2d 882 (1994). The court relied in part on the "long and scholarly opinion" of the federal District Court in *In re DES Cases*, but the factual basis for its conclusion was different in two respects. First, by Boyle's admission, Boyle's market share was 3% rather than 0.5%. Second, Boyle was instrumental in bringing DES to the national market:

> Boyle was one of twelve manufacturers that filed New Drug Applications for permission to market diethylstilbestrol [DES] for use in pregnancy. It and a small number of other pharmaceutical companies were instrumental in getting FDA approval to market DES despite the well known fact that substances given to pregnant women would pass through the placenta into the fetus. In fact, ... as early as 1939, it was shown the administration of DES on rats and mice had malforming effects on the fetus.... Thus, Boyle, by its acts, together with other manufacturers, affirmatively interposed itself into the New York market and "should [have] reasonably expect[ed] the act to have consequences in the state" of New York (CPLR 302(a)(3)(ii)).

at 885.

Was the federal District Court correct in upholding jurisdiction over Boehringer? Over Boyle? Was the New York appellate court correct in upholding jurisdiction over Boyle on the somewhat different factual basis?

7. New York medical treatment case. In Ingraham v. Carroll, 90 N.Y.2d 592, 665 N.Y.S.2d 10, 687 N.E.2d 1293 (1997), defendant was a physician practicing and living in Bennington, Vermont, near the border with New York. Defendant treated plaintiff's wife, a resident of New York, pursuant to a referral by her New York physician. After the death of his wife from cancer, plaintiff brought suit in New York alleging that defendant had been too slow in diagnosing the disease. Although defendant was licenced to practice medicine in New York and saw a number of New York patients referred to him in the same manner as plaintiff's wife had been, defendant saw patients and performed surgery only in Vermont. The Court of Appeals was willing to assume that defendant's conduct "caused injury within New York" as required by NYCPLR § 302(a)(3). But it found that he neither did nor solicited business in New York, § 302(a)(3)(i), nor derived substantial revenue from interstate commerce, § 302(a)(3)(ii). If the New York long-arm statute asserted jurisdiction as far as the due process clause permits, would jurisdiction over defendant have been proper?

8. Maryland hospital case. In Presbyterian University Hospital v. Wilson, 337 Md. 541, 654 A.2d 1324 (1995), Hugh Wilson, a resident of Maryland, was diagnosed as needing a liver transplant. His Maryland doctor called the head of the transplant service at the Presbyterian University Hospital (PUH) in Pittsburgh, Pennsylvania, informing him of Wilson's condition and of Wilson's so-far unsuccessful efforts to obtain insurance covering the transplant. The PUH doctor agreed to admit Wilson despite the lack of coverage. When Wilson arrived, he was refused admission to the hospital because of lack of insurance, but PUH arranged for him to stay at a hostel connected to PUH. Wilson died 11 days after arriving in Pennsylvania while his wife was trying to arrange for insurance under the Maryland Medical Assistance Program (MA).

Wilson's widow sued PUH in Maryland state court for, inter alia, negligence, negligent misrepresentation, breach of contract, and wrongful death. The Court of Appeals of Maryland sustained jurisdiction as consistent with federal due process:

> PUH purposefully availed itself of the benefits and protections of the State of Maryland through its registration as a Maryland MA provider and its designation as a transplant referral center. These contacts were the reasons for Mr. Wilson going to PUH to seek treatment. ... [I]n inviting and arranging for Mr. Wilson to come to PUH, in convincing him to remain in Pennsylvania, and in initiating discussions regarding coverage for Mr. Wilson with various insurance providers in Maryland, PUH established contacts with the State of Maryland which are directly related to the present cause of action.

at 1335.

9. Hong Kong hotel case. In Nowak v. Tak How Investments, Ltd., 94 F.3d 708 (1st Cir.1996), Tak How was a Hong Kong corporation whose sole asset was a Holiday Inn in Hong Kong. The Holiday Inn entered into an arrangement with a Massachusetts corporation under which it agreed to give special rates to employees of that corporation staying at the hotel. In addition, the Holiday Inn advertised in publications, some of which circulated in Massachusetts; and it sent direct mail solicitations to previous hotel guests, some of whom lived in Massachusetts. The wife of one of the corporate employees accompanied her husband on a business trip to Hong Kong and drowned in the hotel swimming pool. In a wrongful death suit filed in Massachusetts, the federal District Court held that Tak How was subject to jurisdiction under the Massachusetts long-arm statute asserting jurisdiction over a case based on "a cause of action ... arising from the person's ... transacting any business" in Massachusetts.

2. FEDERAL LONG-ARM STATUTES

p. 303

NOTES AND QUESTIONS

4a. Pendent personal jurisdiction. A few Courts of Appeals have held that if a plaintiff brings suit under a federal law that authorizes nationwide jurisdiction, "pendent personal jurisdiction" may be exercised over the defendant to decide a joined state law claim even if there are insufficient minimum contacts with the state forum to justify trying the state law claim alone. "Since the court has personal jurisdiction over the defendants [based on nationwide service of process for the federal claim], we can find no constitutional bar to requiring the defendants to defend the entire constitutional case, which includes both federal and state claims arising from the same nucleus of facts, so long as the federal claim is not wholly immaterial or insubstantial." ESAB Group, Inc. v. Centricut, Inc., 126 F.3d 617, 629 (4th Cir.1997). See also IUE AFL–CIO Pension Fund v. Herrmann, 9 F.3d 1049, 1056 (2d Cir.1993); Oetiker v. Jurid Werke, G.m.b.H., 556 F.2d 1, 4–5 (D.C.Cir.1977).

5. Federal Rule of Civil Procedure 4

Please replace the last paragraph on p. 303 with the following:

Rule 4 is directed both to the manner of service of process and to the assertion of *in personam* jurisdiction. Under the Rule as it existed when *Omni Capital* was decided, 4(e) directed the federal courts to follow the state long-arm statute in the absence of a federal statute or rule authorizing broader jurisdiction. ("service may * * * be made under the circumstances and in the manner prescribed in the [state] statute or rule"). The disparate and somewhat incomplete provisions of the old Rule 4, including 4(e), were renumbered and fleshed out in new Rule 4(k), adopted December 1, 1993.

Rule 4(k)(1) establishes the basic framework for exercising territorial jurisdiction over defendants found within the United States. 4(k)(1)(A) provides that the reach of the state's territorial jurisdiction governs in the absence of a contrary federal statute or rule. 4(k)(1)(B) provides that third-party defendants impleaded under Fed.R.Civ.P. 14 and additional parties needed for just adjudication under Rule 19 are subject to *in personam* jurisdiction in federal court, provided they can be served with process within 100 miles of the federal courthouse from which the summons is issued. This so-called "bulge" jurisdiction is available in federal question cases, diversity cases, and any other cases over which the federal court has subject matter jurisdiction. 4(k)(1)(C) and (D) indicate that the federal interpleader statute, and other unspecified federal statutes, authorize *in personam* jurisdiction. Rule 4(k)(2) provides for territorial jurisdiction over defendants found outside the United States. Note how restricted 4(k)(2) is. It allows nationwide aggregation of contacts for purposes of assertion of jurisdiction over a foreign defendant, but only in cases where the claim arises under federal law, and only where there is no state that can exercise jurisdiction over that defendant.

f. CONSENT TO JURISDICTION

2. CONSENT BY CONTRACT

p. 349

NOTES AND QUESTIONS

1. *Carnival Cruise Lines,* **continued.** Congress has revised, and then re-revised, the relevant statute. After the first revision in 1992, the statute read as follows:

> It shall be unlawful for the manager, agent, master or owner of any vessel transporting passengers between ports of the United States or between any such port and a foreign port to insert in any ... contract, or agreement any provision or limitation ... purporting ... to lessen, weaken, or avoid the right of any claimant to a trial by *any* court of competent jurisdiction on the question of liability for such loss or injury, or the measure of damages therefor.

46 U.S.C. § 183c. When *Carnival Cruise Lines* was decided, the italicized word "any" was not in the statute. The Supreme Court held that the statute, as it then read, did not forbid a forum selection clause limiting suit to a particular court of competent jurisdiction. After *Carnival Cruise Lines,* "any" was added to forbid such a clause.

In the second revision, in 1993, "any" was removed. Prior to the passage of the bill removing the word, Representative Studds of Massachusetts explained the bill as it went to the House from Senate:

> [The Senate bill's removal of "any"] clarif[ies] that the tort action cannot be brought in just any district court of the United States, but must be filed in a court located in a district in which the vessel owner is doing business, the vessel is operating, or where the passenger boarded the vessel. For this reason, the word "any" has been deleted. We do not intend by this amendment to restore the standard set by the Supreme Court in its 1991 decision Carnival Cruise Lines versus Shute.

139 Cong. Rec. H10939 (Nov. 22, 1993). After the passage of the amendment, Senator Stevens of Alaska, Senator Breaux of Louisiana, and Senator Hollings of South Carolina took issue with Representative Studd's explanation. They contended that the Senate's removal of "any" was intended precisely to restore the result in *Carnival Cruise Lines.* 140 Cong. Rec. S1847–8 (Feb. 24, 1994).

From the degree of Congressional attention, it is apparent that forum selection clauses are very important to the cruise ship industry. This is more than a fuss over a single word. Recall that Professor Purcell described forum selection clauses as "a substantial obstacle to suit and a powerful force pressing [individuals] to abandon their claims or to discount them substantially." Casebook, p. 349.

A series of cases in the federal District Court for the Eastern District of Louisiana holds that the removal of "any" has restored the result in *Carnival Cruise Lines.* See, e.g., Smith v. Doe, 991 F.Supp. 781 (E.D.La. 1998); Launey v. Carnival Corp., 1997 WL 426095 (E.D.La.1997); Compagno v. Commodore Cruise Line, 1994 WL 462997 (E.D.La.1994). No other District Court appears to have addressed the question.

1a. Economic analysis of forum-selection clauses in consumer contracts. Recall that in *Carnival Cruise Lines* the Supreme Court wrote, "[I]t stands to reason that passengers who purchase tickets containing a forum clause like that at issue in this case benefit in the form of reduced fares reflecting the savings that the cruise line enjoys by limiting the fora in which it may be sued." Casebook, p. 344. Does this really "stand to reason"? How does the Court know that ticket prices in the cruise ship business are cost-driven rather than demand-driven? Further, how does it know that cruise passengers would willingly trade a forum-selection clause for whatever price reduction might result from the clause? Professors Carrington and Haagen write, "This benefit stands to reason only if one makes assumptions that are demonstrably false. The term is not negotiated, the specific market is not competitive, the issue of forum choice is of trivial importance to an individual passenger ex ante, and the unadvised passenger cannot be expected to assign a suitable value to the clause; hence, the savings resulting from the enforcement of the clause went straight to the bottom line of Carnival Lines." Carrington and Haagen, "Contract and Jurisdiction," 1996 Sup.Ct.Rev. 331, 355–56. In a recent case involving a forum-selection clause contained in a passenger cruise ship ticket, Judge Guido Calabresi wrote, "A preliminary analysis leads me to think that upholding forum-selection clauses like the one involved in this case makes very little economic sense. Were we writing on a clean slate, I would want to examine the issue with great care before deciding whether we should do so." Effron v. Sun Line Cruises, Inc., 67 F.3d 7 (2d Cir.1995) (Calabresi, J., concurring).

B. SUBJECT MATTER JURISDICTION

2. FEDERAL COURTS

a. FEDERAL QUESTION JURISDICTION

p. 405

FURTHER NOTE ON 28 U.S.C. § 1331

In Berg v. Leason, 32 F.3d 422 (9th Cir.1994), plaintiff sued for malicious prosecution under California law, basing subject matter jurisdiction on § 1331. To make out a successful claim for malicious prosecution, a plaintiff must show that an earlier suit was brought by the now-defendant against the now-plaintiff without "probable cause" and with malice, and that the earlier suit was terminated on the merits against the now-defendant. Plaintiff in *Berg* contended that defendants had previously filed a malicious suit under the federal Security and Exchange Act and under the federal Racketeer Influenced and Corrupt Organization (RICO) Act. The "probable cause" determination in a malicious prosecution suit is made by determining whether the underlying causes of action in the first suit were legally tenable. Those causes of action were federal, but the Court of Appeals nevertheless declined to find federal question jurisdiction under § 1331: "[T]he task of deciding whether an underlying federal claim was legally tenable does not raise a substantial federal question of federal law." at 425.

Did the Court of Appeals in *Berg* properly apply *Merrell Dow*?

b. DIVERSITY JURISDICTION

p. 411–414

NOTE ON *MAS v. PERRY* AND ASSORTED PROBLEMS OF DIVERSITY JURISDICTION

1. Citizenship

c. Complete diversity. In a diversity case brought under 28 U.S.C. § 1332(a)(3), where citizens of different states are on both sides of the dispute, the additional presence of alien parties on both sides does not defeat complete diversity. Dresser Industries, Inc. v. Underwriters at Lloyd's of London, 106 F.3d 494 (3d Cir.1997). For a thorough discussion of diversity jurisdiction based on alienage, see Johnson, "Why Alienage Jurisdiction? Historical Foundations and Modern Justifications for Federal Jurisdiction over Disputes Involving Noncitizens," 21 Yale J.Int'l L. 1 (1996).

3. Amount in controversy. Effective January, 1997, the amount in controversy in diversity cases was increased to $75,000. Pub.L. 104–317, 110 Stat. 3850 (Oct. 19, 1996).

c. Aggregation of claims. For a useful description of the rules government aggregation and a proposed statute see Rensberger, "The Amount in Controversy: Understanding the Rules of Aggregation," 26 Ariz.St.L.J. 925 (1994).

5. Probate and domestic relations. Consider the following views on the domestic relations exception to diversity jurisdiction:

> [R]ecognizing the increasing federalization of family law as well as past discrimination against these issues, federal courts should treat family law cases like any other diversity cases. ... Domestic relations issues are of paramount importance to the litigants who bring these cases; these litigants deserve as much respect as litigants in any other diversity case.

Cahn, "Family Law, Federalism, and the Federal Courts," 79 Iowa L.Rev. 1073, 1126 (1994).

> Women and the families they sometimes inhabit are not only assumed to be outside the federal courts, they are also assumed not to be related to the "national issues" to which the federal judiciary is to devote its interests. Jurisdictional lines have not been drawn according to the laws of nature by men, who today are seeking to confirm their prestige as members of the most important judiciary in the country. ... Dealing with women—in and out of families, arguing about federal statutory rights of relatively small value—is not how they want to frame their job.

Resnik, " 'Naturally' without Gender: Women, Jurisdiction, and the Federal Courts," 66 N.Y.U.L.Rev. 1682, 1749 (1991). Do you agree?

For an argument in favor of a special category of "*Akenbrandt* abstention," under which federal courts would have jurisdiction but would abstain from deciding "core" domestic relations cases and, in addition, cases raising difficult questions of unresolved state law, see Stein, "The Domestic Relations Exception to Federal Jurisdiction: Rethinking an Unsettled Federal Courts Doctrine," 36 Boston Coll.L.Rev. 669 (1995).

c. SUPPLEMENTAL JURISDICTION

p. 433, 434

NOTE ON SUPPLEMENTAL JURISDICTION

5. Structure of the supplemental jurisdiction statute. c. When jurisdiction may be declined. When the criteria governing remand given in § 1367(c) are inconsistent with those given in *UMW v. Gibbs,* the criteria of § 1367(c) control. Executive Software North America, Inc. v. United States District Court, 24 F.3d 1545 (9th Cir.1994). If neither party requests remand of state-law claims to state court under § 1367(c), the District Court is not required to remand sua sponte. Acri v. Varian Assoc., Inc., 114 F.3d 999 (9th Cir.1997); Myers v. County of Lake, 30 F.3d 847 (7th Cir.), cert. den., 513 U.S. 1058, 115 S.Ct. 666, 130 L.Ed.2d 600 (1994).

7. Proposed revision of § 1367. The American Law Institute, under the direction of Professor John Oakley, has embarked on a Federal Judicial Code Revision Project that will propose revisions to the federal jurisdictional statutes, including § 1367.

8. On beyond § 1367. The American Law Institute has made far-reaching proposals for efficient disposition of complex litigation arising out of mass torts affecting many people in many states. American Law Institute, Complex Litigation: Statutory Recommendations and Analysis (1994). Among other things, the Institute has proposed that removal to federal court be permitted in state-law cases between non-diverse parties if another case arising out of "the same transaction, occurrence, or series of transactions or occurrences" is already in federal court. The proposal contemplates that the cases would thereafter be consolidated in federal court for disposition in a common proceeding. Id., at § 5.01(a). Would removal of such cases be constitutional? For analysis, see the Institute's proposal and Floyd, "The ALI, Supplemental Jurisdiction, and the Federal Constitutional Case," 1995 B.Y.U.L.Rev. 819.

p. 434, after Owen Equipment and Erection Co. v. Kroger and NOTE ON SUPPLEMENTAL JURISDICTION

FREE v. ABBOTT LABORATORIES

United States Court of Appeals for the Fifth Circuit, 1995.
51 F.3d 524.

HIGGINBOTHAM, CIRCUIT JUDGE:

This class action brought under the antitrust laws of the State of Louisiana requires that we decide whether the Judicial Improvements Act of 1990 overrules Zahn v. International Paper Co. 414 U.S. 291, 94 S.Ct. 505, 38 L.Ed.2d 511 (1973). We hold today that it does. We agree with the district court that the claims of the class representatives met the requisite amount in controversy and that it had diversity jurisdiction over their claims, but disagree with its decision to abstain from exercising it. We agree with the district court that it had supplemental jurisdiction over all other members of the class, but disagree with its decision not to exercise it. We vacate the order remanding to state court.

I.

Robin and Renee Free filed suit in a Louisiana state court on October 14, 1993, alleging that Abbott Laboratories, Bristol–Meyers Squibb Company, Inc., and Mead Johnson & Company had conspired to fix infant formula prices. The Frees filed for themselves and for a class of Louisiana consumers. Defendants removed to federal court, and plaintiffs moved to remand.

The federal district court granted the motion to remand. The court held that it lacked federal question jurisdiction and that it had diversity jurisdiction only over the named plaintiffs' claims and not over claims of the other members of the class. The district court declined to exercise supplemental jurisdiction because the claims raised "novel issues of state law."

The district court remanded the named plaintiffs' claims on "the basis of ... the Colorado River/Moses H. Cone doctrine of abstention." [2] It did so to avoid piecemeal litigation and to permit Louisiana to rule on the "novel and complex issues of state law." Defendants both appeal and petition for mandamus, asking that we vacate the order remanding to state court.

II.

28 U.S.C. § 1447(d) shields from review orders remanding for lack of subject matter jurisdiction, see In re Shell Oil Co., 932 F.2d 1518,

2. Colorado River Water Conservation Dist. v. United States, 424 U.S. 800, 96 S.Ct. 1236, 47 L.Ed.2d 483 (1976); Moses H. Cone Memorial Hosp. v. Mercury Constr. Corp., 460 U.S. 1, 103 S.Ct. 927, 74 L.Ed.2d 765 (1983).

1520 (5th Cir.1991), cert. denied, 502 U.S. 1049, 112 S.Ct. 914, 116 L.Ed.2d 814 (1992), or a defect in removal procedure noted by timely motion, see In re Medscope Marine Ltd., 972 F.2d 107, 110 (5th Cir. 1992). See Thermtron Prods. Inc. v. Hermansdorfer, 423 U.S. 336, 96 S.Ct. 584, 46 L.Ed.2d 542 (1976).

Fairly read, the remand order did not rest upon a lack of subject matter jurisdiction or defective removal procedure. The court noted no flaw in the removal procedure, and its decision to abstain follows an explicit finding of subject matter jurisdiction. Our appellate jurisdiction follows. * * *

III. Diversity and Supplemental Jurisdiction

A. Diversity Jurisdiction: The Named Plaintiffs' Claims

The court found it had diversity jurisdiction over the named plaintiffs' claims even though each named and unnamed plaintiff claimed only $20,000, less than the $50,000 minimum for diversity jurisdiction. 28 U.S.C. § 1332(a). The district court found that Louisiana law attributed all of a class's attorney's fees to the named plaintiffs. It held that the claim of the named plaintiffs for $20,000—once swelled by attorney's fees—met the $50,000 amount-in-controversy requirement.

Plaintiffs argue that Louisiana statutes distribute the fees pro rata to all members of the class, with the result that none meets the amount-in-controversy requirement. * * *

We disagree. Defendants pay attorney's fees and damages. The plain text of the first sentence of [Article 595 of the Louisiana Code of Civil Procedure] awards the fees to the "representative parties." * * *

Finally, plaintiffs argue that construing Article 595 to attribute the fees to the named plaintiffs—rather than to distribute them among all the plaintiffs—renders the statute unconstitutional. The argument continues that the federal courts have generally held that Zahn forbids attributing the fees of class members to class representatives. The only circuit court to speak to this question held that attributing a class's attorney's fees only to the named plaintiffs instead of pro rata to each member of the class "would conflict with the policy of Zahn." Goldberg v. CPC Int'l, Inc., 678 F.2d 1365, 1367 (9th Cir.), cert. denied, 459 U.S. 945, 103 S.Ct. 259, 74 L.Ed.2d 202 (1982). Many district courts have followed Goldberg. But Goldberg's reading of Zahn sheds little light on the distinct policy choices behind Louisiana's decision regarding rights of recovery by class members. That a state chooses a set of rules that result in an award in excess of $50,000 frustrates no policy of Zahn. Simply put, under the law of Louisiana the class representatives were entitled to fees. Their rights of recovery were not created by a judge's summing the discrete rights of class members. The district court applied the law of Louisiana. Because it did so, we are persuaded that the individual claims of the class representatives met the requisite jurisdictional amount. We turn now to the question of supplemental jurisdiction over the class members, confronting at its threshold Zahn's current vitality. That is the question of Zahn.

B. Supplemental Jurisdiction: The Unnamed Plaintiffs' Claims

Supplemental jurisdiction over the unnamed plaintiffs' claims has been an open question since Congress passed the Judicial Improvements Act of 1990.

Congress enacted § 1367 against the background of Zahn, in which the Supreme Court had held that the claim of each member of a class action must meet the amount-in-controversy requirement. Zahn, 414 U.S. at 301. Zahn forbade the exercise of supplemental jurisdiction over the claims of class members who did not do so.

Defendants argue that Congress changed the jurisdictional landscape in 1990 by enacting § 1367. Section 1367(a) grants district courts supplemental jurisdiction over related claims generally, and § 1367(b) carves exceptions. Significantly, class actions are not among the exceptions.

Some commentators have interpreted this silence to mean that Congress overruled Zahn and granted supplemental jurisdiction over the claims of class members who individually do not demand the necessary amount in controversy.[5] Some of § 1367's drafters disagree.[6] No appellate court has ruled on the question yet.[7] The district courts are split

---

5. See, e.g., 1 James W. Moore et al., Moore's Federal Practice, ¶ 0.97[5], at 928 (2d ed. 1994); 2 Herbert B. Newberg & Alba Conte, Newberg on Class Actions, § 6.11, at 6–48 (3d ed. 1992); Joan Steinman, Section 1367—Another Party Heard From, 41 Emory L.J. 85, 103 (1992); Thomas C. Arthur & Richard D. Freer, Grasping at Burnt Straws: The Disaster of the Supplemental Jurisdiction Statute, 40 Emory L.J. 963, 981 (1991).

6. See Thomas D. Rowe, Jr., Stephen B. Burbank, & Thomas M. Mengler, Compounding or Creating Confusion About Supplemental Jurisdiction? A Reply to Professor Freer, 40 Emory L.J. 943, 960 n.90 (1991). Professors Rowe, Burbank, and Mengler all had a hand in crafting the supplemental jurisdiction statute. See Rowe, et al., supra, 40 Emory L.J. at 949 n.27; H.R. Rep. No. 734, 101st Cong., 2d Sess. 27, reprinted in 1990 U.S.C.C.A.N. 6860, 6873 n.13.

7. This circuit has twice broached the question, but never answered it. In More v. Intelcon Support Servs., Inc., we noted that § 1367 might affect the Zahn rule, but declined to decide that because the action at issue had been filed before § 1367 took effect. See 960 F.2d 466, 473 (5th Cir. 1992). Later, in Watson v. Shell Oil Co., we reasoned that the Zahn rule would demand dismissal of class members' claims below the jurisdictional threshold. See 979 F.2d 1014, 1021 (5th Cir.1992). However, that case had been filed before § 1367 took effect, and the opinion makes no mention of that statute. See id. at 1021 & n.27. In any event, Watson has been vacated. When this court ordered the case reheard en banc, see 990 F.2d 805 (5th Cir.1993), the panel opinion in Watson was vacated, see 5th Cir. R. 35 (Internal Operating Procedure), and the en banc rehearing never occurred because the parties settled and the appeal was dismissed.

The Third Circuit is the only other circuit to have considered the question. In *Packard v. Provident Nat'l Bank*, the court noted the conflict among authorities on our question, but declined to resolve it. See 994 F.2d 1039, 1045–46 n. 9 (3d Cir.), cert. denied, ___ U.S. ___, 114 S.Ct. 440, 126 L.Ed.2d 373 (1993).

even within this circuit, although the majority appear to hold that Zahn survives the enactment of § 1367.[8]

Perhaps, by some measure transcending its language, Congress did not intend the Judicial Improvements Act to overrule Zahn. The House Committee on the Judiciary considered the bill that became § 1367 to be a "noncontroversial" collection of "relatively modest proposals," not the sort of legislative action that would upset any long-established precedent like Zahn. 1990 U.S.C.C.A.N. at 6861. Plaintiffs argue that the Act was prompted not by a congressional desire for wholesale revisions of the jurisdictional rules, but by the more limited desire to restore traditional understandings of federal jurisdiction, which were upset by Finley v. United States, 490 U.S. 545, 109 S.Ct. 2003, 104 L.Ed.2d 593 (1989). In Finley, the Supreme Court held that federal courts could not exercise pendent-party jurisdiction without an express legislative grant, a grant never thought necessary before. Id. at 556. In short, Congress intended the Act to "essentially restore the pre-Finley understandings of the authorization for and limits on other forms of supplemental jurisdiction," not, arguably, to alter Zahn. 1990 U.S.C.C.A.N. at 6874. A disclaimer in the legislative history strives to make this point clear by stating: "The section is not intended to affect the jurisdictional requirements of 28 U.S.C. § 1332 in diversity-only class actions, as those requirements were interpreted prior to Finley." 1990 U.S.C.C.A.N. at 6875. The passage cites Zahn as a pre-Finley case untouched by the Act. 1990 U.S.C.C.A.N. at 6875 n.17; see also Rowe et al., supra, 40 Emory L.J. at 960 n.90 (stating that this passage was intended to demonstrate that Zahn was to survive the enactment of § 1367).

We cannot search legislative history for congressional intent unless we find the statute unclear or ambiguous. Here, it is neither. The statute's first section vests federal courts with the power to hear supplemental claims generally, subject to limited exceptions set forth in the statute's second section. Class actions are not among the enumerated exceptions.

Omitting the class action from the exception may have been a clerical error.[9] But the statute is the sole repository of congressional

---

8. Compare Henkel v. ITT Bowest Corp., 872 F.Supp. 872 (D.Kan.1994)(holding that § 1367 did not overrule Zahn); Aspe Arquitectos, S.A. de C.V. v. Jamieson, 869 F.Supp. 593, 595 (N.D.Ill.1994)(same); Dirosa v. Grass, 1994 WL 583276 (E.D.La. 1994)(same); * * * with Lindsay v. Kvortek, 865 F.Supp. 264, 276 (W.D.Pa.1994)(determining that § 1367 supersedes Zahn; case did not involve class action); Patterson Enterprises, Inc. v. Bridgestone/Firestone, Inc., 812 F.Supp. 1152, 1154 (D.Kan.1993)(same); and Garza v. National Am. Ins. Co., 807 F.Supp. 1256, 1258 & n. 6 (M.D.La.1992)(same).

9. The impressive array of Professors Burbank, Mengler, and Rowe has observed that "it would have been better had the statute dealt explicitly with this problem, and the legislative history was an attempt to correct the oversight." Rowe et al., supra. 40 Emory L.J. at 960 n.90. They have noted that the supplemental jurisdiction statute is "not a perfect effort." Thomas D. Rowe, Jr., et al., A Coda on Supplemen-

intent where the statute is clear and does not demand an absurd result. See West Virginia Univ. Hosps., Inc. v. Casey, 499 U.S. 83, 111 S.Ct. 1138, 1147, 113 L.Ed.2d 68 (1991)(refusing to permit the Court's "perception of the 'policy' of the statute to overcome its 'plain language' "); United States v. X-Citement Video, Inc., ___ U.S. ___, 115 S.Ct. 464, 467–68, 130 L.Ed.2d 372 (1994)(rejecting lower court's "plain language reading" of a statute where that reading would create a "positively absurd" result). Abolishing the strictures of Zahn is not an absurd result. Justice Brennan's dissent joined by Justices Douglas and Marshall states the counterposition. Some respected commentators would welcome Zahn's demise. See, e.g., 1 Moore et al., supra, ¶ 0.97[5], at 928; Arthur Freer, supra, 40 Emory L.J. at 1008 n.6 ("Abrogating Zahn would hardly be absurd" since doing so would harmonize case law and "enable federal courts to resolve complex interstate disputes in mass tort situations."). But the wisdom of the statute is not our affair beyond determining that overturning Zahn is not absurd. We are persuaded that under § 1367 a district court can exercise supplemental jurisdiction over members of a class, although they did not meet the amount-in-controversy requirement, as did the class representatives.

IV. Abstention and Discretionary Exercise of Supplemental Jurisdiction

Colorado River Abstention is to be used only sparingly, see Colorado River, 424 U.S. at 813, and this case is a poor candidate. The district court acknowledged that "several of the [Colorado River] factors are either neutral or weighing in favor of the exercise of [federal] jurisdiction." It rested its decision on two concerns: that remanding only the class members' claims would split the action, and the novel and complex questions of state law.

The first of these two concerns—the risk of piecemeal litigation—is a problem only under the district court's view of abstention. The second consideration—that novel and complex state law issues govern the action—has more merit. Cf. Moses Cone, 460 U.S. at 23–24 (disfavoring abstention where federal question controls). These state law issues included whether indirect purchasers can state a claim under Louisiana

---

tal Jurisdiction, 40 Emory L.J. 993, 993 (1991).

Some disagree and with inexplicably sharp language, given the reality that most mistakes become "clear" once they are identified. See, e.g., 1 Moore et al., supra, § 0.95[5], at 928 (blaming "Congressional sloth in drafting the supplemental jurisdiction statute" for confusion over whether Zahn survives § 1367); Richard D. Freer, Compounding Confusion and Hampering Diversity: Life After Finley and the Supplemental Jurisdiction Statute, 40 Emory L.J. 445, 471 (1992)(noting that Congress passed § 1367 too quickly to notice some of its problems); Karen N. Moore, The Supplemental Jurisdiction Statute: An Important But Controversial Supplement to Federal Jurisdiction, 41 Emory L.J. 91, 56–58 (1992)(chastising Congress and its legislative advisors for enacting an ambiguous statute); Thomas C. Arthur & Richard D. Freer, Close Enough For Government Work: What Happens When Congress Doesn't Do Its Job, 40 Emory L.J. 1007, 1007 (1991)(calling § 1367(b) a "nightmare of draftsmanship").

antitrust law, and whether the claims in this case were preempted by federal antitrust law.

We agree that these may prove to be difficult questions. Standing alone, however, the novelty or complexity of state law issues is not enough to compel abstention. See, e.g., Rougon v. Chevron, U.S.A., Inc., 575 F.Supp. 95, 97 (M.D.La.1983)(denying motion to remand to state court even though "the issues presented, involving previously undecided matters of Louisiana ... law, are peculiarly suited to disposition by the state courts of Louisiana"). Only " 'exceptional' circumstances, the 'clearest of justifications,' ... can suffice under Colorado River to justify the surrender of [federal] jurisdiction." Moses Cone, 460 U.S. at 25–26 (emphasis omitted). This is not one of those truly rare and exceptional cases in which Colorado River abstention is proper. * * *

In short, the entire case should remain in federal court. The district court had diversity jurisdiction over the named plaintiffs' claims; § 1367 granted it supplemental jurisdiction over the claims of the unnamed plaintiffs; and, considering that it must try the named plaintiffs' claims, it abused its discretion on the facts here in declining supplemental jurisdiction over the unnamed plaintiffs' claims. It is not necessary to decide the problematic contention that the district court also had federal question jurisdiction, and we do not. We VACATE the district court's remand order, and REMAND to the district court for further proceedings. The petition for mandamus is DENIED.

NOTES AND QUESTIONS

1. The court indicates that some of the drafters of § 1367 thought that the statute did not overrule *Zahn*. See note 5 and accompanying text, citing the writings of Professors Rowe, Burbank, and Mengler, who worked on the statute in the late stages of its passage. But in 1990, a Federal Courts Study Committee proposed a supplemental jurisdiction statute that closely resembles the statute ultimately adopted. A working paper of the Study Committee stated explicitly that the proposed statute would overrule *Zahn*:

> [O]ur proposal would overrule the Supreme Court's decision in *Zahn v. International Paper Co.* ... From a policy standpoint, this decision makes little sense, and we therefore recommend that Congress overrule it.

I Federal Courts Study Committee, Working Papers and Subcommittee Reports, July 1, 1990, at 561, n. 33.

2. In Stromberg Metal Works, Inc. v. Press Mechanical, Inc., 77 F.3d 928 (7th Cir.1996), the court found supplemental jurisdiction over a claim by an additional plaintiff joined under Rule 20 in a diversity case even when that plaintiff could not satisfy the amount in controversy requirement. *Free* was not directly on point, for it involved unnamed members of a class action under Rule 23 rather than an additional plaintiff in a non-class action joined under Rule 20. But both cases share the same analytic structure: the failure of § 1367(b) explicitly to exclude from supplemental jurisdiction class mem-

bers under Rule 23 (*Free*) and plaintiffs joined under Rule 20 (*Stromberg*) resulted in supplemental jurisdiction being found under § 1367(a). For further discussion of *Stromberg* and supplemental jurisdiction under Rule 20, see discussion, infra p. 58–59, in this supplement.

3. Is § 1367 the only basis on which federal courts can assert supplemental (or ancillary or pendent) jurisdiction? The answer is probably No. Consider the following two problems:

(a) *Supplemental jurisdiction over claims for set-off*: The casebook, pp. 431–32, discusses set-off. Counterclaims for set-off usually do not arise out of a "common nucleus of operative fact" with the plaintiff's claim. If § 1367 is construed to authorize supplemental jurisdiction only for claims that arise out of a common nucleus of operative fact, either an unrelated counter-claim for set-off cannot be heard or a District Court must rely on some other form of supplemental jurisdiction to hear it.

(b) *Ancillary jurisdiction to enforce settlements*: In Kokkonen v. Guardian Life Insurance Co. of America, 511 U.S. 375, 114 S.Ct. 1673, 128 L.Ed.2d 391 (1994), the District Court entered an unconditional order dismissing plaintiff's claim pursuant to a settlement agreement. When defendant failed to live up to the agreement, plaintiff returned to the federal court. The Supreme Court held that there had to be an independent basis for subject matter jurisdiction to support plaintiff's suit to enforce the agreement. But the Court noted explicitly that if the parties had incorporated into the order of dismissal a condition that the defendant comply with the settlement, the District Court would have had ancillary jurisdiction: "In that event, a breach of the agreement would be a violation of the order, and ancillary jurisdiction to enforce the agreement would therefore exist." at 1677. The Court nowhere mentioned § 1367 in its opinion. For an analysis of *Kokkonen,* see Green, "Justice Scalia and Ancillary Jurisdiction: Teaching a Lame Duck New Tricks in *Kokkonen v. Guardian Life Insurance Company of America,*" 81 Va.L.Rev. 1631 (1995).

d. REMOVAL

p. 439–47

NOTE ON REMOVAL

2. "Artful pleading" and preemption removal. The Supreme Court has significantly narrowed, perhaps nullified, *Moitie*'s troublesome footnote. In Rivet v. Regions Bank of Louisiana, ___ U.S. ___, 118 S.Ct. 921, 139 L.Ed.2d 912 (1998), the Court reaffirmed that the "artful pleading doctrine allows removal where federal law completely preempts a plaintiff's state-law claim." at 925. But it specifically disavowed a reading of the *Moitie* footnote that would allow removal when defendant pleads res judicata to the state court action based on an earlier federal judgment. "The prior federal judgment does not transform the plaintiff's state-law claims into federal claims but rather extinguishes them altogether. ... Under the well-pleaded complaint rule, preclusion thus remains a defensive plea involving no recasting of the plaintiff's complaint, and is therefore not a proper basis for removal. ... '*Moitie*'s enigmatic footnote,' ... we recognize, has caused considerable confusion in the circuit courts. We therefore clarify that *Moitie* did not create a preclusion exception to the rule, fundamental under currently governing legislation, that a defendant cannot remove on the basis of a federal defense." at 926. For an analysis of *Rivet*'s limitation of *Moitie,* see Miller, "Artful Pleading: A Doctrine in Search of Definition," 76 Tex.L.Rev. 1781, particularly 1822–28 (1998).

3. Diversity removal

b. Devices to defeat diversity removal. A plaintiff in a state court suit may join a non-diverse defendant in order to defeat removal unless the joinder is "fraudulent." If joinder is fraudulent, the case may be removed and the fraudulently joined defendant dismissed. But note that a diversity case must be removed within one year of its filing in state court. 28 U.S.C. § 1446(b). See "Procedure," p. 444 of the casebook. The one-year limitation will not be extended even if the defendant seeking to remove could not discover within that time that the joinder was fraudulent. Russaw v. Voyager Life Insurance Co., 921 F.Supp. 723, 725 (M.D.Ala.1996): "[A] defendant has only one year to uncover any fraudulent effort to defeat diversity jurisdiction. If the defendant cannot do so within that time period, then the focus of the litigation should be on the merits rather than the proper forum."

3a. Removal of state court appeals from local administrative decisions. A state court appeal from a decision of a county or municipal administrative agency may be removed if a federal question is raised in the appeal. City of Chicago v. International College of Surgeons, ___ U.S. ___, 118 S.Ct. 523, 139 L.Ed.2d 525 (1997). Justices Ginsburg and Stevens, in dissent, argued that removal in such a case should not be available, for it permits a "cross-system appeal" under which federal courts may "directly superintend local agencies by affirming, reversing or modifying their administrative rulings." at 534–5.

5. Separate and independent claims.

a. Remand. Borough of West Mifflin v. Lancaster, 45 F.3d 780 (3d Cir.1995), holds that the remand language of § 1441(c)("in its discretion, may remand all matters in which state law predominates") provides the standard for remand only when the case has been removed from state court under § 1441(c). When there is supplemental jurisdiction under § 1367, and the case has therefore been removed under the general removal provision of § 1441(a), remand is controlled by § 1367(c). Accord: Kabealo v. Davis, 829 F.Supp. 923 (S.D.Ohio 1993). However, other courts have held that the remand standard of § 1441(c) govern all cases, including those in which removal was based on a combination of §§ 1367 and 1441(a). See, e.g., Moore v. DeBiase, 766 F.Supp. 1311 (D.N.J.1991); Administaff, Inc., v. Kaster, cited in casebook p. 443. For an argument that § 1441(c) should be retained, see "A New Trick from an Old and Abused Dog: Section 1441(c) Lives and Now Permits the Remand of Federal Question Cases," 63 Fordham L.Rev. 1099 (1995).

6. Non-appealability of remand orders. The non-reviewability of remand orders under § 1447(d) is coming under increasing pressure. In some cases, non-reviewability is alive and well. See, e.g., Liberty Mutual Insurance Co. v. Ward Trucking Corp., 48 F.3d 742 (3d Cir.1995), in which defendant removed a diversity case to federal court. The District Court remanded on the ground of insufficient amount in controversy. During discovery, defendant learned that plaintiff had incurred damages of over $150,000, and again removed. The District Court remanded to state court without allowing defendant an opportunity to respond to plaintiff's motion to remand. The Court of Appeals held the remand order non-reviewable.

In other cases, Courts of Appeal have found ways to review remand orders. See, e.g., Free v. Abbott Laboratories, 51 F.3d 524 (5th Cir.1995), supra p. 31 in this supplement, a diversity class action in which the Court of Appeals reviewed a remand order after the District Court had remanded under § 1367(c)(1)(the claim "raise[d] novel or complex issues of state law"). The court construed § 1447(d) to forbid appellate review only when the remand was based on lack of subject matter jurisdiction or on a defect in the removal procedure.

7. Procedure. In Caterpillar v. Lewis, 519 U.S. 61, 117 S.Ct. 467, 136 L.Ed.2d 437 (1996), a diversity suit was improperly removed to federal court, and the federal District Court wrongly denied a timely motion to remand. The non-diverse defendant—whose presence had made removal improper—settled out of the suit before trial. The wrongly removed plaintiff lost on the merits at trial and thereafter renewed his objection to removal. The Supreme Court conceded that removal had been improper and that the District Court had wrongly denied the motion to remand. But "no jurisdictional defect lingered through judgment in the District Court. To wipe out the adjudication post-judgment, and return to the state court a case now satisfying all federal jurisdictional requirements, would impose an exorbitant cost on our dual court system, a cost incompatible with the fair and unprotracted administration of justice." at 477.

A defendant has thirty days from the receipt of the complaint to file a timely notice of removal. 28 U.S.C. § 1446(b). The rule is straightforward in a single-defendant case, but it can become confusing when there are multiple defendants who receive the complaint at different times. For an analysis of the multiple-defendant case, see Hollingsworth, "Section 1446: Remedying the Fifth Circuit's Removal Trap," 49 Baylor L.Rev. 157 (1997).

28 U.S.C. § 1447(c) was amended in 1996 to provide that a motion for remand must be made within 30 days for anything other than a "defect in subject matter jurisdiction." Previously, the 30–day limitation applied only to motions to remand for "procedural defects," a possibly narrow category of motion. Pub.L. 104–219, 110 Stat. 3022 (Oct. 1, 1996).

e. CHALLENGING FEDERAL SUBJECT MATTER JURISDICTION

p. 445

NOTE ON DIRECT CHALLENGE TO FEDERAL SUBJECT MATTER JURISDICTION

A federal court must find that it has subject matter jurisdiction before it can decide any question on the merits. The Supreme Court has disapproved a "doctrine of hypothetical jurisdiction" under which a court could assume that it has subject matter jurisdiction in order to decide the merits when the merits question was easier than the jurisdiction question, and when the result would be the same as if jurisdiction were denied. According to the Court, "Hypothetical jurisdiction produces nothing more than a hypothetical judgment—which comes to the same thing as an advisory opinion, disapproved by this Court from the beginning. ... For a court to pronounce on the meaning or constitutionality of a state or federal law when it has no jurisdiction to do so it, by very definition, for a court to act ultra vires." Steel Company v. Citizens for a Better Environment, ___ U.S. ___, ___, 118 S.Ct. 1003, 1016, 140 L.Ed.2d 210 (1998).

C. VENUE

1. STATE COURTS

p. 446

NOTE ON VENUE IN STATE COURTS

Plaintiff's forum shopping is facilitated by statutes that provide a wide range of forum choices and that restrict a defendant's ability to change venue. For an analysis of forum shopping in Alabama, and a suggestion that Alabama courts should allow defendants to change venue more easily, see Note, "Forum Shopping and Venue Transfers in Alabama," 48 Ala.L.Rev. 671 (1997).

2. FEDERAL COURTS

a. VENUE

p. 451

NOTE ON VENUE IN FEDERAL COURTS

2. The general venue statute, 28 U.S.C. § 1391. Section 1391(a)(3) was amended in October, 1995, to eliminate the reference to plural "defendants." It now provides that venue is proper in a judicial district where "any defendant is subject to personal jurisdiction."

b. CHANGE OF VENUE AND RELATED TOPICS
p. 464, 467–68

NOTE ON *FERENS v. JOHN DEERE*, CHANGE OF VENUE UNDER
§ 1404, DISMISSAL OR TRANSFER FOR LACK OF VENUE
UNDER § 1406(A), AND OTHER TRANSFERS

2. Transfer under § 1404(a). Does forum choice through venue transfer matter? A recent study suggests that it does. Clermont and Eisenberg, "Exorcising the Evil of Forum–Shopping," 80 Cornell L.Rev. 1507 (1995). In a study covering all ninety-four federal districts from 1979 to 1991 and including 2,804,640 cases that terminated in judgments, the authors conclude that plaintiffs' "win rate" in cases that remained in the forum in which they were filed was 58%. In cases transferred to another forum under § 1404(a), plaintiffs' win rate dropped to 29%. The authors recognize that reasons other than favorable or unfavorable forums might account for the difference in win rates. For example, the set of transferred cases may be, on the merits, weaker cases than the set of non-transferred cases. The authors concede that this explanation "contributes," but "probably does not fully explain the effect" of transfer. at 1517. They conclude: "Our empirical investigation suggests that transfer offers the considerable advantage of countering the very real detriments of forum-shopping, and that it does so without undue burden. The new empirical evidence is not definitive, but the transfer critics can find no support in it. Good policy calls, at the least, for preserving the transfer mechanism." at 1530. For an argument that Professors Clermont and Eisenberg have overstated the effect of transfer under § 1404(a) on the outcomes of cases, see Steinberg, "Simplifying the Choice of Forum: A Response to Professor Clermont and Professor Eisenberg," 75 Wash.U.L.Q. 1479 (1997); for a response, see Clermont and Eisenberg, "Simplifying the Choice of Forum: A Reply," 75 Wash.U.L.Q. 1551 (1997).

6. Different federal law. Recent Court of Appeals decisions have followed *Korean Air Lines*, holding that where there is a conflict between the circuits on a question of federal law the transferee court should follow the interpretation of its own circuit. Menowitz v. Brown, 991 F.2d 36 (2d Cir.1993); Eckstein v. Balcor Film Investors, 8 F.3d 1121 (7th Cir.1993)(dictum).

Ragazzo, "Transfer and Choice of Federal Law: The Appellate Model," 93 Mich.L.Rev. 703 (1995), argues that cases should be treated differently depending on whether they are transferred under 28 U.S.C. § 1407 or under §§ 1404 and 1406. Section 1407 allows transfer of mass tort or complex litigation cases to a single federal court for coordinated or consolidated pretrial treatment. It contemplates that cases be transferred back to their original district for trial (although, in fact, this happens in only a minority of § 1407 cases). Sections 1404 and 1406 provide for permanent transfers. Professor Ragazzo argues that in § 1407 cases the federal law of the transferor forum should apply, but that in §§ 1404 and 1406 cases the federal law of the transferee forum should apply. (Recall that *Korean Air Lines*, holding that the federal law of the transferee forum should apply, was a § 1407 case.)

9. "Self-assignment" under 28 U.S.C. § 1407. For many years, transferee courts under § 1407 kept some transferred cases for trial despite the clear language of § 1407(a) providing, "Each action so transferred shall be remanded ... at or before the conclusion of such pretrial proceedings to the district from which it was transferred unless it shall have been previously terminated." The Supreme Court has prohibited such "self-assignments": "[Defendant] may or may not be correct that permitting transferee courts to make self-assignments would be more desirable than [what the § 1407 requires], but the proper venue for resolving that issue remains the floor of Congress." Lexecon Inc. v. Milberg Weiss Bershad Hynes & Lerach, ___ U.S. ___, ___, 118 S.Ct. 956, 964, 140 L.Ed.2d 62 (1998).

D. FORUM NON CONVENIENS
p. 478

NOTE ON *FORUM NON CONVENIENS*

3a. Recent examples of *forum non conveniens* dismissals. In Creative Technology, Ltd. v. Aztech System Pte., Ltd., 61 F.3d 696 (9th Cir.1995), one Singapore company sued another for alleged violations of American copyright law arising out of distribution of competing computer "sound cards" in the United States. The Court of Appeals sustained a *forum non conveniens* dismissal by the District Court, holding: (1) The fact that cases based on American copyright law are within the exclusive jurisdiction of the federal courts means only that American state courts cannot hear them; it does not mean that foreign courts cannot do so. (2) The balance of public and private factors justified dismissal. On the question of public factors, the Court wrote, "This is essentially a dispute between two Singapore corporations as to which of them was the original developer of the disputed sound card technology. This is not a case involving the piracy of American made products or substantively involving American companies." at 704.

In Bhatnagar v. Surrendra Overseas Ltd., 52 F.3d 1220 (3d Cir.1995), plaintiff, a six-year-old girl, was injured aboard an Indian merchant ship in international waters. She was an Indian citizen residing in India, but she had boarded the ship in the United States and had been flown to the United States for emergency medical treatment. The District Court found that "the Indian legal system has a tremendous backlog of cases—so great that it could take up to a quarter of a century to resolve this litigation if it were filed in India." at 1227. The Court of Appeals upheld the refusal of the District Court to dismiss on ground of *forum non conveniens*: "[T]he district court did not commit legal error in concluding that delay can render a putative alternative forum clearly inadequate." at 1230.

Note that in both *Creative Technology* and *Bhatnagar* the Court of Appeals sustained the decision of the District Court, in the one case to dismiss and in the other to deny dismissal. These cases illustrate the fact that *forum non conveniens* accords considerable discretion to the trial court.

5. State or federal law? In American Dredging Co. v. Miller, 510 U.S. 443, 114 S.Ct. 981, 127 L.Ed.2d 285 (1994), the Supreme Court held that in an admiralty suit filed in state court between domestic parties, federal *forum non conveniens* law does not pre-empt Louisiana law. But the Court in *Miller* was careful to indicate that it did not decide whether there should be a uniform federal law of *forum non conveniens* in non-domestic cases:

> [T]he Solicitor General has urged that we limit our holding, that *forum non conveniens* is not part of the uniform law of admiralty, to cases involving domestic entities. We think it unnecessary to do that. Since the parties to this suit are domestic entities it is quite impossible for our holding to be any broader.

at 457.

Chapter 4

THE *ERIE* PROBLEM

A. THE LAW APPLIED IN FEDERAL COURT: THE PROBLEM OF *ERIE RAILROAD v. TOMPKINS*
p. 514

NOTES AND QUESTIONS

2a. Combining *York* and *Byrd*? In Gasperini v. Center for Humanities, Inc., 518 U.S. 415, 116 S.Ct. 2211, 135 L.Ed.2d 659 (1996), plaintiff in a diversity suit based on New York law obtained a jury verdict of $450,000. Defendant sought to overturn the award as excessive. New York trial and appellate courts are required to find a jury award excessive "if it deviates substantially from what would be reasonable compensation." Federal District Courts have the power under Fed.R.Civ.P. 59(a) to order either a new trial, or remittitur of a jury award as an alternative to a new trial, "for any of the reasons for which new trials have heretofore been granted in actions at law in the courts of the United States." The Court of Appeals for the Second Circuit will overturn a jury verdict for excessiveness only if it is so large as to "shock the conscience." at 2217–2221. The Supreme Court, in a 5–4 decision written by Justice Ginsburg, held that the federal courts should apply the New York "deviates substantially" standard in cases based on New York law.

Applying the *York* test, the Court concluded that the choice between the New York "deviates substantially" standard and the federal appellate "shock the conscience" standard was "outcome-affective" in the sense that it " 'would [unfairly discriminate against citizens of the forum State, or] be likely to cause a plaintiff to choose the federal court.' " at 2220 (quoting *Hanna v. Plumer*, brackets in original).

Invoking *Byrd*, the Court then asked whether application of the "deviates substantially" test by a federal court would violate the Seventh Amendment. The Amendment provides that "no fact tried by a jury, shall be otherwise re-examined in any Court of the United States, than according to the rules of the common law." The Court concluded that both federal District Courts and Courts of Appeals have the power to set aside jury verdicts as excessive despite the Seventh Amendment. It held that "New York's dominant interest can be respected without disrupting the federal system" if the District Court applies the "deviates substantially" test to jury verdicts and if the Court of Appeals reviews the District Court decision for abuse of discretion. at 2224–25.

Justice Scalia, in dissent, argued that the New York standard was in direct conflict with Rule 59. As Justice Scalia would read the Rule, it allows the District Judge to order a new trial only when " 'it is quite clear that the jury has reached a seriously erroneous result,' " and that letting the verdict stand would result in a " 'miscarriage of justice.' " at 2239. Because of the direct conflict with New York's "deviates substantially" standard, Rule 59 should control. Justice Ginsburg, for the majority, responded: "It is indeed 'Hornbook' law that a most usual ground for a Rule 59 motion is that 'the damages are excessive.' . . . Whether damages are excessive for the claim-in-suit must be governed by some law. And there is no candidate for that governance other than the law that gives rise to the claim for relief—here, the law of New York." at 2224 n. 22. Note that Justice Ginsburg's response likely means that the standards for granting a new trial under Rule 59 will be different depending on the state or federal law at issue. Should a Federal Rule of Civil Procedure mean something different depending on whether state or federal substantive law is being applied? See discussion of *Walker v. Armco Steel* and related cases in the casebook, pp. 526–33.

Academics have been generally critical of Justice Ginsburg's opinion in *Gasperini*. See, e.g., Floyd, "*Erie* Awry: A Comment on *Gasperini v. Center for Humanities, Inc.*", 1997 B.Y.U.L.Rev.267, 304–5; Freer, "Some Thoughts on the State of *Erie* After *Gasperini*," 76 Tex.L.Rev. 1637, 1663 (1998) ("In *Gasperini*, the Court had another opportunity—perhaps the best in a generation—to make a meaningful contribution to [Rules of Decision Act] analysis, including the role of *Byrd*. Instead, the Court left the field about as murky as it was before."). Compare Rowe, "Not Bad for Government Work: Does Anyone Else Think the Supreme Court is Doing a Halfway Decent Job in Its *Erie–Hanna* Jurisprudence?" 73 Notre D.L.Rev. 963, 966 (1998). For Justice Ginsburg's view, see Ginsburg, "In Celebration of Charles Alan Wright," 76 Tex.L.Rev. 1581, 1583 (1998) ("[Professor Freer] is surely entitled to his view of Gasperini (misguided though it may be!). Understandably, I find more accurate the view of the Second Circuit opinion writer," quoting a letter from Judge Guido Calabresi praising the " 'elegant opinion.' ").

p. 533

NOTE ON STATUTES OF LIMITATIONS, RELATION BACK UNDER RULE 15(c), AND *ERIE*

4. Differential application of state procedural rules to substantive state and federal law? In S.A. Healy Co. v. Milwaukee Metropolitan Sewerage Dist., 60 F.3d 305 (7th Cir.1995) (Posner, J.), a diversity case relying on Wisconsin substantive law, plaintiff sought to use a Wisconsin offer-of-settlement rule. Under the Wisconsin rule, if plaintiff makes an offer of settlement which is refused, and then wins a judgment larger than the rejected offer, plaintiff is entitled to twice his or her taxable costs, plus interest at a rate of 12 percent from the date of the offer. Should the federal District Court follow the Wisconsin rule?

The only comparable federal rule is Fed.R.Civ.P. 68, which applies only to offers of settlement by defendants. The Court of Appeals held that Rule 68 did not occupy the field and therefore did not conflict with the Wisconsin rule. The court also held that the Wisconsin rule was not narrowly limited to a particular substantive area of law, such as contract law, which would have given it a special claim to enforcement in federal court.

Judge Posner then wrote for the Court of Appeals:

> Is the Wisconsin rule so likely to dictate outcomes that it will cause a lot of forum shopping (or, if forum shopping is somehow infeasible, cause like cases to be decided differently) unless it is made applicable to diversity cases and so ceases to be a factor in the choice between state and federal court? Is it so entwined with procedures prescribed by the federal rules that it is likely to impair the integrity of federal procedure if it is applied to diversity cases? If the answer to the first question is "yes" and to the second "no," then we can be reasonably confident that application of the Wisconsin rule in diversity cases would be consistent with the principles of Erie and the Rules Enabling Act. Those in fact are our answers....
>
> The Wisconsin rule favors plaintiffs.... If a rule so favorable to plaintiffs is inapplicable in diversity cases, defendants in such cases will have an added incentive to remove a diversity case to federal district court, just as in the days before the Erie decision, when a more favorable substantive rule of federal common law might induce a defendant to remove a case from state to federal court....

at 311.

Judge Posner's discussion relies heavily on the fact that this is a diversity case involving questions of substantive state law. By negative implication, his discussion suggests that the Wisconsin offer-of-settlement rule should not apply to a case involving a question of substantive federal law. But would the forum-shopping incentives arising out of the Wisconsin offer-of-settlement rule be any less in a case based on federal law? *Erie* and *Guaranty Trust v. York*, 326 U.S. 99, 65 S.Ct. 1464, 89 L.Ed. 2079 try to replicate in federal court the result that would be reached in state court in order to reduce incentives for forum shopping. May we assume that the Wisconsin rule is applied in Wisconsin state court to cases based on federal law? The answer is probably yes. Shouldn't the Wisconsin rule be applied in federal court to cases based on federal law, just as in Wisconsin state court?

B. "REVERSE *ERIE*": FEDERAL LAW IN STATE COURTS

p. 538

NOTE ON FEDERAL LAW IN STATE COURTS

6. Non–FELA cases. In Johnson v. Fankell, 520 U.S. 911, 117 S.Ct. 1800, 138 L.Ed.2d 108 (1997), plaintiff brought a federal civil rights suit in Idaho state court under 42 U.S.C. § 1983 against state officials who asserted a federal defense of "qualified immunity." The trial court rejected the defense and denied their motion to dismiss. Defendants then tried to take an interlocutory appeal, but the Idaho Supreme Court refused to hear it because the ruling did not constitute a "final judgment" under Idaho law. In suits in federal court, defendants are entitled to take interlocutory appeals on qualified immunity rulings in § 1983 cases. The United States Supreme Court held that Idaho state courts were not required to grant an interlocutory appeal. It distinguished *Felder v. Casey* on the ground that, unlike the 120–day statute of limitations in *Felder*, the availability of an interlocutory appeal was not "outcome determinative." at 1805–06. "When pre-emption of state law is at issue, we must respect the 'principles [that] are fundamental to a system of federalism in which the state courts share responsibility for the application and enforcement of federal law.' ... This respect is at its apex when we confront a claim that federal law requires a State to undertake something as fundamental as the restructuring as the operations of its courts." at 1807. Recall *Gasperini v. Center for Humanities*, supra p. 44 in this supplement. Why was the Supreme Court so willing to "restructure the operations" of the federal courts in that case?

C. ASCERTAINING STATE LAW

p. 548

NOTE ON ASCERTAINING STATE LAW

Update on *DeWeerth*. In DeWeerth v. Baldinger, 38 F.3d 1266 (2d Cir.1994), the Court of Appeals reversed the decision of the District Court granting relief under Fed.R.Civ.P. 60(b)(6), thereby reinstating the Court of Appeals' incorrect interpretation of New York law. The Court of Appeals justified its decision as follows:

> It turned out that the *DeWeerth* panel prediction was wrong. However, by bringing this suit, DeWeerth exposed herself to the possibility that her adversaries would argue for a change in the applicable rules of law. By filing her state law claim in a federal forum, she knew that any open question of state law would be decided by a federal court as opposed to a New York state court. The subsequent outcome of the *Guggenheim* decision does not impugn the integrity of the *DeWeerth* decision or the fairness of the process that was accorded DeWeerth. The result in this case would be no different if DeWeerth had filed her claim in state court and Baldinger had removed the action to federal court. The very nature of diversity jurisdiction leaves open the possibility that a state court will subsequently disagree with a federal court's interpretation of state law. However, this aspect of our dual justice system does not mean that all diversity judgments are subject to revision once a state court later addresses the litigated issues. Such a rule would be tantamount to holding that the doctrine of finality does not apply to diversity judgments, a theory that has no basis in *Erie* or its progeny.

at 1273–4. Are you convinced?

In Batts v. Tow–Motor Forklift Co., 66 F.3d 743 (5th Cir.1995), the Court of Appeals for the Fifth Circuit refused to reopen a judgment under Rule 60(b)(6) under circumstances similar to those in *DeWeerth*, relying on the Second Circuit's "well-reasoned opinion."

Compare practice in cases on direct appellate review. In Thomas v. American Home Products, Inc., ___ U.S. ___, 117 S.Ct. 282, 136 L.Ed.2d 201 (1996), the Court of Appeals for the Eleventh Circuit decided a case based on Georgia state law. After the Court of Appeals' decision but before a petition for certiorari was filed in the Supreme Court, a decision of the Georgia Supreme Court made it clear that the Court of Appeals' interpretation of Georgia law was incorrect. The United States Supreme Court granted the petition for certiorari, vacated the judgment of the Court of Appeals, and remanded the case for reconsideration in light of the later decision of the Georgia Supreme Court. See also Lords Landing Village Condominium Council of Unit Owners v. Continental Insurance Co., 520 U.S. 893, 117 S.Ct. 1731, 138 L.Ed.2d 91 (1997) (same). Note that in *DeWeerth*, unlike in *Thomas* and *Lords Landing*, the losing party sought to reopen a judgment after the time for direct appellate review had expired.

D. FEDERAL COMMON LAW

p. 554

NOTES AND QUESTIONS

2a. Recent reluctance to formulate rules of federal common law. In O'Melveny & Myers v. Federal Deposit Insurance Corp., 512 U.S. 79, 114 S.Ct. 2048, 129 L.Ed.2d 67 (1994), the Supreme Court declined to fashion a federal common law rule governing tort liability of attorneys who provide legal services to savings and loans. The Court wrote, "[T]his is not one of those extraordinary cases in which the judicial creation of a federal rule of decision is warranted." at 2056. See also Atherton v. Federal Deposit Insurance Corp., 519 U.S. 213, 117 S.Ct. 666, 136 L.Ed.2d 656 (1997)(quoting *O'Melveny & Myers* and refusing to create a federal common law rule governing liability of officers and directors of federally insured savings institutions). For an analysis of the Supreme Court's reluctance in recent years to create federal common law, see Lund, "The Decline of Federal Common Law," 76 B.U.L.Rev. 895 (1996).

Chapter 5

CLAIMS AND DEFENSES

B. PLEADINGS

1. THE ELEMENTS OF A SUFFICIENT COMPLAINT
p. 591

NOTE ON SUFFICIENCY OF PLEADINGS; BURDEN OF PLEADING, PERSUASION, AND PROOF; AND PRESUMPTIONS

2. Elements of a sufficient complaint. The central function of the complaint is to provide fair notice to the defendant of the nature of plaintiff's case. Fed.R.Civ.P. 8(a)(2) requires that the complaint contain "a short and plain statement of the claim showing that the pleader is entitled to relief ...", but failure to make such "short and plain statement" is usually curable. For example, a complaint may be amended under Fed.R.Civ.P. 15(b) to conform to evidence presented at trial by "express or implied consent of the parties," or over the objection of a party "when the presentation of the merits of the action will be subserved thereby and the objecting party fails to satisfy the court that the admission of such evidence would prejudice the party in maintaining the party's ... defense on the merits." Further, under Fed.R.Civ.P. 54(c) a "final judgment shall grant the relief to which the party in whose favor it is rendered is entitled, even if the party has not demanded such relief in the party's pleadings."

But there are limits beyond which even the forgiving federal pleading rules will not go. In Rodriguez v. Doral Mortgage Corp., 57 F.3d 1168 (1st Cir.1995), plaintiff brought suit against her employer for sexual harassment under Title VII of the federal Civil Rights Act of 1964 and under a Puerto Rican statute known as Law 100. After the conclusion of both parties' evidence, the District Court granted relief to plaintiff on Law 17, a different Puerto Rican statute not asserted as a basis for relief. The Court of Appeals reversed: "[W]e hold that no claim under Law 17 was ever properly before the district court, and that the judgment cannot stand. A federal district court may not, of its own volition, after the parties have rested, recast the complaint and, without notice, predicate its decision on a theory that was neither pleaded nor tried." at 1174. The Court of Appeals then remanded to permit the District Court "in its discretion" to grant a new trial "to allow the plaintiff the opportunity to present and to develop such a claim, subject to any constraints imposed by [Fed.R.Civ.P. 15(b)]." at 1179.

3. Burdens of pleading, persuasion, and proof. In Director, Office of Workers' Compensation Programs v. Greenwich Collieries, 512 U.S. 267, 114 S.Ct. 2251, 129 L.Ed.2d 221 (1994), the Supreme Court defined "burden of proof" as that term is used in the federal Administrative Procedure Act:

> For many years the term "burden of proof" was ambiguous, because the term was used to describe two distinct concepts. Burden of proof was frequently used to refer to what we now call the burden of persuasion—the notion that if the evidence is evenly balanced, the party that bears the burden of persuasion must lose. But it was also used to refer to what we now call the burden of production—a party's obligation to come forward with evidence to support its claim.
>
> * * *
>
> [We] conclude that the drafters of the [Administrative Procedure Act] used the term "burden of proof" to mean the burden of persuasion.

at 2255, 2257.

Note that the Supreme Court in *Greenwich Collieries* defines "burden of proof" as it is used in the following sentence: "Who has the burden of proof?" The answer to that question tells us who bears the risk of nonpersuasion in tie-breaker case. If plaintiff has the burden of proof in this sense, she loses if she must prove her case by a preponderance of the evidence and the evidence in equipoise. The Court does not define "burden of proof" as it is used in the sentence: "What is the burden of proof?" The answer to that question tells us how convincing the evidence must be, and it varies depending on the nature of the case. Common standards require that a civil plaintiff prove a case by the "preponderance of the evidence" (an ordinary case) or by "clear and convincing evidence" (a fraud case).

4. Presumptions and burdens of pleading and production. For a thoughtful discussion of *Hicks* and of the relationship between pleading presumptions and substantive law, see Malamud, "The Last Minuet: Disparate Treatment after *Hicks*," 93 Mich.L.Rev. 2229 (1995).

2. THE PROBLEM OF SPECIFICITY

p. 608

NOTE ON REQUIRING A MORE SPECIFIC STATEMENT OF CLAIM

1. *Leatherman* and pleading in suits against individual officials. The Supreme Court in *Leatherman* explicitly saved out the question of whether a heightened pleading requirement may be imposed on a § 1983 plaintiff suing an individual officer rather than a municipality. How can that be an open question, given the Court's rationale for its holding?

Before the Court's decision in *Leatherman*, several Courts of Appeals required "heightened pleading" by plaintiffs in § 1983 suits against individual officials. See, e.g., Elliott v. Perez, 751 F.2d 1472 (5th Cir.1985). After *Leatherman*, the Fifth Circuit held that plaintiffs in such suits are still required to meet a heightened pleading standard, but in their reply rather than their complaint. The leading case is Schultea v. Wood, 47 F.3d 1427 (5th Cir.1995)(en banc). See also Veney v. Hogan, 70 F.3d 917 (6th Cir.1995)(plaintiff must meet heightened pleading requirement in complaint); Branch v. Tunnell, 14 F.3d 449 (9th Cir.1994)(same). The Fifth Circuit in *Schultea* noted that the burden of pleading the defense of qualified immunity is on the defendant. (See *Gomez v. Toledo*, casebook, p. 577.) If defendant asserts the defense, the question is whether plaintiff can be required to reply to the defense, and, if so, under what standard of particularity. The Court of Appeals wrote:

> When a public official pleads the affirmative defense of qualified immunity in his answer, the district court may, on the official's motion or on its own, require the plaintiff to reply to that defense in detail. By definition, the reply must be tailored to the assertion of qualified immunity and fairly engage its allegations. A defendant has an incentive to plead his defense with particularity because it has the practical effect of requiring particularity in the reply. The Federal Rules of Civil Procedure permit the use of Rule 7 in this manner.

at 1433.

In Crawford–El v. Britton, ___ U.S. ___, ___, 118 S.Ct. 1584, 1596–97, 140 L.Ed.2d 759 (1998), the Supreme Court went beyond *Schultea*, urging federal District Judges to protect individual officials under either Rule 7(a) (as in *Schultea*) or under Rule 12(e):

> When a plaintiff files a complaint against a public official alleging a claim that requires proof of wrongful motive, the trial court must exercise its discretion in a way that protects the substance of the qualified immunity defense. ... The district judge has two primary options prior to permitting any discovery at all. First, the court may order a reply to the defendant's or a third party's answer under Federal Rule of Civil Procedure 7(a), or grant the defendant's motion for a more definite statement under Rule 12(e). Thus, the court may insist that the plaintiff "put forward specific, nonconclusory factual allegations" that establish improper motive causing cognizable injury in order to survive a prediscovery motion for dismissal or summary judgment. This option exists even if the official chooses not to plead the affirmative defense of qualified immunity. Second, if the defendant does plead the immunity defense, the district court should resolve that threshold question before permitting discovery.

2. Additional reading. For useful discussions of *Leatherman*, see Blum, "Heightened Pleading: Is There Life After *Leatherman*?" 44 Cath. U.L.Rev. 59 (1994); Note, "Civil Rights Plaintiffs, Clogged Courts, and the Federal Rules of Civil Procedure: The Supreme Court Takes a Look at Heightened Pleading Standards in Leatherman v. Tarrant County Narcotics and Coordination Unit," 72 N.Car.L.Rev. 1085 (1994). See also Chen, "The Burdens of Qualified Immunity: Summary Judgment and the Role of Facts in Constitutional Tort Law," 47 Am.U.L.Rev. 1 (1997).

p. 612

NOTE ON PLEADING UNDER THE FEDERAL PRIVATE SECURITIES REFORM ACT OF 1995

1. Background. Concerned over the amount and type of securities fraud litigation brought against publicly traded corporations, Congress passed, over President Clinton's veto, the Private Securities Reform Act of 1995. According to the Conference Committee Report:

> Congress has been prompted by significant evidence of abuse in private securities lawsuits to enact reforms to protect investors and maintain confidence in our capital markets. The House and Senate Committees heard evidence that abusive practices committed in private securities litigation include: (1) the routine filing of lawsuits against issuers of securities and others whenever there is a significant change in an issuer's stock price, without regard to any underlying culpability of the issuer, and with only faint hope that the discovery process might lead eventually to some plausible cause of action; (2) the targeting of deep pocket defendants ...; (3) the abuse of the discovery process to impose costs so burdensome that it is often economical for the victimized party to settle; and (4) the manipulation by class action lawyers of the clients whom they purportedly represent.

House Conference Report No. 104–369, Joint Explanatory Statement of the Committee of Conference, 2 U.S.Code Cong. & Admin. News 730; 104th Cong., 1st Sess., 1995.

2. Pleading under the Act. Among other things, the Act requires heightened pleading by the plaintiff. A plaintiff alleging misleading statements "shall specify each statement alleged to have been misleading, and, if an allegation ... is made on information and belief, the complaint shall state with particularity all facts on which the belief is formed." An allegation of fraudulent intent "shall ... state with particularity facts giving rise to a strong inference that the defendant acted with the required state of mind." Pub.L.No. 104–67, Sec. 21D(b)(1) and (2).

Prior to the passage of the Act, the only statute or rule addressing the appropriate standard of pleading was Fed.R.Civ.P. 9(b), which provides that the "circumstances constituting fraud ... shall be stated with particularity," but that "intent, knowledge, and other condition of mind of a person may be averred generally." There was a split among the Courts of Appeals on the application of Rule 9(b) to securities fraud suits. The Second Circuit construed the rule to require that "plaintiffs specifically plead those events which they assert give rise to a strong inference that the defendants had knowledge of the facts [alleged in the complaint] or recklessly disregarded their existence." Ross v. A.H.Robins Co., 607 F.2d 545, 558 (2d Cir.1979), cert. den., 446 U.S. 946, 100 S.Ct. 2175, 64 L.Ed.2d 802 (1980); see also O'Brien v. National Property Analysts Partners, 936 F.2d 674, 676 (2d Cir.1991). The Ninth Circuit refused to follow the Second Circuit, finding that its standard went beyond Rule 9(b)'s undemanding requirement concerning defendant's state of mind (as distinct from its requirements concerning the fraud): "The Second Circuit's test may or may not have the effect of deterring or weeding out 'strike suits,' which various courts have seen as imposing undesirable social and economic costs. ... Whether the test has such an effect is beside the point. We are not permitted to add new requirements to Rule 9(b) simply because we like the effects of doing so." In re GlenFed, Inc., 42 F.3d 1541, 1546 (9th Cir.1994)(en banc).

The Conference Committee Report stated that the language of the Act was "based in part on the pleading standard of the Second Circuit." But it indicated that the Act was intended to go beyond that standard: "Because the Conference Committee intends to strengthen existing pleading requirements, it does not intend to codify the Second Circuit's case law interpreting the pleading standard." 2 U.S.Code & Admin. News 740.

3. Pleading and discovery under the Act. The Act provides that discovery shall be stayed during the pendency of any motion to dismiss for failure to meet the pleading requirements. Sec. 21D(b)(3). The Conference Committee Report explained its desire to eliminate "fishing expeditions": "The cost of discovery often forces innocent parties to settle frivolous securities class actions. According to the general counsel of an investment bank, 'discovery costs account for roughly 80% of total litigation costs in securities fraud cases.'"

Defendants willing to spend the time and money to defend themselves can presumably defeat unmeritorious claims whether or not plaintiffs satisfy heightened pleading standards. A heightened requirement protects individual defendants in securities fraud suits from the nuisance and expense of defending the litigation beyond the pleading stage unless plaintiff can satisfy the higher standard. Compare the availability of heightened pleading requirement against individual governmental officials under § 1983, as recently set forth by the Supreme Court in *Crawford–El v. Britton,* supra p. 55.

4. Litigation under the Act. Early litigation under the Act suggests that the heightened pleading standards will have an appreciable effect on securities fraud litigation. See In re Silicon Graphics, Inc. Securities Litigation, 1996 WL 664639 (N.D.Cal.1996)(dismissing, with leave to amend, for failure to meet the new pleading standard); In re Silicon Graphics, Inc. Securities Litigation, 970 F.Supp. 746 (N.D.Cal.1997) and 1997 WL 337580 (N.D.Cal.1997) (dismissing without leave to amend). One of the attorneys for the plaintiffs said after the dismissal without leave to amend, "If the Ninth Circuit affirms the dismissal of this complaint, private enforcement of the securities laws in this country will be mortally wounded." A defense attorney stated that prior to the Act a complaint such as that in the *Silicon Graphics* case would have survived a motion to dismiss, with disastrous consequences for defendant: "Once you get past the pleading stage in these cases, the plaintiffs can demand that you turn the company upside down and shake. The client is looking at millions and millions of dollars [in attorneys' fees] before it gets to tell its side of the story." Osborne, "Getting Back at Lerach," The Recorder, September 15, 1997.

C. AMENDED AND SUPPLEMENTAL PLEADINGS

1. AMENDED PLEADINGS

p. 641

NOTE ON RULE 15(c) AND RELATION BACK

2. Unnamed or improperly named defendants. a. Unnamed defendants. In Lundy v. Adamar of New Jersey, Inc., 34 F.3d 1173 (3d Cir.1994), plaintiff suffered a heart attack while playing blackjack at defendant Adamar's casino. He and his wife sued the casino for negligent provision of medical services. Adamar brought a third-party complaint against Dr. Carlino who had contracted with Adamar to provide emergency medical treatment to the casino's customers. Plaintiffs later moved to amend the complaint under Rule 15(c) to sue Dr. Carlino directly, but their amended complaint was filed too late under the statute of limitations. Dr. Carlino had received Adamar's third-party complaint (accompanied by plaintiffs' original complaint) within the period specified in Rule 15(c) for relation back.

The question was whether Dr. Carlino, because of his receipt of Adamar's third-party complaint and plaintiffs' original complaint, "knew or should have known that, but for a mistake concerning the identity of the proper party, the action would have been brought against [him]." Fed. R.Civ.P. 15(c)(3). The court denied relation back: "Dr. Carlino would not have been liable under the theory advanced in [plaintiffs'] complaint, ... and we perceive no reason why it should have led Dr. Carlino to believe [plaintiffs] intended to sue him and had failed to do so because of a mistake concerning identity." at 1183.

D. SUBSTANTIALITY OF CLAIMS AND DEFENSES

p. 658–60

NOTE ON RULE 11

4a. Operation of the current rule. Note that Rule 11 is not confined to pleadings. It applies to any "pleading, written motion, or other paper," presented to the court by "signing, filing, submitting, or later advocating." In Bullard v. Chrysler Corp., 925 F.Supp. 1180 (E.D.Tex.1996), an attorney sought to withdraw as co-counsel for plaintiff shortly before trial in a product liability case. He represented to the District Court that he had an unspecified conflict and that his withdrawal would not prejudice plaintiff. Plaintiff's remaining co-counsel successfully moved for Rule 11 sanctions. The court found that the attorney's "conflict" was a threat by Chrysler Corporation that favorable treatment for his clients in other cases against Chrysler would cease if he did not withdraw from this case, and that his late withdrawal would, in fact, prejudice plaintiff.

6. Other power to sanction. In Ted Lapidus, S.A. v. Vann, 112 F.3d 91 (2d Cir.1997), plaintiff moved for sanctions under Rule 11, but the District Court awarded sanctions against 28 U.S.C. § 1927 instead. The Court of Appeals held that § 1927 sanctions were improper in the absence of sufficient notice and opportunity to defend against sanctions imposed under § 1927.

8. Additional reading. For recent articles on Rule 11, see Yablon, "The Good, the Bad, and the Frivolous Case: An Essay on Probability and Rule 11," 44 U.C.L.A.L.Rev. 65 (1996); Schwarzer, "Rule 11: Entering a New Era," 28 Loyola L.A.L.Rev. 7 (1994); Tobias, "The 1993 Revision of Federal Rule 11," 70 Indiana L.J. 171 (1994); Vairo, "Rule 11: Past as Prologue?" 28 Loyola L.A.L.Rev. 39 (1994); Comment, "A Practitioner's Guide to the 1993 Amendment to Federal Rule of Civil Procedure 11," 67 Temple L.Rev. 265 (1994).

Chapter 6

THE SIZE OF THE LITIGATION

A. COLLATERAL REGULATION OF THE SIZE OF THE LITIGATION

1. RES JUDICATA AND COLLATERAL ESTOPPEL

a. PRECLUSION AS BETWEEN THE SAME PARTIES
p. 680, 686, 688

NOTE ON RES JUDICATA BETWEEN THE SAME PARTIES

1. Claim preclusion.

(b) Restatement Second of Judgments § 24 and development of the "entire controversy" doctrine.

In a cluster of four 1995 cases, the New Jersey Supreme Court embraced a surprisingly broad concept of relatedness, creating an "entire controversy" doctrine of claim preclusion. In Circle Chevrolet Co. v. Giordano, 142 N.J. 280, 662 A.2d 509 (1995), Circle Chevrolet leased land for its car dealership under a long-term written lease which included a formula for calculation of rent in the event the lease term was extended. The landowner miscalculated the rent when the lease was extended and, as a result, overcharged Circle Chevrolet. The attorneys representing Circle Chevrolet did not object to the landowner's calculation and discovered their mistake only after several years had passed. Circle, still represented by the same attorneys, then brought suit against the landlord and recovered the overcharge. After the conclusion of the first suit, Circle sued its attorneys for malpractice, seeking recovery of expenses and attorneys' fees incurred in the suit against the landlord. The New Jersey Supreme Court held that Circle should have brought the malpractice suit against its attorneys as part of its suit against the landlord. Having failed to do so, Circle was now barred by claim preclusion: "We ... hold that the entire controversy doctrine applies to a client's legal malpractice claims against his or her attorney, even when the attorney is currently representing the client in an underlying action."

See also Mortgagelinq Corp. v. Commonwealth Land Title Insurance Co., 142 N.J. 336, 662 A.2d 536 (1995); Mystic Isle Development Corp. v. Perskie &

Nehmad, 142 N.J. 310, 662 A.2d 523 (1995); DiTrolio v. Antiles, 142 N.J. 253, 662 A.2d 494 (1995).

New Jersey's "entire controversy" doctrine has been greeted with a mixture of glee and dismay. Professor Stein writes, "This is the stuff of law professors' dreams." Stein, "Foreword," 28 Rutgers L.J. 1 (1996). Professor Hazard writes, "[T]he 'Entire Controversy' doctrine is unintelligible to lawyers, the people who must make the crucial decisions in giving shape to a complex civil litigation. There is no such thing *ex ante*—that is, before the dust in litigation has begun to settle—as *an* entire controversy. Rather, there are immediate and obvious controversies but also secondary and contingent controversies. Most legal controversies, whether primary or secondary, will settle if courts will leave them alone. Moreover, until the immediate and obvious controversies are resolved, by settlement or trial, it cannot be determined whether the secondary and contingent controversies will mature into actual disputes." Hazard, "An Examination Before and Behind the 'Entire Controversy' Doctrine," 28 Rutgers L.J. 7 (1996).

(h) Federal courts' adherence to Restatement Second of Judgments § 24.

Recall Lim v. Central DuPage Hospital, 972 F.2d 758 (7th Cir.1992), bottom of p. 682 in the casebook, in which the Court of Appeals for the Seventh Circuit threatened Rule 11 sanctions for pursuing an antitrust claim that conflicted with the Seventh Circuit caselaw. The litigant withdrew his antitrust claim in the face of this threat. Then, after the United States Supreme Court in a separate case overruled the Seventh Circuit caselaw, the Seventh Circuit held that the litigant was barred by claim preclusion from reinstating his claim.

In McKnight v. General Motors Corp., 511 U.S. 659, 114 S.Ct. 1826, 128 L.Ed.2d 655 (1994)(per curiam), the Supreme Court rapped the knuckles of the Seventh Circuit for behavior similar to that in *Lim*. Plaintiff appealed a District Court dismissal of suit under § 101 of the Civil Rights Act of 1991, arguing that § 101 did not have retroactive application. The rule in the Seventh Circuit was that § 101 applied retroactively, and the Court of Appeals sanctioned the attorney $500 for bringing a frivolous appeal. The Supreme Court reversed the sanction, noting that there were conflicting decisions in several District Courts and that the Supreme Court had not yet ruled on the question: "Filing an appeal was the only way petitioner could preserve the issue pending a possible favorable decision by this Court." at 659.

In separate cases, the Supreme Court decided the merits of the § 101 issue adversely to the position advocated by plaintiff in *McKnight*. Landgraf v. USI Film Products, 511 U.S. 244, 114 S.Ct. 1483, 128 L.Ed.2d 229 (1994); Rivers v. Roadway Express, Inc., 511 U.S. 298, 114 S.Ct. 1510, 128 L.Ed.2d 274 (1994). By the time the Supreme Court issued its opinion in *McKnight* it had already issued opinions in *Landgraf* and *Rivers*. The fact that plaintiff's position on § 101 did not prevail does not mean that his appeal was frivolous.

5. Judicial estoppel. A useful summary, with special attention to the Ninth Circuit, is Moberly, "Playing 'Fast and Loose' or Just Fast?: A Look at Judicial Estoppel in the Ninth Circuit," 33 Gonz.L.Rev. 171 (1997/98).

8. Administrative agency determinations. Recall *University of Tennessee v. Elliott*, 478 U.S. 788, 106 S.Ct. 3220, 92 L.Ed.2d 635 (1986), p. 688 in the casebook, in which the Supreme Court held that an unreviewed state administrative determination does not have preclusive effect in a later federal employment discrimination suit under Title VII of the Civil Rights Act of 1964. In Bradshaw v. Golden Road Motor Inn, Inc., 885 F.Supp. 1370 (D.Nev.1995), plaintiff Bradshaw had been denied unemployment benefits in an unreviewed administrative decision finding that she had been properly discharged from her employment. The defendant employer sought to introduce the administrative decision in a later Title VII employment discrimination suit brought by Bradshaw. *University of Tennessee v. Elliott* clearly did not allow the administrative determination to be used as issue preclusion. The District Judge went further, holding that the administrative decision could not even be admitted as evidence in the Title VII suit:

> Unemployment benefits hearings are designed to be quick and inexpensive. If the decision resulting from such a hearing were given collateral estoppel effect in a federal lawsuit, the parties ... would have every incentive to turn the hearing itself into a full-blown lawsuit. The same incentives would be present, though in weaker form, if the parties knew the decision would be admitted, though not given preclusive effect, in the federal lawsuit.

at *13.

b. PRECLUSION AS AGAINST OTHER PARTIES
p. 704, 706

FURTHER NOTE ON PRECLUSION

2. Settlement to avoid preclusion. In U.S. Bancorp Mortgage Co. v. Bonner Mall Partnership, 513 U.S. 18, 115 S.Ct. 386, 130 L.Ed.2d 233 (1994), the Supreme Court held that vacatur of a lower court decision pursuant to settlement should be allowed only in "exceptional circumstances":

> "Judicial settlements are presumptively correct and valuable to the community as a whole. They are not merely the property of private litigants...." [citation omitted] Congress has prescribed a primary route, by appeal as of right and certiorari, through which parties may seek relief from the legal consequences of judicial judgments. To allow a party who steps off the statutory path to employ the secondary remedy of vacatur as a refined form of collateral attack on the judgment would—quite apart from any considerations of fairness to the parties— disturb the orderly operation of the federal judicial system.

at 392. For discussion written before the Court's decision in *U.S. Bancorp*, see Fisch, "Rewriting History: The Propriety of Eradicating Prior Decisional Law Through Settlement and Vacatur," 76 Cornell L.Rev. 589 (1990); Resnik, "Whose Judgment? Vacating Judgments, Preferences for Settlement, and the Role of Adjudication at the Close of the Twentieth Century," 41 U.C.L.A.L.Rev. 1471 (1994).

3. Preclusion effects of criminal convictions. A federal District Court has recently held that factual findings concerning defendant's conduct at a criminal sentencing hearing may be given preclusive effect in a later civil proceeding even if the defendant was acquitted of that very conduct. Securities and Exchange Commission v. Monarch Funding Corp., 983 F.Supp. 442 (S.D.N.Y.1997). Defendant was convicted on a few criminal charges and was acquitted on the rest. At his sentencing, the judge found that some of the conduct on which the defendant had been acquitted had, in fact, occurred. The judge used that finding to "enhance" the criminal sentence for the charges on which defendant had been convicted. (Under current law, facts supporting the length of a criminal sentence need only be established by a preponderance of the evidence, whereas facts supporting a criminal conviction must be established beyond a reasonable doubt. United States v. Watts, 519 U.S. 148, 117 S.Ct. 633, 136 L.Ed.2d 554 (1997).) The District Court noted that procedural rights at a sentencing hearing are generally narrower than in ordinary civil litigation–for example, the defendant may be denied the right to discovery or to call witnesses. Recognizing the danger in relying on facts established in such a proceeding, the District Court wrote that it "must carefully examine the underlying realities of the sentencing hearing prior to applying collateral estoppel to sentencing findings." at 448.

4. Preclusion against the United States. For a critical analysis of the Supreme Court's "blunt approach" in *Mendoza* and a suggestion that nonmutual issue preclusion should occasionally be available against states, see Comment, "Nonmutual Issue Preclusion against States," 109 Harv. L.Rev. 792 (1996).

Although there is no non-mutual issue preclusion against the United States, holdings in earlier cases do make some difference. In Allbritton v. Commissioner of Internal Revenue, 37 F.3d 183 (5th Cir.1994), the Internal Revenue Service asserted a position that had already been rejected by two Courts of Appeals and several District Courts:

> The government's assessment of deficiencies in the Taxpayers' income taxes, and its appeal based on the same statutory interpretation previously rejected by the Fourth Circuit, the Federal Circuit, and several district courts constitutes 'circuit shopping' at the Taxpayers' expense in the hopes of creating a circuit conflict. ... [W]hile the Commissioner is free by law to relitigate prior lost issues in other circuits, he does so at the risk of incurring the obligation to reimburse the taxpayer. [I]n continuing to litigate this issue despite constant jurisprudence to the contrary, the Commissioner is not substantially justified and should bear all reasonable costs of Taxpayers' litigation [including attorneys' fees].

at 184–85.

p. 716

NOTE ON *MARTIN v. WILKS* AND THE PROBLEM OF PRECLUDING NON–PARTIES

1. *Martin v. Wilks* (update). In In re Birmingham Reverse Discrimination Employment Litigation, 20 F.3d 1525 (11th Cir.1994), cert. denied sub nom. Arrington v. Wilks and Martin v. Wilks, 514 U.S. 1065, 115 S.Ct. 1695, 131 L.Ed.2d 558 (1995), the Court of Appeals decided the merits of the challenge to the 1981 consent decree. The decree set a goal that, "subject to the availability of qualified applicants," the percentages of racial groups in each city job classification should "approximate" their percentages in the civilian labor force. at 1532. The decree required that until the goal was achieved, hiring and promotion of black employees would be done at a prescribed percentages. One provision required that 50 percent of the promotions to Lieutenant in the Fire Department go to black employees until the overall goal was achieved. The Court of Appeals held that this provision violated Title VII of the Civil Rights Act of 1964 and the Fourteenth Amendment.

4. Application of *Martin v. Wilks*. In Richards v. Jefferson County, 517 U.S. 793, 116 S.Ct. 1761, 135 L.Ed.2d 76 (1996), plaintiffs brought a state court class action against Jefferson County, Alabama, on behalf of private taxpayers, challenging the county's occupation tax as unconstitutional. In an earlier suit brought by three county taxpayers and by the City of Birmingham and its finance director, the Supreme Court of Alabama had sustained the tax. The Alabama Supreme Court found that plaintiffs in the second suit had been "adequately represented ... because their interests were 'essentially identical'" to the litigants' interest in the first suit. It therefore held that plaintiffs were bound by the result in the first suit.

The Supreme Court unanimously reversed. It held that plaintiffs had never received notice of the first suit. Further, even if they had received notice, plaintiffs' interests had not been properly represented by the earlier litigants. The three private taxpayers in the first suit had not brought a class action. Nor had the City of Birmingham and its finance director adequately represented private taxpayers. The Court said, "Even if we were to assume ... that by suing in his official capacity, the finance director intended to represent the pecuniary interests of all county taxpayers, and not simply the corporate interests of the city itself, he did not purport to represent the pecuniary interests of *county* taxpayers like petitioners." at 1767. "Because petitioners received neither notice of, nor sufficient representation in, the [earlier] litigation, that adjudication, as a matter of federal due process, may not bind them and thus cannot bar them from challenging an allegedly unconstitutional deprivation of their property." at 1769.

2. RECOGNITION OF JUDGMENTS FROM OTHER JURISDICTIONS

a. INTERSTATE RECOGNITION OF JUDGMENTS
p. 729

NOTE ON FULL FAITH AND CREDIT

1. Recognition of judgments. For a clear description of the operation of the Full Faith and Credit Clause in enforcing judgments, see

Reynolds, "The Iron Law of Full Faith and Credit," 53 Md.L.Rev. 412 (1994).

b. FEDERAL–STATE RECOGNITION OF JUDGMENTS
p. 743, 744

NOTE ON FEDERAL–STATE AND INTERNATIONAL RECOGNITION OF JUDGMENTS

1. Federal-state recognition. (a) The Supreme Court has recently expanded *Marrese* beyond litigated judgments to include court-approved settlements. In Matsushita Electric Industrial Co. v. Epstein, 516 U.S. 367, 116 S.Ct. 873, 134 L.Ed.2d 6 (1996), a disputed tender offer and corporate acquisition resulted in two shareholder class actions in state and federal court. The state court action, filed in Delaware, was based on state law, and the federal court action was based on federal securities statutes. Suits based on federal securities laws are within the exclusive jurisdiction of the federal courts. The state court suit was terminated first, in a judgment incorporating a court-approved settlement. The settlement purported to resolve all state and federal claims against the defendants even though the state court did not have (and indeed could not have had) the federal claims before it.

The Supreme Court held that the state court settlement was entitled to whatever preclusive effect the Delaware courts would have given it. "[W]e conclude that § 1738 is generally applicable in cases in which the state court judgment at issue incorporates a class action settlement releasing claims solely within the jurisdiction of the federal courts." at 878. The Court then analyzed Delaware law and concluded that if otherwise valid the settlement was preclusive as to both the state and federal claims. For discussion of the Supreme Court's decision, see Kahan and Silberman, "*Matsushita* and Beyond: The Role of State Courts in Class Actions Involving Exclusive Federal Claims," 1996 Sup.Ct.Rev. 219.

After remand, the Court of Appeals addressed a question left open by the Supreme Court–whether the settlement violated the due process clause of the Fourteenth Amendment. The Court of Appeals found that the representation of plaintiffs' interests by class counsel in the Delaware had been so inadequate as to violate due process. Epstein v. MCA, Inc., 126 F.3d 1235 (9th Cir.1997). (See, infra p. 86, for further discussion.)

(b) Another troublesome case involving a state court class action settlement is In re General Motors Corp. Pick-Up Truck Fuel Tank Products Liability Litigation, 134 F.3d 133 (3d Cir.1998), in which plaintiffs alleged that fuel tanks of GM pick-up trucks were prone to rupture and to cause fires in accidents. The federal Court of Appeals had earlier reversed and remanded a certification of a "settlement class" by the District Court on the ground that Fed.R.Civ.P. 23 did not permit settlement classes, noting the absence of procedural protections against collusive or severely inadequate settlements. (See, infra p. 102, for materials on settlement class actions, including an excerpt from the earlier opinion in this case.) Rather than proceeding in the District Court on remand, "the parties to the settlement repaired to the 18th Judicial District for the Parish of Iberville, Louisiana, where a similar suit had been pending, restructured their deal, and submitted it to the Louisiana court, which ultimately approved it." at 137. The Court of Appeals declined to enjoin the operation of the state court settlement, based on *Parsons Steel* and *Chick Kam Choo v. Exxon Corp.* (pp. 739, 744, casebook). Not only was the earlier reversal and remand to the District Court not a "judgment." The federal and state courts were also deciding different legal questions: The Court of Appeals had applied Fed.R.Civ.P 23, whereas the Louisiana court was applying the state class action rule. at 145.

(c) In Baker v. General Motors Corp., ___ U.S. ___, 118 S.Ct. 657, 139 L.Ed.2d 580 (1998), the Supreme Court held that 28 U.S.C. § 1738 does not require a federal court to obey a state court decree enjoining a party from testifying in later suits. In the first suit, plaintiff Elwell sued his employer, General Motors Corporation, for wrongful discharge in Michigan state court. During fifteen of his thirty years at GM, Elwell had studied fires in GM vehicles. Elwell and GM settled the state court suit. Pursuant to the settlement, the court entered a judgment enjoining Elwell from "testifying, without the prior written consent of General Motors Corporation, either upon deposition or at trial, as an expert witness, or as a witness of any kind, and from consulting with attorneys or their agents in any litigation ... involving General Motors Corporation[.]"

In a separate suit brought in federal District Court in Missouri, plaintiffs' mother was burned to death in an accident in a General Motors vehicle. Over GM's objection, plaintiffs deposed Elwell and called him as a witness. The Supreme Court held that the Michigan state court decree could not prevent Elwell from testifying:

> Michigan's judgment ... cannot reach beyond the Elwell–GM controversy to control proceedings against GM brought in other States, by other parties, asserting claims the merits of which Michigan has not considered. Michigan has no power over those parties, and no basis for commanding them to become intervenors in the Elwell–GM dispute. ... Most essentially, Michigan lacks authority to control courts elsewhere by precluding them, in actions brought by strangers to the Michigan litigation, from determining for themselves what witnesses are competent to testify and what evidence is relevant and admissible in their search for the truth. ... Michigan's decree could operate against Elwell to preclude him from *volunteering* his testimony. ... But a Michigan court cannot, by entering the injunction to which Elwell and GM stipulated, dictate to a court in another jurisdiction that evidence relevant in [this] case—a controversy to which Michigan is foreign—shall be inadmissible.

118 S.Ct. at 666–7 (emph. in original).

(d) In Rivet v. Regions Bank of Louisiana, ___ U.S. ___, 118 S.Ct. 921, 139 L.Ed.2d 912 (1998), the Supreme Court held that a res judicata defense in state court based on an earlier federal court judgment cannot serve as a basis for removal to federal court. The party wishing to assert res judicata may either assert the defense in state court, or may go to federal court for an injunction against state-court proceedings under the relitigation exception to the Anti–Injunction Act, 28 U.S.C. § 2283. at 926 n. 3. (See discussion, supra p. 41.)

(e) An excellent recent analysis of state-federal preclusion problems is Erichson, "Interjurisdictional Preclusion," 96 Mich.L.Rev. 945 (1998).

2. International recognition. In Matusevitch v. Telnikoff, 877 F.Supp. 1 (D.D.C.1995), plaintiff brought suit in federal District Court to preclude enforcement of a British libel judgment in Maryland, which has adopted the Uniform Foreign–Money Judgment Recognition Act. The District Court held that the British judgment was not entitled to recognition because British law provides too little protection to defendants in libel cases. If applied in the United States, British law would violate a defendant's First and Fourteenth Amendment rights. Thus, "the cause of action on which the judgment is based is repugnant to the public policy of the State." Md.Code Ann., Cts. & Jud. Proc. § 10–704(b)(2); see also Uniform Act, § 4(b)(3), p. 745 in the casebook.

C. JOINDER OF PARTIES

2. BASIC CONCEPTS OF PARTY JOINDER

a. PERMISSIVE JOINDER

p. 789

NOTE ON PERMISSIVE JOINDER OF PARTIES

2. Permissive joinder of parties and supplemental jurisdiction. In federal question cases, a federal District Court has supplemental jurisdiction over all claims forming part of the same case or controversy, even state-law claims by non-diverse parties and by diverse parties alleging $75,000 *or less* in controversy. 28 U.S.C. § 1367(a). (See p. 433 of the casebook for an analysis of § 1367.) In diversity cases, however, matters are not so simple. Section 1367(b) provides that in diversity cases "the district courts shall not have supplemental jurisdiction ... over claims by plaintiffs against persons made parties under Rule ... 20...." It is thus clear that there is no supplemental jurisdiction over state-law claims *against non-diverse defendants* joined under Rule 20. But what about state-law claims *by non-diverse plaintiffs,* or state-law claims *by diverse plaintiffs alleging $75,000 or less,* joined under Rule 20? In enumerating claims over which there is no supplemental jurisdiction, § 1367(b) does not mention these claims. Under the scheme of the statute, the failure to mention a claim in § 1367(b) means that supplemental jurisdiction exists. But this literalistic reading conflicts with deeply rooted principles of complete diversity and amount-in-controversy that prevailed before the enactment of § 1367. (See pp. 411–413 of the casebook.)

One Court of Appeals has found supplemental jurisdiction over a claim brought by an additional plaintiff joined under Rule 20 in a diversity case even when the additional plaintiff could not satisfy the amount in controversy requirement. Stromberg Metal Works, Inc. v. Press Mechanical, Inc., 77 F.3d 928 (7th Cir.1996). District Courts have given conflicting answers to the question. *Compare,* e.g., Garza v. National American Insurance Co., 807 F.Supp. 1256 (M.D.La.1992) (supplemental jurisdiction), and Patterson Enterprises v. Bridgestone/Firestone, Inc., 812 F.Supp. 1152 (D.Kan.1993) (supplemental jurisdiction), *with* Griffin v. Dana Point Condominium Ass'n, 768 F.Supp. 1299 (N.D.Ill.1991) (no supplemental jurisdiction). For discussion, see Hirschfeld, "The $50,000 Question: Does Supplemental Jurisdiction Extend to Claims Between Diverse Parties Which Do Not Meet § 1332's Amount–in–Controversy Requirement?" 68 Temple L.Rev. 107 (1995) (arguing that there should be no supplemental jurisdiction).

b. COMPULSORY JOINDER

p. 797

NOTE ON COMPULSORY JOINDER OF PARTIES

3. Fed.R.Civ.P. 19 and supplemental jurisdiction.

Please replace the first paragraph, running from the bottom of page 797 to the top of page 798, with the following:

The Court of Appeals in *Associated Dry Goods* assumed that 417 Fifth was a party "to be joined if feasible" under Fed.R.Civ.P. 19(a). The Court of Appeals does not specifically say so, but it assumes that 417 Fifth would be aligned as a co-plaintiff with Associated if it were joined under Rule 19. (This alignment of parties is made clear in the opinion of the District Court. See Associated Dry Goods v. Towers Financial Corp., 127 F.R.D. 57, 62 (S.D.N.Y.1989).) But plaintiff Associated could not join 417 Fifth as a co-plaintiff since this would have destroyed complete diversity. There is diversity between plaintiff Associated, a Virginia corporation with its principal place of business in Missouri, and defendant Towers, a Nevada corporation with its principal place of business in New York. 417 Fifth would defeat complete diversity as a co-plaintiff since it is a New York "resident," at 790, with its principal place of business in New York. The court's solution is to require Towers to use Rule 13 to make 417 Fifth a party to Towers' compulsory counterclaim against Associated.

3. DEVICES FOR ADDING PARTIES

b. INTERVENTION

p. 819

FURTHER NOTE ON INTERVENTION

2a. Intervention and standing under Article III. The Courts of Appeals have given different answers to the question whether an intervenor under Fed.R.Civ.P. 24 must have sufficient "standing"—that is, interest in the suit—to satisfy the "case or controversy" requirement of Article III of the Constitution. Compare, e.g., Mausolf v. Babbitt, 85 F.3d 1295 (8th Cir.1996)(Article III standing required), with United States Postal Service v. Brennan, 579 F.2d 188 (2d Cir.1978)(contra). The Supreme Court has noted the question but has declined to answer it. Diamond v. Charles, 476 U.S. 54, 68–9 n. 5, 106 S.Ct. 1697, 90 L.Ed.2d 48 (1986). For discussion of Article III standing, see pp. 765–78 of the casebook.

6. Supplemental jurisdiction. A federal District Court in a diversity case has supplemental jurisdiction over counterclaims against a plaintiff and cross claims against a co-defendant when those claims are made by a defendant intervening as of right under Fed.R.Civ.P. 24(a). See 28 U.S.C. § 1367(b); Development Finance Corp. v. Alpha Housing & Health Care, Inc., 54 F.3d 156 (3d Cir.1995).

4. NOMINAL PARTIES

p. 840

NOTE ON THE REAL PARTY IN INTEREST RULE

For a thorough analysis of the application of Fed.R.Civ.P. 17 and 19 to the insurer who has compensated plaintiff and who seeks reimbursement from the defendant, see Entman, "Compulsory Joinder of Compensating Insurers: Federal Rule of Civil Procedure 19 and the Role of Substantive Law," 45 Case W.Res.L.Rev. 1 (1994).

6. CLASS SUITS

b. USES AND ADMINISTRATION OF CLASS SUITS

p. 891

NOTE ON CLASS SUITS IN PRODUCT LIABILITY AND MASS TORT LITIGATION

In recent years, there has been increasing pressure to use class actions in product liability and mass tort litigation. Such litigation poses enormous problems of administration and fairness. For useful discussions, see Symposium, "Mass Tortes: Serving Up Just Desserts," 80 Cornell L.Rev. 811 (1995); Misko and Goodrich, "Managing Complex Litigation: Class Actions and Mass Torts," 48 Baylor L.Rev. 1001 (1996).

p. 891, after NOTE ON CLASS SUITS IN PRODUCT LIABILITY AND MASS TORT LITIGATION

IN RE RHONE–POULENC RORER, INC.
United States Court of Appeals for the Seventh Circuit, 1995.
51 F.3d 1293.

Posner, Chief Judge:

Drug companies that manufacture blood solids are the defendants in a nationwide class action brought on behalf of hemophiliacs infected by the AIDS virus as a consequence of using the defendants' products. The defendants have filed with us a petition for mandamus, asking us to direct the district judge to rescind his order certifying the case as a class action. We have no appellate jurisdiction over that order. An order certifying a class is not a final decision within the meaning of 28 U.S.C. § 1291; it does not wind up the litigation in the district court. And, in part because it is reviewable (at least in principle—the importance of this qualification will appear shortly) on appeal from the final decision in the case, it has been held not to fit any of the exceptions to the rule that confines federal appellate jurisdiction to final decisions. In short, as the Supreme Court made clear in Coopers & Lybrand v. Livesay, 437 U.S. 463, 98 S.Ct. 2454, 57 L.Ed.2d 351 (1978), and Gardner v. Westinghouse Broadcasting Co., 437 U.S. 478, 480–82, 98 S.Ct. 2451, 57 L.Ed.2d 364 (1978), it is not an appealable order. Those decisions involved the denial rather than the grant of motions for class certification, but the grant is no more final than the denial and no more within any of the exceptions to the final-decision rule. Hoxworth v. Blinder, Robinson & Co., 903 F.2d 186, 208 (3d Cir.1990); 7B Charles Alan Wright, Arthur A. Miller & Mary Kay Kane, Federal Practice and Procedure § 1802, pp. 484–86 (2d ed. 1986). Still, even nonappealable orders can be challenged by asking the court of appeal to mandamus the district court. * * * For obvious reasons, * * * mandamus is issued only in extraordinary cases. Otherwise, interlocutory orders would be appealable routinely, but with "appeal" renamed "mandamus." Kerr v. United States District Court, 426 U.S. 394, 403, 96 S.Ct. 2119, 48 L.Ed.2d 725 (1976); Eisenberg v. United States District Court, 910 F.2d 374, 375 (7th Cir.1990).

How to cabin this too-powerful writ which if uncabined threatens to unravel the final-decision rule? By taking seriously the two conditions for the grant of a writ of mandamus. The first is that the challenged order not be effectively reviewable at the end of the case—in other words, that it inflict irreparable harm. Kerr v. United States, supra, 426 U.S. at 403; In re Sandahl, 980 F.2d 1118, 1119 (7th Cir.1992); Eisenberg v. United States District Court, supra, 910 F.2d at 375. The petitioner "must ordinarily demonstrate that something about the order, or its circumstances, would make an end-of-case appeal effectual or leave legitimate interests unduly at risk." In re Recticel Foam Corp., 859 F.2d 1000, 1005–06 (1st Cir.1988). Second, the order must so far exceed the proper bounds of judicial discretion as to be legitimately considered usurpative in character, or in violation of a clear and indisputable legal right, or, at the very least, patently erroneous. Gulfstream Aerospace Corp. v. Mayacamas Corp., 485 U.S. 271, 289, 108 S.Ct. 1133, 99 L.Ed.2d 296 (1988); * * *

The set of orders in which both conditions are satisfied is small. It certainly is not coterminous with the set of orders certifying suits as class actions. For even though such orders often, perhaps typically, inflict irreparable injury on the defendants (just as orders denying class certification often, perhaps typically, inflict irreparable injury on the members of the class), irreparable injury is not sufficient for mandamus; there must also be an abuse of discretion that can fairly be characterized as gross, very clear, or unusually serious. But it is not an empty set. The point of cases like Coopers & Lybrand is that irreparable harm is not enough to make class certification orders automatically appealable under 28 U.S.C. § 1291, not that mandamus is never appropriate in a class certification setting. There is a big difference between saying that all class certification rulings are appealable as of right because they are final within the meaning of section 1291 (the position rejected in Coopers & Lybrand) and saying that a handful are—the handful in which the district judge committed a clear abuse of discretion. Mandamus has occasionally been granted to undo class certifications, see, e.g., In re Fibreboard Corp., 893 F.2d 706 (5th Cir.1990), and we are not aware that any case has held that mandamus will never be granted in such cases. See In re Catawba Indian Tribe, 973 F.2d 1133, 1137 (4th Cir.1992); DeMasi v. Weiss, 669 F.2d 114, 117–19 and n. 6 (3d Cir.1982). The present case, as we shall see, is quite extraordinary when all its dimensions are apprehended. We shall also see that when mandamus is sought to protect the Seventh Amendment's right to a jury trial in federal civil cases, as in this case, the requirement of proving irreparable harm is relaxed.

The suit to which the petition for mandamus relates, *Wadleigh v. Rhone–Poulenc Rorer, Inc.*, arises out of the infection of a substantial fraction of the hemophiliac population of this country by the AIDS virus because the blood supply was contaminated by the virus before the nature of the disease was well understood or adequate methods of screening the blood supply existed. The AIDS virus (HIV—human immunodeficiency virus) is transmitted by the exchange of bodily fluids, primarily semen and blood. Hemophiliacs depend on blood solids that contain the clotting factors whose absence defines their disease. These blood solids are concentrated from blood obtained from many donors. If just one of the donors is infected by the AIDS virus the probability that the blood solids manufactured in part from his blood will be infected is very high unless the blood is treated with heat to kill the virus. * * *

First identified in 1981, AIDS was diagnosed in hemophiliacs beginning in 1982, and by 1984 the medical community agreed that the virus was transmitted by blood as well as by semen. That year it was demonstrated that treatment with heat could kill the virus in the blood supply and in the following year a reliable test for the presence of the virus in blood was developed. By this time, however, a large number of hemophiliacs had become infected. Since 1984 physicians have been advised to place hemophiliacs on heat-treated blood solid, and since 1985 all blood donated for the manufacture of blood solids has been screened and supplies discovered to be HIV-positive have been discarded. Supplies that test negative still are heat-treated, because the test is not infallible and in particular may fail to detect the virus in persons who became infected within six months before taking the test.

The plaintiffs have presented evidence that 2,000 hemophiliacs have died of AIDS and that half or more of the remaining U.S. hemophiliac population of 20,000 may be HIV-positive. Unless there are dramatic breakthroughs in the treatment of HIV or AIDS, all infected persons will die from the disease. The reason so many are infected even though the supply of blood for the manufacture of blood solids (as for transfusions) has been safe since the mid–80s is that the disease has a very long incubation period; the median period for hemophiliacs may be as long as 11 years. Probably most of the hemophiliacs who are now HIV-positive, or have AIDS, or have died of AIDS were infected in the early 1980s, when the blood supply was contaminated.

Some 300 lawsuits, involving some 400 plaintiffs, have been filed, 60 percent of them in state courts, 40 percent in federal district courts under the diversity jurisdiction, seeking to impose tort liability on the defendants for the transmission of HIV to hemophiliacs in blood solids manufactured by the defendants. Obviously these 400 plaintiffs represent only a small fraction of the hemophiliacs (or their next of kin, in cases in which the hemophiliac has died) who are infected by HIV or have died of AIDS. One of the 300 cases is Wadleigh, filed in September 1993, the case that the district judge certified as a class action. Thirteen other cases have been tried already in various courts around the country, and the defendants have won twelve of them. All the cases brought in federal court (like Wadleigh)—cases brought under the diversity jurisdiction—have been consolidated for pretrial discovery in the Northern District of Illinois by the panel on multidistrict litigation.

The plaintiffs advance two principal theories of liability. The first is that before anyone had heard of AIDS or HIV, it was known that Hepatitis B, a lethal disease through less so than HIV–AIDS, could be transmitted either through blood transfusions or through injection of blood solids. The plaintiffs argue that due care with respect to the risk of infection with Hepatitis B required the defendants to take measures to purge that virus from their blood solids, whether by treating the blood they bought or by screening the donors—perhaps by refusing to deal with paid donors, known to be a class at high risk of being infected with Hepatitis B. The defendants' failure to take effective measures was, the plaintiffs claim, negligent. Had the defendants not been negligent, the plaintiffs further argue, hemophiliacs would have been protected not only against Hepatitis B but also, albeit fortuitously or as the plaintiffs put it "serendipitously," against HIV.

The plaintiffs' second theory of liability is more conventional. It is that the defendants, again negligently, dragged their heels in screening donors and taking other measures to prevent contamination of blood solids by HIV when they learned about the disease in the early 1980s.
* * *

The district judge did not think it feasible to certify Wadleigh as a class action for the adjudication of the entire controversy between the plaintiffs and the defendants. Fed.R. Civ.P. 23(b)(3). The differences in the date of infection alone of the thousands of potential class members would make such a procedure infeasible. Hemophiliacs infected before anyone knew about the contamination of blood solids by HIV could not rely on the second theory of liability, while hemophiliacs infected after the blood supply became safe (not perfectly safe, but nearly so) probably were not infected by any of the defendants' products. Instead the judge certified the suit "as a class action with respect to particular issues" only. Fed.R.Civ.P. 23(c)(4)(A). He explained this decision in an opinion which implied that he did not envisage the entry of a final judgment but rather the rendition by a jury of a special verdict that would answer a number of questions bearing, perhaps decisively, on whether the defendants are negligent under either of the theories sketched above. If the special verdict found no negligence under either theory, that presumably would be the end of all the cases unless other theories of liability proved viable. If the special verdict found negligence, individual members of the class would then file individual tort suits in state and federal district courts around the nation and would use the special verdict, in conjunction with the doctrine of collateral estoppel, to block relitigation of the issue of negligence.

With all due respect for the district judge's commendable desire to experiment with an innovative procedure for streamlining the adjudication of this "mass tort," we believe that his plan so far exceeds the permissible bounds of discretion in the management of federal litigation as to compel us to intervene and order decertification. * * *

Consider the situation that would obtain if the class had not been certified. The defendants would be facing 300 suits. More might be filed, but probably only a few more, because the statutes of limitations in the various states are rapidly expiring for potential plaintiffs. * * *

Three hundred is not a trivial number of lawsuits. The potential damages in each one are great. But the defendants have won twelve of the first thirteen, and, if this is a representative sample, they are likely to win most of the remaining ones as well. Perhaps in the end, if class action treatment is denied (it has been denied in all the other hemophiliac HIV suits in which class certification has been sought), they will be compelled to pay damages in only 25 cases, involving a potential liability of perhaps no more than $125 million altogether. These are guesses, of course, but they are at once conservative and usable for the limited purpose of comparing the situation that will face the defendants if the class certification stands. All of a sudden they will face thousands of plaintiffs. Many may already be barred by the statute of limitations, as we have suggested, though its further running was tolled by the filing of Wadleigh as a class action. American Pipe & Construction Co. v. Utah, 414 U.S. 538, 554, 94 S.Ct. 756, 38 L.Ed.2d 713 (1974). (If the class is decertified, the statute of limitations will start running again. Glidden v. Chromalloy American Corp., 808 F.2d 621, 627 (7th Cir.1986); * * *.)

Suppose that 5,000 of the potential class members are not yet barred by the statute of limitations. And suppose the named plaintiffs in Wadleigh win the class portion of this case to the extent of establishing the defendants' liability under either of the two negligence theories. It is true that this would only be prima facie liability, that the defendants would have various defenses. But they could not be confident that the defenses would prevail. They might, therefore, easily be facing $25 billion in potential liability (conceivably more), and with bankruptcy. They may not wish to roll these dice. That is putting it mildly. They will be under intense pressure to settle. * * * Judge Friendly, who was not given to hyperbole, called settlements induced by a small probability of an immense judgment in a class action "blackmail settlements." Henry J. Friendly, Federal Jurisdiction: A General View 120 (1973). Judicial concern about them is legitimate, not "sociological," as it was derisively termed in In re Sugar Antitrust Litigation, 559 F.2d 481, 483 n. 1 (9th Cir.1977).

* * *

We do not want to be misunderstood as saying that class actions are bad because they place pressure on defendants to settle. That pressure is a reality, but it must be balanced against the undoubted benefits of the class action that have made it an authorized procedure for employment by federal courts. We have yet to consider the balance. All that our discussion to this point has shown is that the first condition for the grant of mandamus—that the challenged ruling not be effectively reviewable at the end of the case—is fulfilled. The ruling will inflict irreparable harm; the next question is whether the ruling can fairly be described as usurpative. We have formulated this second condition as narrowly, as stringently, as can be, but even so formulated we think it is fulfilled. We do not mean to suggest that the district judge is engaged in a deliberate power-grab. We have no reason to suppose that he wants to preside over an unwieldy class action. We believe that he was responding imaginatively and in the best of faith to the challenge that mass torts, graphically illustrated by the avalanche of asbestos litigation, pose for the federal courts. But the plan that he has devised for the HIV-hemophilia litigation exceeds the bounds of allowable judicial discretion. Three concerns, none of them necessarily sufficient in itself but cumulatively compelling, persuade us to this conclusion.

The first is a concern with forcing these defendants to stake their companies on the outcome of a single jury trial, or be forced by fear of the risk of bankruptcy to settle even if they have no legal liability, when it is entirely feasible to allow a final, authoritative determination of their liability for the colossal misfortune that has befallen the hemophiliac population to emerge from a decentralized process of multiple trials, involving different juries, and different standards of liability, in different jurisdictions; and when, in addition, the preliminary indications are that the defendants are not liable for the grievous harm that has befallen the members of the class. These qualifications are important. In most class actions—and those the ones in which the rationale for the procedure is most compelling—individual suits are infeasible because the claim of each class member is tiny relative to the expense of litigation. That plainly is not the situation here. A notable feature of this case, and one that has not been remarked upon or encountered, so far as we are aware, in previous cases, is the demonstrated great likelihood that the plaintiffs' claims, despite their human appeal, lack legal merit. This is the inference from the defendants' having won 92.3 percent ($^{12}/_{13}$) of the cases to have gone to judgment. * * *

For this consensus or maturing of judgment the district judge proposes to substitute a single trial before a single jury instructed in accordance with no actual law of any jurisdiction—a jury that will receive a kind of Esperanto instruction, merging the negligence standards of the 50 states and the District of Columbia. One jury, consisting of six persons (the standard federal civil jury nowadays consists of six regular jurors and two alternates), will hold the fate of an industry in the palm of its hand. This jury, jury number fourteen, may disagree with twelve of the previous thirteen juries—and hurl the industry into bankruptcy. That kind of thing can happen in our system of civil justice (it is not likely to happen, because the industry is likely to settle—whether or not it really is liable) without violating anyone's legal rights. But it need not be tolerated when the alternative exists of submitting an issue to multiple juries constituting in the aggregate a much larger and more diverse sample of decision-makers. That would not be a feasible option if the stakes to each class member were too slight to repay the cost of suit, even though the aggregate stakes are very large and would repay the costs of a consolidated proceeding. But this is not the case with regard to the HIV-hemophilia litigation. Each plaintiff if successful is apt to receive a judgment in the millions. With the aggregate stakes in the tens or hundreds of millions of dollars, or even in the billions, it is not a waste of judicial resources to conduct more than one trial, before more than six jurors, to determine whether a major segment of the international pharmaceutical industry is to follow the asbestos manufacturers into Chapter 11.

We have hinted at the second reason for concern that the district judge exceeded the bounds of permissible judicial discretion. He proposes to have a jury determine the negligence of the defendants under a legal standard that does not actually exist anywhere in the world. One is put in mind of the concept of "general" common law that prevailed in the era of Swift v. Tyson. The assumption is that the common law of the 50 states and the District of Columbia, at least so far as bears on a claim of negligence against drug companies, is basically uniform and can be abstracted in a single instruction. It is no doubt true that at some level of generality the law of negligence is one, not only nationwide but worldwide. Negligence is a failure to take due care, and due care a function of the probability and magnitude of accident and the costs of avoiding it. A jury can be asked whether the defendants took due care. And in many cases such differences as there are among the tort rules of the different states would not affect the outcome. The Second Circuit was willing to assume dubitante that this was true of the issues certified for class determination in the Agent Orange litigation. In re Diamond Shamrock Chemicals Co., 725 F.2d 858, 861 (2d Cir.1984).

We doubt that it is true in general, and we greatly doubt that it is true in a case such as this in which one of the theories pressed by the plaintiffs, the "serendipity" theory, is novel. If one instruction on negligence will serve to instruct the jury on the legal standard of every state of the United States applicable to a novel claim, implying that the claim despite its controversiality would be decided identically in all 50 states and the District of Columbia, one wonders what the Supreme Court thought it was doing in the Erie case when it held that it was unconstitutional for federal courts in diversity cases to apply general common law rather than the common law of the state whose law would apply if the case were being tried in state rather than federal court. Erie R.R. v. Tompkins, 304 U.S. 64, 78–80, 58 S.Ct. 817, 82 L.Ed. 1188 (1938). * * * "The common law is not a brooding omnipresence in the sky, but the articulate voice of some sovereign or quasi sovereign that can be identified." Southern Pacific Co. v. Jensen, 244 U.S. 205, 222, 37 S.Ct. 524, 61 L.Ed. 1086 (1917)(Holmes, J. dissenting). The voices of the quasi-sovereigns that are the states of the United States sing negligence with a different pitch.

* * *

The diversity jurisdiction of the federal courts is, after Erie, designed merely to provide an alternative forum for the litigation of state-law claims, not an alternative system of substantive law for diversity cases. But under the district judge's plan the thousands of members of the plaintiff class will have their rights determined, and the four defendant manufacturers will have their duties determined, under a law that is merely an amalgam, an averaging, of the nonidentical negligence laws of 51 jurisdictions. No one doubts that Congress could constitutionally prescribe a uniform standard of liability for manufacturers of blood solids. It might we suppose promulgate pertinent provisions of the Restatement (Second) of Torts. The point of Erie is that Article III of the Constitution does not empower the federal courts to create such a regime for diversity cases.

* * *

The third respect in which we believe that the district judge has exceeded his authority concerns the point at which his plan of action proposes to divide the trial of the issues that he has certified for class-action treatment from the other issues involved in the thousands of actual and potential claims of representatives and members of the class. Bifurcation and even finer divisions of lawsuits into separate trials are authorized in federal district courts. Fed.R.Civ.P. 42(b); Sellers v. Baisier, 792 F.2d 690, 694 (7th Cir.1986). And a decision to employ the procedure is reviewed deferentially. Berry v. Deloney, 28 F.3d 604, 610 (7th Cir.1994); * * *. However, as we have been at pains to stress recently, the district judge must carve at the joint. Hydrite Chemical Co. v. Calumet Lubricants Co., 47 F.3d 887 (7th Cir.1995); cf. McLaughlin v. State Farm Mutual Automobile Ins. Co., 30 F.3d 861, 870–71 (7th Cir.1994). Of particular relevance here, the judge must not divide issues between separate trials in such a way that the same issue is reexamined by different juries. * * * [M]ost of the separate "cases" that compose this class action will be tried, after the initial trial in the Northern District of Illinois, in different courts, scattered throughout the country. The right to a jury trial in federal civil cases, conferred by the Seventh Amendment, is a right to have juriable issues determined by the first jury impaneled to hear them (provided there are no errors warranting a new trial), and not reexamined by another finder of fact. This would be obvious if the second finder of fact were a judge. Byrd v. Blue Ridge Rural Electric Cooperative, Inc., 356 U.S. 525, 537–38, 78 S.Ct. 893, 2 L.Ed.2d 953 (1958); Davenport v. DeRobertis, 844 F.2d 1310, 1313–14 (7th Cir.1988); Hunter v. Allis–Chalmers Corp., 797 F.2d 1417, 1421 (7th Cir.1986). But it is equally true if it is another jury. Gasoline Products Co. v. Champlin Refining Co., 283 U.S. 494, 500, 51 S.Ct. 513, 75 L.Ed. 1188 (1931); McDaniel v. Anheuser–Busch, Inc., 987 F.2d 298, 305 (5th Cir.1993); Alabama v. Blue Bird Body Co., 573 F.2d 309, 318 (5th Cir.1978). * * *

The plan of the district judge in this case is inconsistent with the principle that the findings of one jury are not to be reexamined by a second, or third, or nth jury. The first jury will not determine liability. It will determine merely whether one or more of the defendants was negligent under one of the two theories. The first jury may go on to decide the additional issues with regard to the named plaintiffs. But it will not decide them with regard to the other class members. Unless the defendants settle, a second (and third, and fourth, and hundredth, and conceivably thousandth) jury will have to decide, in individual follow-on litigation by class members not named as plaintiffs in the Wadleigh case, such issues as comparative negligence—did any class members knowingly continue to use unsafe blood solids after they learned or should have learned of the risk of contamination with HIV?—and proximate causation. Both issues overlap the issue of the defendants' negligence. Comparative negligence entails, as the name implies, a comparison of the degree of negligence of plaintiff and defendant. See, e.g., Alaska Stat. § 09.17.080; ILCS 735 5/2–1116; N.J. Stat. § 2A:15–5.1; Ohio Rev. Code § 2315.19; Utah Code § 78'38. Proximate causation is found by determining whether the harm to the plaintiff followed in some sense naturally, uninterruptedly, and with reasonable probability from the negligent act of the defendant. It overlaps the issue of the defendants' negligence even when the state's law does not (as many states do) make the foreseeability of the risk to which the defendant subjected the plaintiff an explicit ingredient of negligence. See, e.g., Powell v. Drumheller, 539 Pa. 484, 653 A.2d 619 (1995) * * *. How the resulting inconsistency between juries could be prevented escapes us.

The protection of the right conferred by the Seventh Amendment to trial by jury in federal civil cases is a traditional office of the writ of mandamus. Beacon Theatres v. Westover, 359 U.S. 500, 510–11, 79 S.Ct. 948, 3 L.Ed.2d 988 (1959); Dairy Queen, Inc. v. Wood, 369 U.S. 469, 472, 82 S.Ct. 894, 8 L.Ed.2d 44 (1962); * * *. When the writ is used for that purpose, strict compliance with the stringent conditions on the availability of the writ (including the requirement of proving irreparable harm) is excused. * * * But the looming infringement of Seventh Amendment rights is only one of our grounds for believing this to be a case in which the issuance of a writ of mandamus is warranted. The others as we have said are the undue and unnecessary risk of a monumental industry-busting error in entrusting the determination of potential multibillion dollar liabilities to a single jury when the results of the previous cases indicate that the defendants' liability is doubtful at best and the questionable constitutionality of trying a diversity case under a legal standard in force in no state. We need not consider whether any of these grounds standing by itself would warrant mandamus in this case. Together they make a compelling case.

We know that an approach similar to that proposed by [the district judge] has been approved for asbestos litigation. See in particular Jenkins v. Raymark Industries, Inc., 782 F.2d 468 (5th Cir.1986); In re School Asbestos Litigation, 789 F.2d 996 (3d Cir.1986). Most federal courts, however, refuse to permit the use of the class action device in mass-tort cases, even asbestos cases. Thomas E. Willging, Trends in

Asbestos Litigation 93–98 (Federal Judicial Center 1987); cf. In re Fibreboard Corp., supra; In re Joint Eastern & Southern District Asbestos Litigation, 982 F.2d 721 (2d Cir.1992). Those courts that have permitted it have been criticized, and alternatives have been suggested which recognize that a sample of trials makes more sense than entrusting the fate of an industry to a single jury. See, e.g., Michael J. Saks & Peter David Blanck, "Justice Improved: The Unrecognized Benefits of Aggregation and Sampling in the Trial of Mass Torts," 44 Stan.L.Rev. 815 (1992). The number of asbestos cases was so great as to exert a well-nigh irresistible pressure to bend the normal rules. No comparable pressure is exerted by the HIV-hemophilia litigation. That litigation can be handled in the normal way without undue inconvenience to the parties or to the state or federal courts.

* * * The petition for a writ of mandamus is granted, and the district judge is directed to decertify the plaintiff class.

ROVNER, CIRCUIT JUDGE dissenting:

The majority today takes the extraordinary step of granting defendants' petition for a writ of mandamus and directing the district court to rescind its order certifying the plaintiff class. Although certification orders like this one are not immediately appealable (see Coopers & Lybrand v. Livesay, 437 U.S. 463, 98 S.Ct. 2454, 57 L.Ed.2d 351 (1978)), the majority seizes upon our mandamus powers to effectively circumvent that rule. Because, in my view, our consideration of [the district judge's] decision to certify an issue class under Fed.R.Civ.P. 23(c)(4) should await an appeal from the final judgment in Wadleigh, I would deny the writ.

* * *

I find the majority's reasoning troubling in several respects. First, it means that the preliminary requirement for mandamus—the lack of an alternative means of obtaining relief—will be satisfied by virtually every class certification order, which then authorizes the court to assess the relative merits of the order to determine whether it is "usurpative." The majority's complaint about [the district judge's] order—that it will make a settlement more likely than if defendants' negligence were to be determined by separate juries in individual trials—is true of most every order certifying a large plaintiff class. Certification orders almost always increase the likelihood of settlement by expanding the scope of defendants' exposure. Yet that does not make the order any less reviewable if defendants resist the temptation to settle and litigate to final judgment. See In re Sugar Antitrust Litigation, 559 F.2d 481, 483 n. 1 (9th Cir.1977). Indeed, in concluding that certification orders are not immediately appealable under 28 U.S.C. § 1291, the Supreme Court observed that any order certifying a large plaintiff class "may so increase the defendant's potential damages liability and litigation costs that he may find it economically prudent to settle and to abandon a meritorious defense." Coopers & Lybrand, 437 U.S. at 476. Yet that did not stop the Court from finding that "orders granting class certification are interlocutory" and thus not immediately appealable as of right. Id. But the majority here would override Coopers' edict, making certification orders reviewable on mandamus simply because the likelihood of a settlement makes the order unreviewable at the end of the case. * * *

I also am wary of the majority's application of a "settlement theory" in this case, as defendants did not offer that rationale in support of their petition. Their failure to do so is important because the Supreme Court has required the party seeking mandamus to bear the burden of establishing that it lacks an alternative means of obtaining relief. See, e.g., Mallard, 490 U.S. at 309; In re Catawba Indian Tribe, 973 F.2d at 1136; In re Recticel Foam Corp., 859 F.2d 1000, 1006 (1st Cir.1988). Nowhere in their petition or in their briefs to this court did defendants suggest that [the district judge's] order would prompt them to settle. Instead, defendants argued that irreparable harm would result from the class trial itself, as well as from the satellite litigation it would spawn. The possibility of a settlement was raised for the first time by the court itself at oral argument. Generally, arguments not raised in a party's brief, but only an oral argument, are waived. See, e.g., United States v. Rodriguez, 888 F.2d 519, 524 (7th Cir.1989). But even assuming that we may consider the argument, I fail to see how counsel's vague statements at oral argument about the possibility of a settlement can be said to satisfy defendants' substantial burden of establishing that they will suffer irreparable harm. The only "evidence" supporting counsel's assertion has been supplied by the majority's own statistical conjecturing, to which plaintiffs have had no opportunity to respond. * * *

Furthermore, even if the possibility of a settlement were relevant to the first mandamus requirement, and even if it had been asserted by defendants in support of their petition, I still cannot agree with the majority's premise that [the district judge's] order in fact will prompt a settlement. Contrary to the clear implication of the majority's opinion * * *, the class portion of the anticipated trial in this case would not go so far as to establish defendants' liability to a class of plaintiffs; it would instead resolve only a question of whether defendants were negligent in disturbing tainted clotting factor at any particular point in time. Even if defendants were faced with an adverse class verdict, then, a plaintiff still would be required to clear a number of hurdles before he would be entitled to a judgment. For example, defendants no doubt would contest at that stage whether a particular plaintiff could establish proximate causation or whether his or her claim is in any event barred by the statute of limitations. Thus, contrary to the majority's implication, a class verdict in favor of plaintiffs would not automatically entitle each member of the class to a seven figure judgment. * * * The defendants will thus have ample opportunity to settle should they lose the class trial. And that would seem to me an advisable strategy in light of the success they have had in earlier cases. That factor distinguishes this case from a more standard class action, where a non-bifurcated trial would resolve all relevant issues and conclusively establish liability to the class. Perhaps that explains why defendants' own arguments in support of their petition are based on the assumption that a class trial would ensue, rather than on the proposition that a settlement would follow inevitably from [the district judge's] order.[3]

Finally, although the availability of review on direct appeal after final judgment makes it unnecessary for me to discuss the merits of the certification order, the majority's arguments addressed to the propriety of forcing "defendants to stake their companies on the outcome of a single jury trial" or of allowing a single jury to "hold the fate of an industry in the palm of its hand" seem to me at odds with Fed.R.Civ.P. 23 itself. * * * That rule expressly permits class treatment of such claims when its requirements are met, regardless of the magnitude of potential liability. And I see nothing in Rule 23, or in any of the relevant cases, that would make likelihood of success on the merits a prerequisite for class certification. * * * The majority's preference for avoiding a class trial and for submitting the negligence issue "to multiple juries constituting in the aggregate a much larger and more diverse sample of decision-makers" * * * is a rationale for amending the rule, not for avoiding its application in a specific case. * * *

I must concede that I too have doubts about whether the class trial proposed by [the district judge] will succeed, and I sympathize with many of the apprehensions of my brothers. But in my view, the law requires that [the district judge's] plan be given the opportunity to

---

[3]. As an alternative to its settlement theory, the majority suggests that the irreparable harm requirement is relaxed in this case because the certification order infringes defendants' Seventh Amendment right to a jury trial. But the circumstances here are unlike those in Beacon Theatres, Inc. v. Westover, 359 U.S. 500, 79 S.Ct. 948, 3 L.Ed.2d 988 (1959), and Dairy Queen, Inc. v. Wood, 369 U.S. 469, 82 S.Ct. 894, 8 L.Ed.2d 44 (1962), which the majority cites to support its position. In those cases, mandamus issued after the district court had decided to try equitable claims to the court before trying related legal claims to a jury. Because the court's findings on the equitable claims would have effectively denied defendants their right in jury resolution of issues common to their legal claims, the Supreme Court granted mandamus to protect defendants' right to a jury trial. Beacon Theatres, 359 U.S. at 510–11; Dairy Queen, 369 U.S. at 472–73; see also Will v. Calvert Fire Ins. Co., 437 U.S. 655, 665 n. 7, 98 S.Ct. 2552, 57 L.Ed.2d 504 (1978). The Court believed that there was no need to await an appeal from a final judgment in that circumstance to remedy an obvious violation of the Seventh Amendment. See First Nat'l Bank of Waukesha v. Warren, 796 F.2d 999, 1004 (7th Cir. 1986). Here, by contrast, the district court's certification order does not present such an obvious Seventh Amendment problem as it will not deprive defendants of their right to have a jury resolve any issue. Instead, the Seventh Amendment violation the majority envisions might appear, if at all, only in a phase II trial. It is thus a possible but by no means imminent consequence of the certification order. And if any constitutional problem were to materialize, it would be reviewable either by this court after the class trial or by other courts reviewing phase II trials. In either event, the reviewing court would then have a record to examine, rather than speculating about a potential constitutional violation, as the majority does here. * * * I thus cannot agree that the mere possibility of a constitutional violation somehow eliminates the first mandamus requirement.

82 PLEADING AND PROCEDURE Ch. 6

succeed. Class certification orders are, after all, conditional orders subject to modification or revocation as the circumstances warrant. Fed.R.Civ.P. 23(c)(1); Coopers & Lybrand, 437 U.S. at 469; * * *.

NOTE ON CLASS CERTIFICATION

1. Appealability of class certification ruling. Ordinarily, a District Court's order certifying or declining to certify a class is a non-appealable interlocutory order. See Coopers & Lybrand v. Livesay, 437 U.S. 463, 98 S.Ct. 2454, 57 L.Ed.2d 351 (1978), p. 1368 in the casebook. The Court of Appeals in *Rhone-Poulenc* acknowledges the *Coopers & Lybrand* rule, but finds that mandamus is available because the order both inflicted irreparable harm and was a clear abuse of discretion. How convincing is Judge Posner's argument that the class certification constitutes irreparable harm because it threatens defendants with bankruptcy?

Judge Posner hypothesizes a potential liability of $25 billion, and a resulting "intense pressure to settle." It is by no means clear that $25 billion figure is realistic. Judge Rovner, in dissent, states that the numbers come from "the majority's own statistical conjecturing." Elaborating on that theme, *The American Lawyer*, "Posner's Bearish Dissent," (May 1995), p. 73, reports that Judge Posner first raised the possibility of bankruptcy at oral argument. He suggested that there might be a total of 10,000 claimants each collecting $10 million, for a total liability of $100 billion. Plaintiffs' lawyer declined to agree to these, or any other, numbers. In Judge Posner's opinion, the hypothesized liability has been reduced by one quarter, to $25 billion. But there is no evidence in the record, and no contention by counsel at oral argument, to support that figure. Further, if class certification posed a serious threat of bankruptcy, one would expect the Court of Appeals' decision decertifying the class to have had some effect on the stock price of the companies. In fact, as one stock analyst noted, "The stocks didn't react to the judgment.... The case came and went unnoted." Quoted in *The American Lawyer*, id.

2. Proposed amendment that would permit interlocutory appeal. An amendment has been proposed to Fed.R.Civ.P. 23 that would permit interlocutory appeals of class certification decisions by the District Court. Proposed Rule 23(f) provides:

> APPEALS: A court of appeals may in its discretion permit an appeal from an order of a district court granting or denying class action certification under this rule if application is made to it within ten days after entry of the order. An appeal does not stay proceedings in the district court unless the district court of the court of appeals so orders.

66 U.S.L.W. 4323 (April 24, 1998.) If not disapproved by Congress, the amendment will go into effect on December 1, 1998.

3. Class decertification in the tobacco litigation. In Castano v. American Tobacco Co., 84 F.3d 734 (5th Cir.1996), the Court of Appeals for the Fifth Circuit decertified a nation-wide class in litigation against American cigarette manufacturers. The class in *Castano* had been certified by the District Court as "(a) All nicotine-dependent persons in the United States, its territories, possessions and the Commonwealth of Puerto Rico, who have purchased and smoked cigarettes manufactured by the defendants; (b) the estates, representatives, and administrators of these nicotine-dependent cigarette smokers; and (c) the spouses, children, relatives and 'significant others' of these nicotine-dependent cigarette smokers and their heirs or survivors." "Nicotine-dependent" people were defined as "(a) all cigarette smokers who have been diagnosed by a medical practitioner as nicotine-dependent; and/or (b) all regular cigarette smokers who were or have been advised by a medical practitioner that smoking has had or will have adverse health consequences who thereafter do not or have not quit smoking." at 737 and n. 1.

The Court of Appeals gave three reasons for decertifying the class. First, the District Court failed to consider sufficiently the impact of different state laws.

> The district court's review of state law variances can hardly be considered extensive; it conducted a cursory review of state law variations and gave short shrift to the defendants' arguments concerning variations. * * * The class members were exposed to nicotine through different products, for different amounts of time, and over different time periods. Each class member's knowledge about the effects of smoking differs, and each plaintiff began smoking for different reasons. Each of these factual differences impacts the application of legal rules such as causation, reliance, comparative fault, and other affirmative defenses.
>
> Variations in state law magnify the differences. In a fraud claim, some states require justifiable reliance on a misrepresentation, while others require reasonable reliance. States impose varying standards to determine when there is a duty to disclose facts. Products liability law also differs among states. Some states do not recognize strict liability. Among the states that have adopted the Restatement, there are variations. Differences in affirmative defenses also exist. Assumption of risk is a complete defense to a products claim in some states. Some states utilize "pure" comparative fault; others follow a "greater fault bar"; and still others use an "equal fault bar." Negligent infliction of emotional distress also involves wide variations. Some states do not recognize the cause of action at all. Others require a physical impact.
>
> Despite these overwhelming individual issues, common issues might predominate. We are, however, left to speculate [because of the District Court's failure consider these questions in detail].

at 743 (citations and some paragraphing omitted).

Second, in conducting its "predominance inquiry" the District Court did not sufficiently consider how the trial would be conducted.

> The premise of the [district] court's opinion is ... a conclusion that class treatment of common issues would significantly advance the individual trials. Absent knowledge of how addiction-as-injury cases would actually be tried, however, it was impossible for the court to know whether the common issues would be a "significant" portion of the individual trials. The court just assumed that because the common issues would play a part in every trial, they must be significant.

at 744.

Third, independent of the first two grounds for decertification, the class failed the "superiority requirement" of Rule 23(b)(3).

> [H]istorically, certification of mass tort litigation has been disfavored. The traditional concern over the rights of defendants in mass tort class actions is magnified in the instant case. Our specific concern is that a mass tort cannot be properly certified without a prior track record of trials from which the district court can draw the information necessary to make the predominance and superiority requirements required by rule 23.
>
> * * *
>
> Fairness may demand that mass torts with few prior verdicts or judgments be litigated first in small units—even single-plaintiff, single-defendant trials—until general causation, typical injuries, and levels of damages become established.
>
> * * *
>
> Even assuming arguendo that the tort system will see many more addiction-as-injury claims, a conclusion that certification will save judicial resources is premature at this stage of the litigation.... Only after the courts have more experience with this type of case can a court certify issues in a way that preserves judicial resources.

at 746–49.

4. Class certification in other cases. For a decision criticizing and distinguishing *Rhone–Poulenc,* see In re Copley Pharmaceutical, Inc., "Albuterol" Products Liability Litigation, 161 F.R.D. 456 (D.Wyo.1995) (refusing to decertify class); see also In re Copley Pharmaceutical, Inc., 158 F.R.D. 485 (D.Wyo.1994) (certifying class). For a decision reversing the District Court's certification of a nationwide class of recipients of allegedly defective penile implants, see In re American Medical Systems, Inc., 75 F.3d 1069 (6th Cir.1996).

p. 911, 914, 915

FURTHER NOTE ON THE USES AND ADMINISTRATION OF CLASS SUITS

2a. Choice to certify as a 23(b)(1), (b)(2), or (b)(3) class. Some suits qualify as class actions under more than one provision of Rule 23. Recall that class actions certified under 23(b)(1) and (b)(2) do not require special rule-based notice and do not allow "opt-out" by members of the class. Class actions certified under 23(b)(3), on the other hand, require "the best notice practicable under the circumstances, including individual notice to all members who can be identified through reasonable effort," and members of the class have the right to opt out of the class. 23(c)(2). What notice and opt-out provisions apply to an action that qualifies under more than one provision of the rule? Lower federal courts have developed a "predominance" test, under which the court certifies the kind of class action that predominates. See. e.g., Arnold v. United Artists Theatre Circuit, Inc., 158 F.R.D. 439, 450–53 (N.D.Cal.1994)(certifying a (b)(2) class despite the presence of damage claims). See also H. Newberg and A. Conte, 1 Newberg on Class Actions (3d ed. 1992) § 4.14; Note, "The Class Action Dilemma: The Certification of Classes Seeking Equitable Relief and Monetary Damages after *Ticor Title Insurance Co. v. Brown*," 43 Ford.L.Rev. 1745 (1995).

In Brown v. Ticor Title Insurance Co., 982 F.2d 386 (9th Cir.1992), a nationwide class action had been certified under Rule 23(b)(1) and (b)(2) despite the presence of damage claims. The suit was settled without any payment of damages, over the objection of class members Wisconsin and Arizona, objecting on behalf of themselves and of their citizens who were class members. Brown then brought a separate suit for damages against the same defendants, representing Arizona and Wisconsin citizens. Relying on Phillips Petroleum Co. v. Shutts, casebook p. 361, the Court of Appeals held that the foreclosing the plaintiff class from bringing a damage suit would violate due process because they had not been able to opt out of the earlier class action. The Supreme Court granted certiorari, but later dismissed. Ticor Title Insurance v. Brown, 511 U.S. 117, 114 S.Ct. 1359, 128 L.Ed.2d 33 (1994)(dismissing cert. as improvidently granted). As presented, *Ticor* posed only the constitutional question of due process, and the Court preferred a case in which it had the possibility of basing its decision on Rule 23.

Plaintiffs in *Ticor* did not contend that they had not received notice of the class action. Their argument appears to have been, rather, that they had a constitutional right to opt out *simpliciter*. What about the case, not presented by *Ticor*, in which damage claims were resolved in a (b)(1) or (b)(2) class action, and in which a class member did not receive notice? Is that person barred from a later suit for damages against the same defendant?

The Supreme Court recently tried again to reach the "opt-out" question. In Adams v. Robertson, 676 So.2d 1265 (Ala.1995), the Alabama Supreme Court approved certification and settlement of a Rule 23(b)(1) and (b)(2) class action where all plaintiffs suffered monetary damage. (The Alabama class action rule is the same as the federal rule.) No plaintiffs were permitted to opt out, and the settlement resulted in monetary compensation for very few members of the class. The Supreme Court granted certiorari to decide whether constitutional due process had been violated, but dismissed certiorari as improvidently granted when it learned that the federal issue had not been properly raised in the state court proceedings below. Adams v. Robertson, 520 U.S. 83, 117 S.Ct. 1028, 137 L.Ed.2d 203 (1997).

3. "Adequacy" of representation. The adequacy of class plaintiffs' counsel may in practical fact be more important than the adequacy of the named representatives of the class, but it is difficult to dislodge a class counsel even when he or she has displeased the named representatives. In Maywalt v. Parker & Parsley Petroleum Co., 155 F.R.D. 494, 496 (S.D.N.Y. 1994), four out of the five named class representatives of the plaintiff class sought a judicial order that would have replaced the class counsel. The District Court refused to order the substitution absent some showing of impropriety. The fact that a majority of the named members of the class were dissatisfied did not mean that class counsel had failed to represent properly the interests of the class as a whole. "Class counsel must act in a way which best represents the interests of 'the entire class and is not dependent on the special desires of the named plaintiffs' " (quoting Parker v. Anderson, 667 F.2d 1204 (5th Cir.), cert. den., 459 U.S. 828, 103 S.Ct. 63, 74 L.Ed.2d 65 (1982)).

In Epstein v. MCA, Inc., 126 F.3d 1235 (9th Cir.1997), plaintiffs sued in federal District Court in California based solely on federal law claims. Plaintiffs had been unnamed parties in a separate Delaware state court class action arising out of the same events, in which both state and federal claims had been settled. The Supreme Court held that the Delaware state court settlement was entitled to preclusive effect in federal court, even as to federal claims over which the Delaware court did not have subject matter jurisdiction. Matsushita Electric Industrial Co. v. Epstein, 516 U.S. 367, 116 S.Ct. 873, 134 L.Ed.2d 6 (1996). After remand from the Supreme Court, plaintiffs in *Epstein v. MCA* argued that there had been inadequate representation by class counsel in the Delaware suit. After finding that this question had been left open by the Supreme Court, the Court of Appeals agreed with plaintiffs:

> [T]he only "vigorous" and "tenacious" work ... that Delaware counsel performed on behalf of the Epstein plaintiffs was to convince the [Delaware] court to adopt their adversary's position and view the federal claims as essentially worthless. This was not merely "inadequate" representation, it was hostile representation that served the interests of counsel in getting a fee, but did not serve the interests of the MCA shareholders in getting a settlement based upon a thorough and fair assessment of their [federal] claims. To bind the Epstein plaintiffs to the Delaware judgment under these circumstances would violate their due process rights to have their interests adequately represented at all times.

at 1255. For an argument that the court's holding threatens unduly to impede class action settlements and to spawn wasteful litigation over adequacy of representation, see Kahan and Silberman, "The Inadequate Search for 'Adequacy' in Class Actions: A Critique of *Epstein v. MCA, Inc.*," 73 N.Y.U.L.Rev. 765 (1998). Would the holding not also threaten the conclusiveness of judgments in litigated class suits?

5. Notice. If a defendant obtains summary judgment against a plaintiff class before notice has been sent out to unnamed class members, the judgment will be binding only on the named plaintiffs. Post-judgment notice to unnamed members of the class will not be allowed to take the place and serve the purpose of pre-judgment notice, and the unnamed members of the class will not be bound by the judgment. Schwarzschild v. Tse, 58 F.3d 430 (9th Cir.1995); Postow v. OBA Federal Savings and Loan Ass'n, 627 F.2d 1370 (D.C.Cir.1980).

7. Appellate review of certification. A proposed amendment to Fed.R.Civ.P. 23 would permit interlocutory appeals of class certification decisions by the District Court. See supra p. 82.

9a. Subject matter jurisdiction in diversity class actions. Zahn v. International Paper Co., 414 U.S. 291, 94 S.Ct. 505, 38 L.Ed.2d 511 (1973), held that each member of a plaintiff class must allege the requisite jurisdictional amount in diversity cases. A recent Court of Appeals decision has held that the new supplemental jurisdictional statute, 28 U.S.C. § 1367, has overruled *Zahn*. Free v. Abbott Laboratories, 51 F.3d 524 (5th Cir. 1995), supra this supplement, p. 31. If *Free* is good law, named plaintiffs in a diversity class action must satisfy the jurisdictional amount, but unnamed members of the plaintiff class need not do so.

c. SETTLEMENT OF CLASS SUITS
P. 922, after FURTHER NOTE ON CLASS SUITS

AMCHEM PRODUCTS, INC. v. WINDSOR

United States Supreme Court, 1997.
___ U.S. ___, 117 S.Ct. 2231, 138 L.Ed.2d 689.

JUDGES: GINSBURG, J., delivered the opinion of the Court, in which REHNQUIST, C.J., and SCALIA, KENNEDY, SOUTER, and THOMAS, JJ., joined. BREYER, J., filed an opinion concurring in part and dissenting in part, in which STEVENS, J., joined. O'CONNOR, J., took no part in the consideration or decision of the case.

JUSTICE GINSBURG delivered the opinion of the court.

This case concerns the legitimacy under Rule 23 of the Federal Rules of Civil Procedure of a class-action certification sought to achieve global settlement of current and future asbestos-related claims. The class proposed for certification potentially encompasses hundreds of thousands, perhaps millions, of individuals tied together by this commonality: each was, or some day may be, adversely affected by past exposure to asbestos products manufactured by one or more of 20 companies. Those companies, defendants in the lower courts, are petitioners here.

The United States District Court for the Eastern District of Pennsylvania certified the class for settlement only, finding that the proposed settlement was fair and that representation and notice had been adequate. That court enjoined class members from separately pursuing asbestos-related personal-injury suits in any court, federal or state, pending the issuance of a final order. The Court of Appeals for the Third Circuit vacated the District Court's orders, holding that the class certification failed to satisfy Rule 23's requirements in several critical respects. We affirm the Court of Appeals' judgment.

I

A

The settlement-class certification we confront evolved in response to an asbestos-litigation crisis. See Georgine v. Amchem Products, Inc., 83 F.3d 610, 618, and n. 2 (C.A.3 1996) (citing commentary). A United States Judicial Conference Ad Hoc Committee on Asbestos Litigation, appointed by THE CHIEF JUSTICE in September 1990, described facets of the problem in a 1991 report:

"[This] is a tale of danger known in the 1930s, exposure inflicted upon millions of Americans in the 1940s and 1950s, injuries that began to take their toll in the 1960s, and a flood of lawsuits beginning in the 1970s. On the basis of past and current filing data, and because of a latency period that may last as long as 40 years for some asbestos related diseases, a continuing stream of claims can be expected. The final toll of asbestos related injuries is unknown. Predictions have been made of 200,000 asbestos disease deaths before the year 2000 and as many as 265,000 by the year 2015.

"The most objectionable aspects of asbestos litigation can be briefly summarized: dockets in both federal and state courts continue to grow; long delays are routine; trials are too long; the same issues are litigated over and over; transaction costs exceed the victims' recovery by nearly two to one; exhaustion of assets threatens and distorts the process; and future claimants may lose altogether." Report of The Judicial Conference Ad Hoc Committee on Asbestos Litigation 2–3 (Mar. 1991).

Real reform, the report concluded, required federal legislation creating a national asbestos dispute-resolution scheme ... To this date, no congressional response has emerged.

In the face of legislative inaction, the federal courts—lacking authority to replace state tort systems with a national toxic tort compensation regime—endeavored to work with the procedural tools available to improve management of federal asbestos litigation. Eight federal judges, experienced in the superintendence of asbestos cases, urged the Judicial Panel on Multidistrict Litigation (MDL Panel), to consolidate in a single district all asbestos complaints then pending in federal courts. Accepting the recommendation, the MDL Panel transferred all asbestos cases then filed, but not yet on trial in federal courts to a single district, the United States District Court for the Eastern District of Pennsylvania; pursuant to the transfer order, the collected cases were consolidated for pretrial proceedings before Judge Weiner. See In re Asbestos Products Liability Litigation (No. VI), 771 F.Supp. 415, 422–424 (JPML 1991). The order aggregated pending cases only; no authority resides in the MDL Panel to license for consolidated proceedings claims not yet filed.

B

After the consolidation, attorneys for plaintiffs and defendants formed separate steering committees and began settlement negotiations. Ronald L. Motley and Gene Locks—later appointed, along with Motley's law partner Joseph F. Rice, to represent the plaintiff class in this action—co-chaired the Plaintiffs' Steering Committee. Counsel for the Center for Claims Resolution (CCR), the consortium of 20 former asbestos manufacturers now before us as petitioners, participated in the Defendants' Steering Committee. Although the MDL order collected, transferred, and consolidated only cases already commenced in federal courts, settlement negotiations included efforts to find a "means of resolving ... future cases." ...

In November 1991, the Defendants' Steering Committee made an offer designed to settle all pending and future asbestos cases by providing a fund for distribution by plaintiffs' counsel among asbestos-exposed individuals. The Plaintiffs' Steering Committee rejected this offer, and negotiations fell apart. CCR, however, continued to pursue "a workable administrative system for the handling of future claims."

To that end, CCR counsel approached the lawyers who had headed the Plaintiffs' Steering Committee in the unsuccessful negotiations, and a new round of negotiations began; that round yielded the mass settlement agreement now in controversy. At the time, the former heads of the Plaintiffs' Steering Committee represented thousands of plaintiffs with then-pending asbestos-related claims—claimants the parties to this suit call "inventory" plaintiffs. CCR indicated in these discussions that it would resist settlement of inventory cases absent "some kind of protection for the future." ...

Settlement talks thus concentrated on devising an administrative scheme for disposition of asbestos claims not yet in litigation. In these negotiations, counsel for masses of inventory plaintiffs endeavored to represent the interests of the anticipated future claimants, although those lawyers then had no attorney-client relationship with such claimants.

Once negotiations seemed likely to produce an agreement purporting to bind potential plaintiffs, CCR agreed to settle, through separate agreements, the claims of plaintiffs who had already filed asbestos-related lawsuits. In one such agreement, CCR defendants promised to pay more than $200 million to gain release of the claims of numerous inventory plaintiffs. After settling the inventory claims, CCR, together with the plaintiffs' lawyers CCR had approached, launched this case, exclusively involving persons outside the MDL Panel's province—plaintiffs without already pending lawsuits.[3]

C

The class action thus instituted was not intended to be litigated. Rather, within the space of a single day, January 15, 1993, the settling parties—CCR defendants and the representatives of the plaintiff class described below—presented to the District Court a complaint, an answer, a proposed settlement agreement, and a joint motion for conditional class certification.

---

3. It is basic to comprehension of this proceeding to notice that no transferred case is included in the settlement at issue, and no case covered by the settlement existed as a civil action at the time of the MDL Panel transfer.

The complaint identified nine lead plaintiffs, designating them and members of their families as representatives of a class comprising all persons who had not filed an asbestos-related lawsuit against a CCR defendant as of the date the class action commenced, but who (1) had been exposed—occupationally or through the occupational exposure of a spouse or household member—to asbestos or products containing asbestos attributable to a CCR defendant, or (2) whose spouse or family member had been exposed. Untold numbers of individuals may fall within this description. All named plaintiffs alleged that they or a member of their family had been exposed to asbestos-containing products of CCR defendants. More than half of the named plaintiffs alleged that they or their family members had already suffered various physical injuries as a result of the exposure. The others alleged that they had not yet manifested any asbestos-related condition. The complaint delineated no subclasses; all named plaintiffs were designated as representatives of the class as a whole.

The complaint invoked the District Court's diversity jurisdiction and asserted various state-law claims for relief....

A stipulation of settlement accompanied the pleadings; it proposed to settle, and to preclude nearly all class members from litigating against CCR companies, all claims not filed before January 15, 1993, involving compensation for present and future asbestos-related personal injury or death. An exhaustive document exceeding 100 pages, the stipulation presents in detail an administrative mechanism and a schedule of payments to compensate class members who meet defined asbestos-exposure and medical requirements. The stipulation describes four categories of compensable disease: mesothelioma; lung cancer; certain "other cancers" (colon-rectal, laryngeal, esophageal, and stomach cancer); and "non-malignant conditions" (asbestosis and bilateral pleural thickening). Persons with "exceptional" medical claims—claims that do not fall within the four described diagnostic categories—may in some instances qualify for compensation, but the settlement caps the number of "exceptional" claims CCR must cover.

For each qualifying disease category, the stipulation specifies the range of damages CCR will pay to qualifying claimants. Payments under the settlement are not adjustable for inflation. Mesothelioma claimants—the most highly compensated category—are scheduled to receive between $20,000 and $200,000. The stipulation provides that CCR is to propose the level of compensation within the prescribed ranges; it also establishes procedures to resolve disputes over medical diagnoses and levels of compensation.

Compensation above the fixed ranges may be obtained for "extraordinary" claims. But the settlement places both numerical caps and dollar limits on such claims. The settlement also imposes "case flow maximums," which cap the number of claims payable for each disease in a given year.

Class members are to receive no compensation for certain kinds of claims, even if otherwise applicable state law recognizes such claims. Claims that garner no compensation under the settlement include claims by family members of asbestos-exposed individuals for loss of consortium, and claims by so-called "exposure only" plaintiffs for increased risk of cancer, fear of future asbestos-related injury, and medical monitoring. "Pleural" claims, which might be asserted by persons with asbestos-related plaques on their lungs but no accompanying physical impairment, are also excluded. Although not entitled to present compensation, exposure-only claimants and pleural claimants may qualify for benefits when and if they develop a compensable disease and meet the relevant exposure and medical criteria. Defendants forgo defenses to liability, including statute of limitations pleas.

Class members, in the main, are bound by the settlement in perpetuity, while CCR defendants may choose to withdraw from the settlement after ten years. A small number of class members—only a few per year—may reject the settlement and pursue their claims in court. Those permitted to exercise this option, however, may not assert any punitive damages claim or any claim for increased risk of cancer. Aspects of the administration of the settlement are to be monitored by the AFL–CIO and class counsel. Class counsel are to receive attorneys' fees in an amount to be approved by the District Court.

D

On January 29, 1993, as requested by the settling parties, the District Court conditionally certified, under Federal Rule of Civil Procedure 23(b)(3), an encompassing opt-out class. The certified class included persons occupationally exposed to defendants' asbestos products, and members of their families, who had not filed suit as of January 15. Judge Weiner appointed Locks, Motley, and Rice as class counsel, noting that "the Court may in the future appoint additional counsel if it is deemed necessary and advisable." At no stage of the proceedings, however, were additional counsel in fact appointed. Nor was the class ever divided into subclasses. In a separate order, Judge Weiner assigned to Judge Reed, also of the Eastern District of Pennsylvania, "the task of conducting fairness proceedings and of determining whether the proposed settlement is fair to the class." See 157 F.R.D. at 258. Various class members raised objections to the settlement stipulation, and Judge Weiner granted the objectors full rights to participate in the subsequent proceedings. Ibid.[7]

* * *

---

[7]. These objectors, now respondents before this Court, include three groups of individuals with overlapping interests, designated as the "Windsor Group," the New

Objectors raised numerous challenges to the settlement. They urged that the settlement unfairly disadvantaged those without currently compensable conditions in that it failed to adjust for inflation or to account for changes, over time, in medical understanding. They maintained that compensation levels were intolerably low in comparison to awards available in tort litigation or payments received by the inventory plaintiffs. And they objected to the absence of any compensation for certain claims, for example, medical monitoring, compensable under the tort law of several States. Rejecting these and all other objections, Judge Reed concluded that the settlement terms were fair and had been negotiated without collusion. He also found that adequate notice had been given to class members and that final class certification under Rule 23(b)(3) was appropriate.

As to the specific prerequisites to certification, the District Court observed that the class satisfied Rule 23(a)(1)'s numerosity requirement, a matter no one debates. The Rule 23(a)(2) and (b)(3) requirements of commonality and preponderance were also satisfied, the District Court held, in that

> the members of the class have all been exposed to asbestos products supplied by the defendants and all share an interest in receiving prompt and fair compensation for their claims, while minimizing the risks and transaction costs inherent in the asbestos litigation process as it occurs presently in the tort system. Whether the proposed settlement satisfies this interest and is otherwise a fair, reasonable and adequate compromise of the claims of the class is a predominant issue for purposes of Rule 23(b)(3).

The District Court held next that the claims of the class representatives were "typical" of the class as a whole, a requirement of Rule 23 (a)(3) and that, as Rule 23(b)(3) demands, the claims of the class the class settlement was "superior" to other methods of adjudication.

Strenuous objections had been asserted regarding the adequacy of representation, a Rule 23(a)(4) requirement. Objectors maintained that class counsel and class representatives had disqualifying conflicts of interests. In particular, objectors urged, claimants whose injuries had become manifest and claimants without manifest injuries should not have common counsel and should not be aggregated in a single class. Furthermore, objectors argued, lawyers representing inventory plaintiffs should not represent the newly-formed class.

Jersey "White Lung Group, "and the "Cargile Group." Margaret Balonis, an individual objector, is also a respondent before this Court. Balonis states that her husband, Casimir, was exposed to asbestos in the late 1940s and was diagnosed with mesothelioma in May 1994, after expiration of the opt-out period. The Balonises sued CCR members in Maryland state court, but were charged with civil contempt for violating the federal District Court's anti-suit injunction. Casimir Balonis died in October 1996.

Satisfied that class counsel had ably negotiated the settlement in the best interests of all concerned, and that the named parties served as adequate representatives, the District Court rejected these objections. Subclasses were unnecessary, the District Court held, bearing in mind the added cost and confusion they would entail and the ability of class members to exclude themselves from the class during the three-month opt-out period. Reasoning that the representative plaintiffs "have a strong interest that recovery for all of the medical categories be maximized because they may have claims in any, or several categories," the District Court found "no antagonism of interest between class members with various medical conditions, or between persons with and without currently manifest asbestos impairment." Declaring class certification appropriate and the settlement fair, the District Court preliminarily enjoined all class members from commencing any asbestos-related suit against the CCR defendants in any state or Federal court.

E

The Court of Appeals, in a long, heavily detailed opinion by Judge Becker, first noted several challenges by objectors to justiciability, subject-matter jurisdiction, and adequacy of notice....

On class-action prerequisites, the Court of Appeals referred to an earlier Third Circuit decision, In re General Motors Corp. Pick–Up Truck Fuel Tank Products Liability Litigation, 55 F.3d 768 (CA3), cert. denied, 516 U.S. __ (1995) (hereinafter GM Trucks), which held that although a class action maybe certified for settlement purposes only, Rule 23(a)'s requirements must be satisfied as if the case were going to be litigated. 55 F.3d at 799–800. The same rule should apply, the Third Circuit said, to class certification under Rule 23(b)(3). While stating that the requirements of Rule 23(a) and (b)(3) must be met "without taking into account the settlement," the Court of Appeals in fact closely considered the terms of the settlement as it examined aspects of the case under Rule 23 criteria.

* * *

The Third Circuit, after intensive review, ultimately ordered decertification of the class and vacation of the District Court's anti-suit injunction....

We granted certiorari, 519 U.S. __ (1996), and now affirm.

* * *

III

* * *

In the decades since the 1966 revision of Rule 23, class action practice has become ever more "adventuresome" as a means of coping with claims too numerous to secure their "just, speedy, and inexpensive determination" one by one. The development reflects concerns about the efficient use of court resources and the conservation of funds to compensate claimants who do not line up early in a litigation queue....

Among current applications of Rule 23(b)(3), the "settlement only" class has become a stock device. See, e.g., T. Willging, L. Hooper, & R. Niemic, Empirical Study of Class Actions in Four Federal District Courts: Final Report to the Advisory Committee on Civil Rules 61–62 (1996) (noting large number of such cases in districts studied). Although all Federal Circuits recognize the utility of Rule 23(b)(3) settlement classes, courts have divided on the extent to which a proffered settlement affects court surveillance under Rule 23's certification criteria.

In GM Trucks and in the instant case, the Third Circuit held that a class cannot be certified for settlement when certification for trial would be unwarranted. Other courts have held that settlement obviates or reduces the need to measure a proposed class against the enumerated Rule 23 requirements....

A proposed amendment to Rule 23 would expressly authorize settlement class certification, in conjunction with a motion by the settling parties for Rule 23(b)(3) certification, "even though the requirements of subdivision (b)(3) might not be met for purposes of trial." Proposed Amendment to Fed.Rule Civ.Proc. 23(b), 117 S.Ct. No. 1 CXIX, CLIV to CLV (Aug. 1996) (Request for Comment). In response to the publication of this proposal, voluminous public comments—many of them opposed to, or skeptical of, the amendment—were received by the Judicial Conference Standing Committee on Rules of Practice and Procedure. The Committee has not yet acted on the matter. We consider the certification at issue under the rule as it is currently framed.

IV

We granted review to decide the role settlement may play, existing Rule 23, in determining the propriety of class certification....

We agree with petitioners to this limited extent: settlement is relevant to a class certification. The Third Circuit's opinion bears modification in that respect. But, as we earlier observed, the Court of Appeals in fact did not ignore the settlement; instead, that court homed in on settlement terms in explaining why it found the absentees' interests inadequately represent. The Third Circuit's close inspection of the settlement in that regard was altogether proper.

Confronted with a request for settlement-only class certification, a district court need not inquire whether the case, if tried, would present intractable management problems, see Fed.Rule Civ.Proc. 23(b)(3)(D), for the proposal is that there be no trial. But other specifications of the rule—those designed to protect absentees by blocking unwarranted or overbroad class definitions—demand undiluted, even heightened, attention in the settlement context. Such attention is of vital importance, for a court asked to certify a settlement class will lack the opportunity, present when a case is litigated, to adjust the class, informed by the proceedings as they unfold. See Fed.Rule Civ.Proc. 23(c), (d).

And, of overriding importance, courts must be mindful that the rule as now composed sets the requirements they are bound to enforce. Federal Rules take effect after an extensive deliberative process involving many reviewers: a Rules Advisory Committee, public commenters, the Judicial Conference, this Court, the Congress. See 28 U.S.C. §§ 2073, 2074. The text of a rule thus proposed and reviewed limits judicial inventiveness. Courts are not free to amend a rule outside the process Congress ordered, a process properly tuned to the instruction that rules of procedure "shall not abridge ... any substantive right." § 2072(b).

Rule 23(e), on settlement of class actions, reads in entirety: "A class action shall not be dismissed or compromised without the approval of the court, and notice of the proposed dismissal or compromise shall be given to all members of the class in such manner as the court directs." This prescription was designed to function as an additional requirement, not a superseding direction, for the "class action" to which Rule 23(e) refers is one qualified for certification under Rule 23(a) and(b).... Subdivisions (a) and (b) focus court attention on whether a proposed class has sufficient unity so that absent members can fairly be bound by decisions of class representatives. That dominant concern persists when settlement, rather than trial, is proposed.

The safeguards provided by the Rule 23(a) and (b) class-qualifying criteria, we emphasize, are not impractical impediments—checks shorn of utility—in the settlement class context. First, the standards set for the protection of absent class members serve to inhibit appraisals of the chancellor's foot kind—class certifications dependent upon the court's gestalt judgment or overarching impression of the settlement's fairness.

Second, if a fairness inquiry under Rule 23(e) controlled certification, eclipsing Rule 23(a) and (b), and permitting class designation despite the impossibility of litigation, both class counsel and court would be disarmed. Class counsel confined to settlement negotiations could not use the threat of litigation to press for a better offer, see Coffee, Class Wars: The Dilemma of the Mass Tort Class Action, 95 Colum.L.Rev. 1380 (1995), and the court would face a bargain proffered for its approval without benefit of adversarial investigation, see, e.g., Kamilewicz v. Bank of Boston Corp., 100 F.3d 1348, 1352 (C.A.7 1996) (Easterbrook, J., dissenting from denial of rehearing en banc) (parties "may even put one over on the court, in a staged performance"), cert. denied, 520 U.S. ___ (1997).

Federal courts, in any case, lack authority to substitute for Rule 23's certification criteria a standard never adopted—that if a settlement is "fair," then certification is proper. Applying to this case criteria the rulemakers set, we conclude that the Third Circuit's appraisal is essentially correct. Although that court should have acknowledged that settlement is a factor in the calculus, a remand is not warranted on that account. The Court of Appeals' opinion amply demonstrates why—with or without a settlement on the table—the sprawling class the District Court certified does not satisfy Rule 23's requirements.

A

We address first the requirement of Rule 23(b)(3) that "[common] questions of law or fact ... predominate over any questions affecting only individual members." ...

The predominance requirement stated in Rule 23(b)(3), we hold, is not met by the factors on which the District Court relied. The benefits asbestos-exposed persons might gain from the establishment of a grand-scale compensation scheme is a matter fit for legislative consideration, but it is not pertinent to the predominance inquiry. That inquiry trains on the legal or factual questions that qualify each class member's case as a genuine controversy, questions that preexist any settlement.

The Rule 23(b)(3) predominance inquiry tests whether proposed classes are sufficiently cohesive to warrant adjudication by representation. See 7A Wright, Miller, & Kane 518–519. The inquiry appropriate under Rule 23(e), on the other hand, protects unnamed class members "from unjust or unfair settlements affecting their rights when the representatives become faint hearted before the action is adjudicated or are able to secure satisfaction of their individual claims by a compromise." See 7B Wright, Miller, & Kane § 1797, at 340–341. But it is not the mission of Rule 23(e) to assure the class cohesion that legitimizes representative action in the first place. If a common interest in a fair compromise could satisfy the predominance requirement of Rule 23(b)(3), that vital prescription would be stripped of any meaning in the settlement context.

The District Court also relied upon this commonality: "The members of the class have all been exposed to asbestos products supplied by the defendants...." Even if Rule 23(a)'s commonality requirement may be satisfied by that shared experience, the predominance criterion is far more demanding. Given the greater number of questions peculiar to the several categories of class members, and to individuals within each category, and the significance of those uncommon questions, any overarching dispute about the health consequences of asbestos exposure cannot satisfy the Rule 23(b)(3) predominance standard.

The Third Circuit highlighted the disparate questions undermining class cohesion in this case:

Class members were exposed to different asbestos-containing products, for different amounts of time, in different ways, and over different periods. Some class members suffer no physical injury or have only asymptomatic pleural changes, while others suffer from lung cancer, disabling asbestosis, or from mesothelioma.... Each has a different history of cigarette smoking, a factor that complicates the causation inquiry.

The [exposure-only] plaintiffs especially share little in common, either with each other or with the presently injured class members. It is unclear whether they will contract asbestos-related disease and, if so, what disease each will suffer. They will also incur different medical expenses because their monitoring and treatment will depend on singular circumstances and individual medical histories.

Differences in state law, the Court of Appeals observed, compound these disparities. See id., at 627 (citing Phillips Petroleum Co. v. Shutts, 472 U.S. 797, 823, 86 L. Ed. 2d 628, 105 S.Ct. 2965 (1985)).

No settlement class called to our attention is as sprawling as this one.... As the Third Circuit's opinion makes plain, the certification in this case does not follow the counsel of caution. That certification cannot be upheld, for it rests on a conception of Rule 23(b)(3)'s predominance requirement irreconcilable with the rule's design.

B

Nor can the class approved by the District Court satisfy Rule 23(a)(4)'s requirement that the named parties "will fairly and adequately protect the interests of the class." ...

As the Third Circuit pointed out, named parties with diverse medical conditions sought to act on behalf of a single giant class rather than on behalf of discrete subclasses. In significant respects, the interests of those within the single class are not aligned. Most saliently, for the currently injured, the critical goal is generous immediate payments. That goal tugs against the interest of exposure-only plaintiffs in ensuring an ample, inflation-protected fund for the future....

The disparity between the currently injured and exposure-only categories of plaintiffs, and the diversity within each category are not made insignificant by the District Court's finding that petitioners' assets suffice to pay claims under the settlement. Although this is not a "limited fund" case certified under Rule 23(b)(1)(B), the terms of the settlement reflect essential allocation decisions designed to confine compensation and to limit defendants' liability....

The settling parties, in sum, achieved a global compromise with no structural assurance of fair and adequate representation for the diverse groups and individuals affected. Although the named parties alleged a range of complaints, each served generally as representative for the whole, not for a separate constituency.... The Third Circuit found no assurance here—either in the terms of the settlement or in the structure of the negotiations—that the named plaintiffs operated under a proper understanding of their representational responsibilities. That assessment, we conclude, is on the mark.

C

Impediments to the provision of adequate notice, the Third Circuit emphasized, rendered highly problematic any endeavor to tie to a settlement class persons with no perceptible asbestos-related disease at the time of the settlement. Many persons in the exposure-only category, the Court of Appeals stressed, may not even know of their exposure, or realize the extent of the harm they may incur. Even if they fully appreciate the significance of class notice, without current afflictions may not have the information or foresight needed to decide, intelligently, whether to stay in or opt out.

Family members of asbestos-exposed individuals may themselves fall prey to disease or may ultimately have ripe claims for loss of consortium. Yet large numbers of people in this category—future spouses and children of asbestos victims—could not be alerted to their class membership. And current spouses and children of the occupationally exposed may know nothing of that exposure.

Because we have concluded that the class in this case cannot satisfy the requirements of common issue predominance and adequacy of representation, we need not rule, definitively, on the notice given here. In accord with the Third Circuit, however, we recognize the gravity of the question whether class action notice sufficient under the Constitution and Rule 23 could ever be given to legions so unselfconscious and amorphous.

V

The argument is sensibly made that a nationwide administrative claims processing regime would provide the most secure, fair, and efficient means of compensating victims of asbestos exposure. Congress, however, has not adopted such a solution. And Rule 23, which must be interpreted with fidelity to the Rules Enabling Act and applied with the interests of absent class members in close view, cannot carry the large load CCR, class counsel, and the District Court heaped upon it. As this case exemplifies, the rulemakers' prescriptions for class actions may be endangered by "those who embrace [Rule 23] too enthusiastically just as [they are by] those who approach [the rule] with distaste." C. Wright, Law of Federal Courts 508 (5th ed. 1994)....

For the reasons stated, the judgment of the Court of Appeals for the Third Circuit is

Affirmed.

Justice O'Connor took no part in the consideration or decision of this case.

JUSTICE BREYER, with whom JUSTICE STEVENS joins, concurring in part and dissenting in part.

Although I agree with the Court's basic holding that "settlement is relevant to a class certification," I find several problems in its approach that lead me to a different conclusion. First, I believe that the need for settlement in this mass tort case, with hundreds of thousands of lawsuits, is greater than the Court's opinion suggests. Second, I would give more weight than would the majority to settlement-related issues for purposes of determining whether common issues predominate. Third, I am uncertain about the Court's determination of adequacy of representation, and do not believe it appropriate for this Court to second-guess the District Court on the matter without first having the Court of Appeals consider it. Fourth, I am uncertain about the tenor of an opinion that seems to suggest the settlement is unfair. And fifth, in the absence of further review by the Court of Appeals, I cannot accept the majority's suggestions that "notice" is inadequate.

These difficulties flow from the majority's review of what are highly fact-based, complex, and difficult matters that are inappropriate for initial review before this Court. The law gives broad leeway to district courts in making class certification decisions, and their judgments are to be reviewed by the Court of Appeals only for abuse of discretion. See Califano v. Yamasaki, 442 U.S. 682, 703, 61 L.Ed.2d 176, 99 S.Ct. 2545 (1979). Indeed, the District Court's certification decision rests upon more than 300 findings of fact reached after five weeks of comprehensive hearings. Accordingly, I do not believe that we should in effect set aside the findings of the District Court. That court is far more familiar with the issues and litigants than is a court of appeals or are we, and therefore has "broad power and discretion ... with respect to matters involving the certification" of class actions. Reiter v. Sonotone Corp., 442 U.S. 330, 345, 60 L.Ed.2d 931,99 S.Ct. 2326 (1979); cf. Cooter & Gell v. Hartmarx Corp., 496 U.S. 384, 402, 110 L.Ed.2d 359, 110 S.Ct. 2447 (1990) (district court better situated to make fact-dependent legal determinations in Rule 11 context).

* * *

I

First, I believe the majority understates the importance of settlement in this case. Between 13 and 21 million workers have been exposed to asbestos in the workplace—over the past 40 or 50 years—but the most severe instances of such exposure probably occurred three or four decades ago. See Report of The Judicial Conference Ad Hoc Committee on Asbestos Litigation, pp. 6–7 (Mar. 1991) (Judicial Conference Report); App. 781782, 801; B. Castleman, Asbestos: Medical and Legal Aspects 787–788 (4th ed. 1996). This exposure has led to several thousand lawsuits, about 15% of which involved claims for cancer and about 30%

for asbestosis. See In re Joint Eastern and Southern Dist. Asbestos Litigation, 129 B.R. 710, 936–937 (E and S.D.N.Y.1991) (Joint Litigation). About half of the suits have involved claims for pleural thickening and plaques—the harmfulness of which is apparently controversial. (One expert below testified that they "don't transform into cancer" and are not "predictors of future disease," App. 781.) Some of those who suffer from the most serious injuries, however, have received little or no compensation.... These lawsuits have taken up more than 6% of all federal civil filings in one recent year, and are subject to a delay that is twice that of other civil suits. Judicial Conference.

Delays, high costs, and a random pattern of noncompensation led the Judicial Conference Ad Hoc Committee on Asbestos Litigation to transfer all federal asbestos personal-injury cases to the Eastern District of Pennsylvania in an effort to bring about a fair and comprehensive settlement....

Although the transfer of the federal asbestos cases did not produce a general settlement, it was intertwined with and led to a lengthy year-long negotiation between the co-chairs of the Plaintiff's Multi–District Litigation Steering Committee (elected by the Plaintiff's Committee Members and approved by the District Court) and the 20 asbestos defendants who are before us here. These "protracted and vigorous" negotiations led to the present partial settlement, which will pay an estimated $1.3 billion and compensate perhaps 100,000 class members in the first 10 years....

The District Court, when approving the settlement, concluded that it improved the plaintiffs' chances of compensation and reduced total legal fees and other transaction costs by a significant amount. Under the previous system, according to the court, "the sickest of victims often go uncompensated for years while valuable funds go to others who remain unimpaired by their mild asbestos disease." The court believed the settlement would create a compensation system that would make more money available for plaintiffs who later develop serious illnesses.

I mention this matter because it suggests that the settlement before us is unusual in terms of its importance, both to many potential plaintiffs and to defendants, and with respect to the time, effort, and expenditure that it reflects. All of which leads me to be reluctant to set aside the District Court's findings without more assurance than I have that they are wrong. I cannot obtain that assurance through comprehensive review of the record because that is properly the job of the Court of Appeals and that court, understandably, but as we now hold, mistakenly, believed that settlement was not a relevant (and, as I would say, important) consideration.

Second, the majority, in reviewing the District Court's determination that common "issues of fact and law predominate," says that the predominance "inquiry trains on the legal or factual questions that qualify each class member's case as a genuine controversy, questions that preexist any settlement." I find it difficult to interpret this sentence in a way that could lead me to the majority's conclusion. If the majority means that these pre-settlement questions are what matters, then how does it reconcile its statement with its basic conclusion that "settlement is relevant" to class certification, or with the numerous lower court authority that says that settlement is not only relevant, but important?

* * *

Third, the majority concludes that the "representative parties" will not "fairly and adequately protect the interests of the class." Rule 23(a)(4). It finds a serious conflict between plaintiffs who are now injured and those who may be injured in the future because "for the currently injured, the critical goal is generous immediate payments," a goal that "tugs against the interest of exposure-only plaintiffs in ensuring an ample, inflation-protected fund for the future."

I agree that there is a serious problem, but is a problem that often exists in toxic tort cases.... And it is a problem that potentially exists whenever a single defendant injures several plaintiffs, for a settling plaintiff leaves fewer assets available for the others. With class actions, at least, plaintiffs have the consolation that a district court, thoroughly familiar with the facts, is charged with the responsibility of ensuring that the interests of no class members are sacrificed.

But this Court cannot easily safeguard such interests through review of a cold record. "What constitutes adequate representation is a question of fact that depends on the circumstances of each case." Wright, Miller, & Kane, 7A Federal Practice and Procedure, § 1765, at 271. * * *

The difficulties inherent in both knowing and understanding the vast number of relevant individual fact-based determinations here counsel heavily in favor of deference to district court decisionmaking in Rule 23 decisions. Or, at the least, making certain that appellate court review has taken place with the correct standard in mind.

Fourth, I am more agnostic than is the majority about the basic fairness of the settlement. The District Court's conclusions rested upon complicated factual findings that are not easily cast aside....

Finally, I believe it is up to the District Court, rather than this Court, to review the legal sufficiency of notice to members of the class....

II

The issues in this case are complicated and difficult. The District Court might have been correct. Or not. Subclasses might be appropriate. Or not. I cannot tell. And I do not believe that this Court should be in the business of trying to make these fact-based determinations. That is a job suited to the district courts in the first instance, and the courts of appeal on review. But there is no reason in this case to believe that the Court of Appeals conducted its prior review with an understanding that the settlement could have constituted a reasonably strong factor in favor of class certification. For this reason, I would provide the courts below with an opportunity to analyze the factual questions involved in certification by vacating the judgment, and remanding the case for further proceedings.

NOTE ON SETTLEMENT CLASSES

1. What is a "settlement class"? Rule 23, as currently drafted, does not mention a "settlement class." But federal courts in recent years have frequently approved their use. They have been described as follows:

> The settlement class device ... is a judicially crafted procedure. Usually, the request for a settlement class is presented to the court by both plaintiff(s) and defendant(s); having provisionally settled the case before seeking certification, the parties move for simultaneous class certification and settlement approval. Because this process is removed from the normal, adversarial, litigation mode, the class is certified for settlement purposes, not for litigation. Sometimes ... the parties reach a settlement while the case is in litigation posture, only then moving the court, with the defendants' stipulation as to the class's compliance with the Rule 23 requisites, for class certification and settlement approval. In any event, the court disseminates notice of the proposed settlement and fairness hearing at the same time it notifies class members of the pendency of class action determination. Only when the settlement is about to be finally approved does the court formally certify the class, thus binding the interests of its members by the settlement.

In re GMC Pick–Up Truck Fuel Tank Products Liability Litigation, 55 F.3d 768, 777–78 (3d Cir.1995)(rejecting proposed settlement).

The settlement class device has great attraction in mass tort cases. A suitable settlement can so reduce litigation costs that defendants can save money even while the plaintiff class as a whole can obtain a larger recovery. But how can one determine that the settlement is fair in the sense that at least some of the savings achieved through settlement are coming to the class members? And how can one determine that it is fair as among subclasses in the overall class? The difficulties in making such determinations are said to include: (1) "[T]he court cannot properly discharge its duty to protect the interests of the absentees during the disposition of the action. Because the class has not yet been defined, the court lacks the information necessary to determine the identity of the absentees and the likely extent of liability, damages, and expenses of preparing for trial. ... Moreover, the court performs its role as supervisor/protector without the benefit of a full adversarial briefing on the certification issues. With less information about the class, the judge cannot as effectively monitor for collusion, individual settlements, buy-offs (where some individuals use the class action device to benefit themselves at the expense of absentees), and other abuses." (2) "[S]ettlement classes create especially lucrative opportunities for putative class attorneys to generate fees for themselves without any effective monitoring by class members who have not yet been apprised of the pendency of the action." *GMC Pick–Up Truck Litigation*, at 813–14, 815–17.

2. Should a settlement class meet the same criteria for certification as a litigation class? Some settlement classes would be certifiable whether the case is litigated or settled. Others, however, present such problems of management, potential conflict among class members, and the like, that the class could never be certified for litigation under the standards of Rule 23(b)(3). Should the standards for certification be different depending on whether the case is litigated or settled? The Court of Appeals in *Amchem* had held that standards for class certification must be the same in each instance. The Supreme Court disagreed, saying that if management problems that would defeat class certification in a litigated case could be reduced by settlement, that difference could be taken into account in deciding whether to certify a settlement class. But, in the view of the Court, other criteria for certification—primarily those concerning the definition of the class and subclasses within it—merit heightened scrutiny in certification of a settlement class.

3. Should the Court have waited for a change in Rule 23? The Court in *Amchem* noted that the Standing Committee on Rules of Practice and Procedure had recently proposed a change in Rule 23 that, if adopted, would allow certification of settlement classes more easily than litigation classes. Under the proposed rule, a 23(b)(3) class could be certified for settlement "even though the requirements of subdivision (b)(3) might not be met for purposes of trial." Proposed Rule 23(b)(4). One hundred forty-four law professors have objected to the proposed change. They argue, among other things, that the change would invite collusion between class counsel for plaintiff and counsel for the defendant, and that it gives too much discretion to the District Judge. The fate of the proposed change is, as of this writing, uncertain.

4. Limited ability of the District Judge to assess the fairness of a proposed settlement. Even in the best of circumstances—in a case where the class has been certified under the standard criteria for a litigation class and where the case has proceeded far enough for its outlines to emerge fairly clearly—it is difficult for a District Judge to assess the fairness of a proposed settlement. The problems are compounded in a settlement class action. In part, the question is one of knowledge. The judge is never in a position to know as much about the case as the lawyers who present the case for approval of the settlement, and this particularly so in a settlement class action. And, in part, the question is one of standards. If a proposed settlement is within the range of settlement solutions in which each side shares some of the "surplus" created by settlement, it is very difficult—some would say impossible—to characterize one settlement as more fair than another. See, e.g., Hazard, "The Settlement Black Box," 75 B.U.L.Rev. 1257 (1995). Are the limits on the judge's ability to assess fairness the reason the Court in *Amchem* was so concerned that there had been "no structural assurance of fair and adequate representation of the diverse groups and individuals affected"?

5. The settlement in *Amchem*. For assessments of the fairness of the (now disapproved) settlement in *Amchem*, see Koniak, "Feasting While the Widow Weeps: *Georgine v. Amchem Products, Inc.*," 80 Cornell L.Rev. 1045 (1995); Menkel–Meadow, "Ethics and the Settlement of Mass Torts: When the Rules Meet the Road," 80 Cornell L.Rev. 1159 (1995). For more general discussion, see Coffee, "Class Wars: The Dilemma of the Mass Tort Class Action," 95 Colum.L.Rev. 1343 (1995); Symposium, "Mass Tortes: Serving Up Just Desserts," 80 Cornell L.Rev. 811 (1995)(including the articles by Professors Koniak and Menkel–Meadow); Comment, "Back to the Drawing Board: The Settlement Class Action and the Limits of Rule 23," 109 Harv.L.Rev. 828 (1996).

6. *Amchem* revisited? The Supreme Court has granted certiorari in *Flanagan v. Ahearn*, another asbestos settlement class action case. After this case was remanded to the Court of Appeals for reconsideration in light of *Amchem*, the Court of Appeals adhered to its prior approval of the settlement, noting inter alia that this case involved a class certified under Fed.R.Civ.P. 23(b)(1) rather than 23(b)(3), as in *Amchem*. Flanagan v. Ahearn, 134 F.3d 668 (5th Cir.1998), cert. granted sub nom. Ortiz v. Fibreboard Corp., ___ U.S. ___, 118 S.Ct. 2339, ___ L.Ed.2d ___ (1998).

7. More favorable assessment of class action settlements. Two professors with first-hand experience in the administration of class action settlements have a more favorable view than many of their academic colleagues. See Green, "What Will We Do When Adjudication Ends? We'll Settle in Bunches: Bringing Rule 23 into the Twenty–First Century," 44 U.C.L.A.L.Rev. 1773 (1997)(Professor Green was guardian ad litem in *Ahearn v. Fibreboard Corp.*, an asbestos class settlement); Vairo, "Georgine, The Dalkon Shield Claimants Trust, and the Rhetoric of Mass Tort Claims Resolution," 31 Loyola L.A.L.Rev. 79 (1997)(Professor Vairo served as a trustee and chairperson of the Dalkon Shield Claimants Trust. She writes, "My experience ... suggests that aggregated solutions to mass tort cases are the preferred alternative to traditional one-on-one litigation.").

8. Additional reading. There has been an enormous outpouring of articles on class actions. See, e.g., Shapiro, "Class Actions: The Class as Party and Client," 73 Notre Dame L.Rev.913 (1998); Symposium, "Rule 23 at the Crossroads," 39 Ariz.L.Rev. 407 (1997); Symposium, "The Institute of Judicial Administration Research Conference on Class Actions," 71 N.Y.U.L.Rev. 1 (1996); Symposium, "Summing Up Procedural Justice: Exploring the Tension Between Collective Processes and Individual Rights in the Context of Settlement and Litigating Classes," 30 U.C.Davis L.Rev. 786 (1997).

"FISTFULS OF COUPONS:
MILLIONS FOR CLASS–ACTION LAWYERS,
SCRIP FOR PLAINTIFFS"

The New York Times,
May 26, 1995
by Barry Meier

Mary Tolja recently learned that she was a winner in a class-action lawsuit brought against the Ford Motor Company on behalf of 65,000 owners of possibly leaky 1983–86 Mustang convertibles. She is less than elated.

While plaintiffs' lawyers expect to receive about $1 million in fees and expenses, Ms. Tolja, like many others in the class, can't imagine a use for her award—a $400 nontransferable coupon good for a year toward a new Ford.

"To me, these coupons are not worth 2 cents," Ms. Tolja, a retired school administrator in Sonoma, Calif., said. "I'm not going to buy a new Ford; I already have a new Honda."

That kind of disdain is spreading as more corporate defendants in class actions are working out settlements in which consumers are paid off in scrip while their lawyers walk away with millions. The awards—for discounts on a defendant's products or for other nonmonetary benefits like car safety inspections—have ranged from $4,000 off a new BMW to a $25 reduction in airline fares to a free box of Cheerios.

Some noncash settlements have proved of value when, among other things, a coupon is readily convertible into cash. But as Congress is weighing broad changes in civil litigation rules, some critics see the settlements as a glaring example of what is wrong with a system whose prime beneficiaries often turn out to be lawyers.

At their worst, critics say, the cases represent a mass of small, sometimes marginal claims packaged by lawyers for the sole purpose of snaring fat fees. Even when the complaints have merit, the lawyers compromise their clients' interests, the critics contend, by colluding with big corporate defendants who see a cheap way to end protracted litigation and use the coupons to increase their sales.

"Some of these settlements are a joke," said Brian Wolfman, a lawyer with Public Citizen, a public interest group in Washington that has objected to proposed settlements in several noncash cases, including the Mustang suit.

Federal and state courts have started to scrutinize the settlements more closely and have recently thrown out several proposed agreements. In a case involving allegations of safety defects in the Ford Bronco II, in which safety inspections and videotapes were offered as awards, a Federal judge said that plaintiffs' lawyers had settled for so little that the deal created the appearance of a sellout. Ford, which is not appealing the decision, says the vehicle is safe and plans to legally defend it.

"Courts are starting to realize what a scam and hypocrisy these types of settlements can be," said Beverly Moore, the editor of Class Action Report, a Washington publication.

For their part, lawyers involved in settlements with Ford and others say they have nothing to apologize for. They work hard for their fees in often difficult cases, they say, and get the best deals for clients. Even in cases that involve awards as minimal as a box of cereal, the lawyers say they protect the public by putting corporate America on notice.

"I look at a lawsuit as trying to get something of value for the client, and in some of these cases the wrongdoing does not give rise to easy cash recovery," said Melvyn I. Weiss, a leading class-action lawyer with Milberg, Weiss, Bershad, Hynes & Lerach of New York.

Even critics of nonmonetary pacts agree that they can work to every one's benefit if structured properly. A financially weak company facing numerous claims can avoid bankruptcy by paying out scrip rather than cash. When coupons are not convertible into cash, they can still have value if the scrip involves a small-ticket item like a video game, as it did in a case involving Nintendo, or if it represents a high percentage of a product's cost, legal experts say.

But sometimes, critics assert, plaintiffs' lawyers and defendant companies inflate the value of settlements by overestimating how many class members will use coupons. Some companies may have tried to cut costs further by making scrip hard to redeem.

"These scrip settlements tend to be used by lawyers who are not zealous on behalf of the class," said John Coffee, a professor at the Columbia University School of Law.

There are benefits to noncash settlements that make them particularly attractive to corporate defendants. For one thing, they close the door to future claims on the same issue by consumers who have not opted out of the class.

Also, scrip is effectively "soft money" that does not come off a company's bottom line, but may serve to provide incentives to increase product sales, said Lew Goldfarb, the assistant general counsel for the Chrysler Corporation, which has used coupons in one case.

The Mustang lawsuit may provide a case study of some of the shortcomings of coupon settlements.

In that case, the lawyers first asserted that the vehicles were dangerous, asserting that there was a structural defect in the frame. That approach was based on a single accident, the cause of which was never proved, said Robert S. Kilborne 4th, one of the lawyers.

Mr. Kilborne said he and his colleagues could not find other similar accidents. They did hear, however, of problems relating to leaks, so they focused on a claim that the same defect lets wind and rain into the passenger compartment.

While Ford has denied there is any structural defect in the older Mustangs, the company did change the vehicle's frame design in 1987 and offered owners a $600 retrofit kit, court papers indicate.

Ms. Tolja and other owners said they would have liked the kit or the money to buy one. But Mr. Kilborne said Ford would settle the case only with a nontransferable coupon. He noted that the proposed settlement had been approved as fair by a California court.

"They were not interested in a cash settlement at all," Mr. Kilborne said, referring to Ford. "We were trying to get 100 bucks, even 50."

Jon Harmon, a Ford spokesman, declined to comment on the settlement plan.

Some law firms are particularly active in noncash deals. Mr. Weiss's firm, for example, has been involved in three such cases recently. They involve allegations of steering troubles in Mercedes–Benz S-class cars made in 1992 and 1993, defective Pentium computer chips made by the Intel Corporation and the pesticide-related problems of breakfast cereals sold by General Mills Inc. Fees and expenses proposed or awarded to Milberg, Weiss and other firms in those cases: more than $19 million.

To determine fees, lawyers sometimes negotiate directly with the defendant. More often, they apply to the court, seeking payment for hours spent on the case, increased by a bonus that doubles or triples their normal rate to reflect the case's complexity or risk.

While lawyers may reap small fortunes, the cases are sometimes quickly resolved without witnesses being deposed. In a case with Chrysler involving defective heater coils in Renault Encore and Alliance cars made in 1983–87, lawyers for both sides hammered out a settlement proposal after about 20 hours of face-to-face meetings, said Mary Rosseel–Jones, a Chrysler lawyer. Plaintiffs' lawyers fees and expenses in that case: $1.65 million.

One of the most contentious coupon cases now unfolding involves the General Motors Corporation.

A Texas appeals court last year and a Federal appeals panel this April rejected a $1,000 coupon deal for 6.4 million owners of older G.M. pickup trucks that may explode after side-impact collisions, agreeing with critics who called the plan a "sophisticated marketing program" to sell trucks. The Federal panel also questioned whether the G.M. coupons could be readily transferred.

Ed Lechtzin, a G.M. spokesman, said the company and plaintiffs' lawyers were appealing both rulings. G.M. says the trucks are safe but declined to comment on the coupon aspect of the case.

And in the Bronco II case, Federal District Judge Morey L. Sear in New Orleans threw out a settlement proposed in March that would have covered 645,000 owners of Bronco II's made in 1983–90, saying the plan provided "effectively zero" value to those who fear the vehicle is prone to rollovers.

Ford has paid $113.4 million to settle 334 death and injury claims involving the Bronco II.

* * *

After a string of hollow settlements, some critics of coupons wonder why lawyers cannot come up with better deals.

It is a question that also occurs to Ms. Tolja, who objected to the Mustang settlement.

"The whole idea that the lawyer collects a million and the person collects nothing," she said, "is the most asinine thing that I have ever heard."

For a description of a settlement of an Alabama state court class action against a bank, in which a Maine customer's account was credited $2.19 as her recovery but was debited $145.65 as her share of the class counsel's fee, see Koniak and Cohen, "Under Cloak of Settlement," 82 Va.L.Rev. 1051, 1057–68, 1270–80 (1996)(be sure to read the "epilogue"). For a discussion of in-kind settlements, see Comment, "In–Kind Class Action Settlements," 109 Harv.L.Rev. 810 (1996).

For a post-*Amchem* decertification of a settlement class and disapproval of the proposed settlement, see Clement v. American Honda Finance Corp., 176 F.R.D. 15 (D.Conn.1997). The nationwide class action claimed that automobile lease agreements offered by defendants were unfair and misleading, violating both federal and state law. Under the proposed settlement, unnamed class members would have received non-transferable coupons worth $75 or $150 toward a new lease with defendants; the three named class members would each have received $2,500; class counsel would have received a fee of $140,000. The court wrote, "The plaintiffs' argument that [defendant] AHFC's substantial losses justify the fee award is illusory. AHFC would not suffer harm as a result of this settlement, but rather would benefit substantially from the additional cars it would sell or lease with each coupon redeemed.... A $140,000 attorneys' fee award is a settlement that benefits the named plaintiffs and defendants, but not the individual class members is more than just suspect. It is wholly inappropriate."

Chapter 7
THE PRETRIAL STAGE

B. DISCLOSURE OF THE EVIDENCE
p. 929, 935, 937, 938, 939

INTRODUCTORY NOTE ON DISCOVERY

1. Discovery Tools

   b. Formal discovery.

   (1) Depositions. In Emerson Electric Co. v. Superior Court, 16 Cal.4th 1101, 68 Cal.Rptr.2d 883, 946 P.2d 841 (1997), the California Supreme Court held that a plaintiff in a product liability case can be compelled in a videotaped deposition to re-enact how the injury occurred.

   c. Additional reading. Useful recent articles on discovery include Dickerson, "The Law and Ethics of Civil Depositions," 57 Md.L.Rev. 273 (1998); Hazard, "Discovery and the Role of the Judge in Civil Law Jurisdictions," 73 Notre Dame L.Rev. 1017 (1998); Symposium, "Conference on Discovery Rules," 39 B.C.L.Rev. 517 (1998), particularly Subrin, "Fishing Expeditions Allowed: Historical Background of the 1938 Federal Discovery Rules," at 691.

3. The Federal Discovery Rules

   c. Rule 30. Depositions.

   (2) Means of recording. In Riley v. Murdock, 156 F.R.D. 130 (E.D.N.C.1994), the court upheld a switch from stenographic and audio recording to videotape recording. The deposing party sought the change on the ground that during the initial session the deponent had received coaching and had been evasive, and that the videotape would show what was happening.

   (3) Conduct of the deposition. In Smith v. Diamond Offshore Drilling, Inc., 168 F.R.D. 582 (S.D.Tex.1996), surveillance tapes were made of a personal injury plaintiff without his knowledge. The court held that the existence of the tapes had to be made known to the plaintiff before he was deposed, but that the tapes themselves did not have to be provided until after the deposition was concluded. Other courts have held that even the existence of surveillance tapes need not be disclosed until after the deposition. See, e.g., Ward v. CSX Transportation, Inc., 161 F.R.D. 38 (E.D.N.C. 1995).

   h. Rule 35. Physical and mental examination of persons. In Sacramona v. Bridgestone/Firestone, Inc., 152 F.R.D. 428 (D.Mass.1993), plaintiff was injured by an exploding tire rim. During discovery, defendants learned that plaintiff was a former intravenous drug user and a bisexual who engaged in unprotected sex. Defendants sought to compel a blood test for HIV on the ground that the likelihood of plaintiff's being HIV positive was greater than for the general population, and that if plaintiff were HIV positive his life expectancy and hence his recoverable damages would be reduced. The court held that under Rule 26(b)(1) the relevance of the blood test to plaintiff's cause of action was "too attenuated," and that under Rule 35(a) there was not "good cause" to order the test.

j. Rule 37. Orders compelling disclosure or discovery, and sanctions. (2) Sanctions. In Federal Deposit Insurance Corp. v. Conner, 20 F.3d 1376 (5th Cir.1994), the court held that dismissal of plaintiff's action was not warranted by plaintiff's failure to obey a discovery order unless defendant could show substantial prejudice. Where the disobedience took place early in discovery and did not seriously interfere with defendant's preparation of the case, an award of attorneys' fees was a sufficient sanction.

In Chilcutt v. United States, 4 F.3d 1313 (5th Cir.1993), the attorney for the United States failed to provide relevant documents. After repeatedly denying that the documents existed, the attorney finally provided them four days before trial. The Court of Appeals upheld as sanctions: (1) a finding of prima facie liability against the government; and (2) a requirement that the government's attorney compensate plaintiff's attorneys' fees out of his own pocket.

In a highly unusual case, United States v. Lundwall, 1 F.Supp.2d 249 (S.D.N.Y.1998), defendants were criminally charged under 18 U.S.C. § 1503 with destruction of documents sought in civil discovery. Section 1503 provides that "whoever ... corruptly ... obstructs or impedes ... the due administration of justice, shall [be guilty of a federal crime]." The statute had never before been held to apply to destruction of documents in a civil case, but the court found that such conduct was within its scope. "This case ... goes beyond civil discovery abuse remedial through civil sanctions. ... [Defendants] are charged with seeking to impair a pending court proceeding through the intentional destruction of documents sought in, and highly relevant to, that proceeding."

k. Inherent power to impose sanctions. In cases where sanctions are not provided in the Federal Rules, the court has "inherent power" to impose sanctions. But such power is used sparingly. For example, in Shepherd v. American Broadcasting Companies, Inc., 62 F.3d 1469, 1472 (D.C.Cir.1995), the Court of Appeals reversed a default judgment entered as a sanction for alteration of a document, improper interrogatory verification, witness harassment, and other discovery abuses. The Court held that a default judgment could be entered as a sanction under the District Court's inherent power "only if it finds, first, by clear and convincing evidence—a preponderance is not sufficient—that the abusive behavior occurred; and, second, that a lesser sanction would not sufficiently punish and deter the abusive conduct while allowing a full and fair trial on the merits."

3. Controversy over disclosure requirement in the 1993 amendments to the Federal Rules. For a good description of the process leading to the adoption of the new mandatory disclosure provision of Rule

26(a)(1), as well as a brief description of the history of federal rulemaking, see Carrington, "Learning from the Rule 26 Brouhaha: Our Courts Need Real Friends," 156 F.R.D. 295 (1994). For an overall assessment of the 1993 discovery amendments, see "Symposium on Recent Changes in the Rules of Pretrial Fact Development: What Do They Disclose about Litigation and the Legal Profession?" 46 Fla.L.Rev. 1 (1994).

3a. Recent state discovery reforms. Arizona, Illinois, and Colorado have recently revised their discovery rules. Arizona and Illinois require litigants to disclose fully the facts of their cases without being specifically asked to do so. See, e.g., Ariz.R.Civ.P. 26.1(a)(1)("each party shall disclose in writing to every other party ... the factual basis of the claim or defense"); (2–5)(shall disclose the names and addresses of expected witnesses, of persons with relevant knowledge or information, of persons who have given statements, and of expert witnesses); (8)(shall disclose the existence, location and description of tangible evidence); and (9)(shall disclose a list of documents relevant to the subject matter of the action). This disclosure is significantly broader than that required under Fed.R.Civ.P. 26(a)(1). Colorado requires an initial disclosure roughly comparable to that required under the federal rules. For generally favorable evaluation of the experience in these states, see "Symposium: Innovations in Discovery," 16 Rev. of Litig. 249 (1997).

2. TRIAL PREPARATION PRIVILEGES

a. THE ATTORNEY–CLIENT AND WORK PRODUCT PRIVILEGES

p. 958

NOTE ON THE WORK–PRODUCT PRIVILEGE

See E. Epstein, The Attorney–Client Privilege and the Work–Product Doctrine (3d ed.1996).

In Bartley v. Isuzu Motors Ltd., 158 F.R.D. 165 (D.Colo.1994), plaintiff was injured when his Isuzu Trooper skidded on ice and he was thrown out the window. Defendant sought discovery of documents and depositions in other Isuzu accident cases. These materials were held by plaintiff but had originally been collected by the litigation clearinghouse of the American Trial Lawyers' Association. The Magistrate Judge found that the materials were not work product because they had been prepared by third parties and had not been prepared in anticipation of this litigation.

The 1993 amendments to Rule 26 concerning expert witnesses have made incursions into the classic work product rule. An expert who is expected to testify must now provide a written report to the other side, including "a complete statement of all opinions to be expressed and the basis and reasons therefore" and "the data or other information considered by the witness in forming the opinions." Fed.R.Civ.P. 26(a)(2)(B). To the extent that an attorney has supplied work product materials to an expert to use in forming the expert's opinions, those materials are discoverable. According to the Advisory Committee notes, "Litigants should no longer be able to argue that materials furnished to their experts to be used in forming their opinions—whether or not ultimately relied on by the expert—are privileged or otherwise protected from disclosure when such persons are testifying or being deposed." For thorough discussions, see Karn v. Ingersoll Rand, 168 F.R.D. 633 (N.D.Ind.1996); Haworth, Inc. v. Herman Miller, Inc., 162 F.R.D. 289 (W.D.Mich.1995).

p. 959, after NOTE ON THE WORK PRODUCT PRIVILEGE

SWIDLER & BERLIN v. UNITED STATES

United States Supreme Court, 1998.
___ U.S. ___, 118 S.Ct. 2081, ___ L.Ed.2d ___.

CHIEF JUSTICE REHNQUIST delivered the opinion of the court.

Petitioner, an attorney, made notes of an initial interview with a client shortly before the client's death. The Government, represented by the Office of Independent Counsel, now seeks his notes for use in a criminal investigation. We hold that the notes are protected by the attorney-client privilege.

This dispute arises out of an investigation conducted by the Office of the Independent Counsel into whether various individuals made false statements, obstructed justice, or committed other crimes during investigations of the 1993 dismissal of employees from the White House Travel Office. Vincent W. Foster, Jr., was Deputy White House Counsel when the firings occurred. In July, 1993, Foster met with petitioner James Hamilton, an attorney at petitioner Swidler & Berlin, to seek legal representation concerning possible congressional or other investigations of the firings. During a 2-hour meeting, Hamilton took three pages of handwritten notes. One of the first entries in the notes is the word "Privileged." Nine days later, Foster committed suicide.

In December 1995, a federal grand jury, at the request of the Independent Counsel, issued subpoenas to petitioners Hamilton and Swidler & Berlin for, inter alia, Hamilton's handwritten notes of his meeting with Foster. Petitioners filed a motion to quash, arguing that the notes were protected by the attorney client privilege and by the work product privilege. The District Court, after examining the notes in camera, concluded they were protected from disclosure by both doctrines and denied enforcement of the subpoenas.

The Court of Appeals for the District of Columbia Circuit reversed. *In re Sealed Case,* 124 F.3d 230 (1997). * * * The Court of Appeals thought that the risk of posthumous revelation, when confined to the criminal context, would have little to no chilling effect on client communication, but that the costs of protecting communications after death were high. It therefore concluded that the privilege was not absolute in such circumstances, and that instead, a balancing test should apply.

* * * It thus held that there is a posthumous exception to the privilege for communications whose relative importance to particular criminal litigation is substantial. * * *

Petitioners sought review in this Court [.] * * * We granted certiorari, 523 U.S. ___, 118 S.Ct. 1358, 140 L.Ed.2d 509 (1998), and we now reverse.

The attorney client privilege is one of the oldest recognized privileges for confidential communications. *Upjohn Co. v. United States,* 449 U.S. 383, 389, 101 S.Ct. 677, 682, 66 L.Ed.2d 584 (1981); *Hunt v. Blackburn*, 128 U.S. 464, 470, 9 S.Ct. 125, 127, 32 L.Ed. 488 (1888). The privilege is intended to encourage "full and frank communication between attorneys and their clients and thereby promote broader public interests in the observance of law and the administration of justice." *Upjohn*, supra, at 389, 101 S.Ct. at 682. The issue presented here is the scope of that privilege; more particularly, the extent to which the privilege survives the death of the client. Our interpretation of the privilege's scope is guided by "the principles of the common law ... as interpreted by the courts ... in the light of reason and experience." Fed.Rule Evid. 501; *Funk v. United States*, 290 U.S. 371, 54 S.Ct. 212, 78 L.Ed. 369 (1933).

The Independent Counsel argues that the attorney-client privilege should not prevent disclosure of confidential communications where the client has died and the information is relevant to a criminal proceeding. There is some authority for this position. One state appellate court, *Cohen v. Jenkintown Cab Co.*, 238 Pa.Super. 456, 357 A.2d 689 (1976), and the Court of Appeals below have held the privilege may be subject to posthumous exceptions in certain circumstances. In Cohen, a civil case, the court recognized that the privilege generally survives death, but concluded that it could make an exception where the interest of justice was compelling and the interest of the client in preserving the confidence was insignificant. * * *

But other than these two decisions, cases addressing the existence of the privilege after death—most involving the testamentary exception—uniformly presume the privilege survives, even if they do not so hold. See, e.g., *Mayberry v. Indiana,* 670 N.E.2d 1262 (Ind.1996); *Morris v. Cain*, 39 La. Ann. 712, 1 So. 797 (1887); *People v. Modzelewski*, 611 N.Y.S.2d 22, 203 A.D.2d 594 (1994). Several State Supreme Court decisions expressly hold that the attorney-client privilege extends beyond the death of the client, even in the criminal context. See *In re John Doe Grand Jury Investigation*, 408 Mass. 480, 481–483, 562 N.E.2d 69, 70 (1990); *State v. Doster*, 276 S.C. 647, 650–651, 284 S.E.2d 218, 219 (1981); *State v. Macumber*, 112 Ariz. 569, 571, 544 P.2d 1084, 1086 (1976). In John Doe Grand Jury Investigation, for example, the Massachusetts Supreme Court concluded that survival of the privilege was "the clear implication" of its early pronouncements that communications subject to the privilege could not be disclosed at any time. * * * The court further noted that survival of the privilege was "necessarily implied" by cases allowing waiver of the privilege in testamentary disputes. * * *

Such testamentary exception cases consistently presume the privilege survives. See, e.g., *United States v. Osborn,* 561 F.2d 1334, 1340 (C.A.9 1977); *DeLoach v. Myers,* 215 Ga. 255, 259–260, 109 S.E.2d 777, 780–781 (1959); *Doyle v. Reeves,* 112 Conn. 521, 152 A. 882 (1931); Russell v. Jackson, 9 Hare. 387, 68 Eng. Rep. 558 (V.C.1851). They view testamentary disclosure of communications as an exception to the privilege: "[T]he general rule with respect to confidential communications ... is that such communications are privileged during the testator's lifetime and, also, after the testator's death unless sought to be disclosed in litigation between the testator's heirs." * * * The rationale for such disclosure is that it furthers the client's intent.[2]

Indeed, in *Glover v. Patten*, 165 U.S. 394, 406–408, 17 S.Ct. 411, 416, 41 L.Ed. 760 (1897), this Court, in recognizing the testamentary exception, expressly assumed that the privilege continues after the individual's death. The Court explained that testamentary disclosure was permissible because the privilege, which normally protects the client's interests, could be impliedly waived in order to fulfill the client's testamentary intent. Id., at 407–408, 17 S.Ct., at 416 (quoting *Blackburn v. Crawfords,* 3 Wall. 175, 18 L.Ed. 186 (1865), and Russell v. Jackson, supra).

The great body of this caselaw supports, either by holding or considered dicta, the position that the privilege does survive in a case such as the present one. Given the language of Rule 501, at the very least the burden is on the Independent Counsel to show that "reason and experience" require a departure from this rule.

The Independent Counsel contends that the testamentary exception supports the posthumous termination of the privilege because in practice most cases have refused to apply the privilege posthumously. He further argues that the exception reflects a policy judgment that the interest in settling estates outweighs any posthumous interest in confidentiality. He then reasons by analogy that in criminal proceedings, the interest in determining whether a crime has been committed should trump client confidentiality, particularly since the financial interests of the estate are not at stake.

But the Independent Counsel's interpretation simply does not square with the caselaw's implicit acceptance of the privilege's survival and with the treatment of testamentary disclosure as an "exception" or

---

2. About half the States have codified the testamentary exception by providing that a personal representative of the deceased can waive the privilege when heirs or devisees claim through the deceased client (as opposed to parties claiming against the estate, for whom the privilege is not waived). See, e.g., Ala.Rule Evid. 502 (1996); Ark.Code Ann. § 16–41–101, Rule 502 (Supp.1997); Neb.Rev.Stat. § 27–503, Rule 503 (1995). * * *

an implied "waiver." And the premise of his analogy is incorrect, since cases consistently recognize that the rationale for the testamentary exception is that it furthers the client's intent, see, e.g., *Glover, supra.* There is no reason to suppose as a general matter that grand jury testimony about confidential communications furthers the client's intent.

Commentators on the law also recognize that the general rule is that the attorney-client privilege continues after death. See, e.g., 8 Wigmore, Evidence § 2323 (McNaughton rev. 1961); Frankel, The Attorney–Client Privilege After the Death of the Client, 6 Geo.J.Legal Ethics 45, 78–79 (1992); 1 J. Strong, McCormick on Evidence § 94, p. 348 (4th ed. 1992). Undoubtedly, as the Independent Counsel emphasizes, various commentators have criticized this rule, urging that the privilege should be abrogated after the client's death where extreme injustice would result, as long as disclosure would not seriously undermine the privilege by deterring client communication. See, e.g., C. Mueller & L. Kirkpatrick, 2 Federal Evidence § 199, at 380–381 (2d ed. 1994); Restatement (Third) of the Law Governing Lawyers § 127, Comment d (Proposed Final Draft No. 1, Mar. 29, 1996). But even these critics clearly recognize that established law supports the continuation of the privilege and that a contrary rule would be a modification of the common law. See, e.g., Mueller & Kirkpatrick, supra, at 379; Restatement of the Law Governing Lawyers, supra, § 127, Comment c; 24 C. Wright & K. Graham, Federal Practice and Procedure § 5498, p. 483 (1986).

Despite the scholarly criticism, we think there are weighty reasons that counsel in favor of posthumous application. Knowing that communications will remain confidential even after death encourages the client to communicate fully and frankly with counsel. While the fear of disclosure, and the consequent withholding of information from counsel, may be reduced if disclosure is limited to posthumous disclosure in a criminal context, it seems unreasonable to assume that it vanishes altogether. Clients may be concerned about reputation, civil liability, or possible harm to friends or family. Posthumous disclosure of such communications may be as feared as disclosure during the client's lifetime.

The Independent Counsel suggests, however, that his proposed exception would have little to no effect on the client's willingness to confide in his attorney. He reasons that only clients intending to perjure themselves will be chilled by a rule of disclosure after death, as opposed to truthful clients or those asserting their Fifth Amendment privilege. This is because for the latter group, communications disclosed by the attorney after the client's death purportedly will reveal only information that the client himself would have revealed if alive.

The Independent Counsel assumes, incorrectly we believe, that the privilege is analogous to the Fifth Amendment's protection against self-incrimination. But as suggested above, the privilege serves much broader purposes. Clients consult attorneys for a wide variety of reasons, only one of which involves possible criminal liability. Many attorneys act as counselors on personal and family matters, where, in the course of obtaining the desired advice, confidences about family members or financial problems must be revealed in order to assure sound legal advice. The same is true of owners of small businesses who may regularly consult their attorneys about a variety of problems arising in the course of the business. These confidences may not come close to any sort of admission of criminal wrongdoing, but nonetheless be matters which the client would not wish divulged.

The contention that the attorney is being required to disclose only what the client could have been required to disclose is at odds with the basis for the privilege even during the client's lifetime. In related cases, we have said that the loss of evidence admittedly caused by the privilege is justified in part by the fact that without the privilege, the client may not have made such communications in the first place. See *Jaffee*, 518 U.S., at 12, 116 S.Ct., at 1929; *Fisher v. United States*, 425 U.S. 391, 403, 96 S.Ct. 1569, 1577, 48 L.Ed.2d 39 (1976). This is true of disclosure before and after the client's death. Without assurance of the privilege's posthumous application, the client may very well not have made disclosures to his attorney at all, so the loss of evidence is more apparent than real. In the case at hand, it seems quite plausible that Foster, perhaps already contemplating suicide, may not have sought legal advice from Hamilton if he had not been assured the conversation was privileged.

The Independent Counsel additionally suggests that his proposed exception would have minimal impact if confined to criminal cases, or, as the Court of Appeals suggests, if it is limited to information of substantial importance to a particular criminal case.[3] However, there is no case authority for the proposition that the privilege applies differently in criminal and civil cases, and only one commentator ventures such a suggestion, see Mueller & Kirkpatrick, supra, at 380–381. In any event, a client may not know at the time he discloses information to his attorney whether it will later be relevant to a civil or a criminal matter, let alone whether it will be of substantial importance. Balancing ex post the importance of the information against client interests, even limited to criminal cases, introduces substantial uncertainty into the privilege's application. For just that reason, we have rejected use of a balancing test in defining the contours of the privilege. See Upjohn, 449 U.S., at 393, 101 S.Ct., at 684; Jaffee, supra, at 17–18, 116 S.Ct., at 1932.

In a similar vein, the Independent Counsel argues that existing exceptions to the privilege, such as the crime-fraud exception and the

---

3. Petitioner, while opposing wholesale abrogation of the privilege in criminal cases, concedes that exceptional circumstances implicating a criminal defendant's constitutional rights might warrant breaching the privilege. We do not, however, need to reach this issue, since such exceptional circumstances clearly are not presented here.

testamentary exception, make the impact of one more exception marginal. However, these exceptions do not demonstrate that the impact of a posthumous exception would be insignificant, and there is little empirical evidence on this point.[4] The established exceptions are consistent with the purposes of the privilege, see *Glover*, 165 U.S., at 407–408, 17 S.Ct., at 416; *United States v. Zolin*, 491 U.S. 554, 562–563, 109 S.Ct. 2619, 2625–2626, 105 L.Ed.2d 469 (1989), while a posthumous exception in criminal cases appears at odds with the goals of encouraging full and frank communication and of protecting the client's interests. A "no harm in one more exception" rationale could contribute to the general erosion of the privilege, without reference to common law principles or "reason and experience."

Finally, the Independent Counsel, relying on cases such as *United States v. Nixon*, 418 U.S. 683, 710, 94 S.Ct. 3090, 3108, 41 L.Ed.2d 1039 (1974), and *Branzburg v. Hayes*, 408 U.S. 665, 92 S.Ct. 2646, 33 L.Ed.2d 626 (1972), urges that privileges be strictly construed because they are inconsistent with the paramount judicial goal of truth seeking. But both Nixon and Branzburg dealt with the creation of privileges not recognized by the common law, whereas here we deal with one of the oldest recognized privileges in the law. And we are asked, not simply to "construe" the privilege, but to narrow it, contrary to the weight of the existing body of caselaw.

It has been generally, if not universally, accepted, for well over a century, that the attorney-client privilege survives the death of the client in a case such as this. While the arguments against the survival of the privilege are by no means frivolous, they are based in large part on speculation—thoughtful speculation, but speculation nonetheless—as to whether posthumous termination of the privilege would diminish a client's willingness to confide in an attorney. In an area where empirical information would be useful, it is scant and inconclusive.

---

4. Empirical evidence on the privilege is limited. Three studies do not reach firm conclusions on whether limiting the privilege would discourage full and frank communication. Alexander, The Corporate Attorney Client Privilege: A Study of the Participants, 63 St. John's L.Rev. 191 (1989); Zacharias, Rethinking Confidentiality, 74 Iowa L.Rev. 352 (1989); Comment, Functional Overlap Between the Lawyer and Other Professionals: Its Implications for the Privileged Communications Doctrine, 71 Yale L.J. 1226 (1962). These articles note that clients are often uninformed or mistaken about the privilege, but suggest that a substantial number of clients and attorneys think the privilege encourages candor. Two of the articles conclude that a substantial number of clients and attorneys think the privilege enhances open communication, Alexander, supra, at 244–246, 261, and that the absence of a privilege would be detrimental to such communication, Comment, 71 Yale L. J., supra, at 1236. The third article suggests instead that while the privilege is perceived as important to open communication, limited exceptions to the privilege might not discourage such communication, Zacharias, supra, at 382, 386. Similarly, relatively few court decisions discuss the impact of the privilege's application after death. This may reflect the general assumption that the privilege survives—if attorneys were required as a matter of practice to testify or provide notes in criminal proceedings, cases discussing that practice would surely exist.

Rule 501's direction to look to "the principles of the common law as they may be interpreted by the courts of the United States in the light of reason and experience" does not mandate that a rule, once established, should endure for all time. Funk v. United States, 290 U.S. 371, 381, 54 S.Ct. 212, 215, 78 L.Ed. 369 (1933). But here the Independent Counsel has simply not made a sufficient showing to overturn the common law rule embodied in the prevailing caselaw. Interpreted in the light of reason and experience, that body of law requires that the attorney client privilege prevent disclosure of the notes at issue in this case. The judgment of the Court of Appeals is

Reversed.

JUSTICE O'CONNOR, with whom JUSTICE SCALIA and JUSTICE THOMAS join, dissenting.

Although the attorney-client privilege ordinarily will survive the death of the client, I do not agree with the Court that it inevitably precludes disclosure of a deceased client's communications in criminal proceedings. In my view, a criminal defendant's right to exculpatory evidence or a compelling law enforcement need for information may, where the testimony is not available from other sources, override a client's posthumous interest in confidentiality.

We have long recognized that "[t]he fundamental basis upon which all rules of evidence must rest—if they are to rest upon reason—is their adaptation to the successful development of the truth." *Funk v. United States*, 290 U.S. 371, 381, 54 S.Ct. 212, 215, 78 L.Ed. 369 (1933). In light of the heavy burden that they place on the search for truth, see *United States v. Nixon*, 418 U.S. 683, 708–710, 94 S.Ct. 3090, 3107–3109, 41 L.Ed.2d 1039 (1974), "[e]videntiary privileges in litigation are not favored, and even those rooted in the Constitution must give way in proper circumstances," *Herbert v. Lando* 441 U.S. 153, 175, 99 S.Ct. 1635, 1648, 60 L.Ed.2d 115 (1979). Consequently, we construe the scope of privileges narrowly. See *Jaffee v. Redmond*, 518 U.S. 1, 19, 116 S.Ct. 1923, 1932–1933, 135 L.Ed.2d 337 (1996) (SCALIA, J., dissenting); see also *University of Pennsylvania v. EEOC*, 493 U.S. 182, 189, 110 S.Ct. 577, 582, 107 L.Ed.2d 571 (1990). We are reluctant to recognize a privilege or read an existing one expansively unless to do so will serve a "public good transcending the normally predominant principle of utilizing all rational means for ascertaining truth." *Trammel v. United States*, 445 U.S. 40, 50, 100 S.Ct. 906, 912, 63 L.Ed.2d 186 (1980) (internal quotation marks omitted).

The attorney-client privilege promotes trust in the representational relationship, thereby facilitating the provision of legal services and ultimately the administration of justice. See *Upjohn Co. v. United States*, 449 U.S. 383, 389, 101 S.Ct. 677, 682, 66 L.Ed.2d 584 (1981). The systemic benefits of the privilege are commonly understood to outweigh the harm caused by excluding critical evidence. A privilege should operate, however, only where "necessary to achieve its purpose," see *Fisher v. United States*, 425 U.S. 391, 403, 96 S.Ct. 1569, 1577, 48 L.Ed.2d 39 (1976), and an invocation of the attorney-client privilege should not go unexamined "when it is shown that the interests of the administration of justice can only be frustrated by [its] exercise," *Cohen v. Jenkintown Cab Co.*, 238 Pa.Super. 456, 464, 357 A.2d 689, 693–694 (1976).

I agree that a deceased client may retain a personal, reputational, and economic interest in confidentiality. But, after death, the potential that disclosure will harm the client's interests has been greatly diminished, and the risk that the client will be held criminally liable has abated altogether. Thus, some commentators suggest that terminating the privilege upon the client's death "could not to any substantial degree lessen the encouragement for free disclosure which is [its] purpose." 1 J. Strong, McCormick on Evidence § 94, p. 350 (4th ed. 1992); see also Restatement (Third) of the Law Governing Lawyers § 127, Comment d (Proposed Final Draft No. 1, Mar. 29, 1996). This diminished risk is coupled with a heightened urgency for discovery of a deceased client's communications in the criminal context. The privilege does not "protect[ ] disclosure of the underlying facts by those who communicated with the attorney," Upjohn, supra, at 395, 101 S.Ct., at 685, and were the client living, prosecutors could grant immunity and compel the relevant testimony. After a client's death, however, if the privilege precludes an attorney from testifying in the client's stead, a complete "loss of crucial information" will often result, see 24 C. Wright & K. Graham, Federal Practice and Procedure § 5498, p. 484 (1986).

As the Court of Appeals observed, the costs of recognizing an absolute posthumous privilege can be inordinately high. See *In re Sealed Case*, 124 F.3d 230, 233–234 (C.A.D.C.1997). Extreme injustice may occur, for example, where a criminal defendant seeks disclosure of a deceased client's confession to the offense. See *State v. Macumber*, 112 Ariz. 569, 571, 544 P.2d 1084, 1086 (1976); cf. *In the Matter of John Doe Grand Jury Investigation*, 408 Mass. 480, 486, 562 N.E.2d 69, 72 (1990) (Nolan, J., dissenting). In my view, the paramount value that our criminal justice system places on protecting an innocent defendant should outweigh a deceased client's interest in preserving confidences. See, e.g., *Schlup v. Delo*, 513 U.S. 298, 324–325, 115 S.Ct. 851, 865, 130 L.Ed.2d 808 (1995); *In re Winship*, 397 U.S. 358, 371, 90 S.Ct. 1068, 1076, 25 L.Ed.2d 368 (1970) (Harlan, J., concurring). * * * Given that the complete exclusion of relevant evidence from a criminal trial or investigation may distort the record, mislead the factfinder, and undermine the central truth-seeking function of the courts, I do not believe that the attorney-client privilege should act as an absolute bar to the disclosure of a deceased client's communications. When the privilege is asserted in the criminal context, and a showing is made that the communications at issue contain necessary factual information not otherwise available, courts should be permitted to assess whether interests in fairness and accuracy outweigh the justifications for the privilege.

A number of exceptions to the privilege already qualify its protections, and an attorney "who tells his client that the expected communications are absolutely and forever privileged is oversimplifying a bit." 124 F.3d, at 235. In the situation where the posthumous privilege most frequently arises—a dispute between heirs over the decedent's will—the privilege is widely recognized to give way to the interest in settling the estate. See *Glover v. Patten*, 165 U.S. 394, 406–408, 17 S.Ct. 411, 416, 41 L.Ed. 760 (1897). This testamentary exception, moreover, may be invoked in some cases where the decedent would not have chosen to waive the privilege. For example, "a decedent might want to provide for an illegitimate child but at the same time much prefer that the relationship go undisclosed." 124 F.3d, at 234. * * *

Finally, the common law authority for the proposition that the privilege remains absolute after the client's death is not a monolithic body of precedent. Indeed, the Court acknowledges that most cases merely "presume the privilege survives," and it relies on the case law's "implicit acceptance" of a continuous privilege. Opinions squarely addressing the posthumous force of the privilege "are relatively rare." See 124 F.3d, at 232. And even in those decisions expressly holding that the privilege continues after the death of the client, courts do not typically engage in detailed reasoning, but rather conclude that the cases construing the testamentary exception imply survival of the privilege. See, e.g., Glover, supra, at 406–408, 17 S.Ct., at 416; see also Wright & Graham, supra, § 5498, at 484 ("Those who favor an eternal duration for the privilege seldom do much by way of justifying this in terms of policy").

Moreover, as the Court concedes, there is some authority for the proposition that a deceased client's communications may be revealed, even in circumstances outside of the testamentary context. California's Evidence Code, for example, provides that the attorney-client privilege continues only until the deceased client's estate is finally distributed, noting that "there is little reason to preserve secrecy at the expense of excluding relevant evidence after the estate is wound up and the representative is discharged." Cal. Evid. Code Ann. § 954, and comment, p. 232, § 952 (West 1995). And a state appellate court has admitted an attorney's testimony concerning a deceased client's communications after "balanc[ing] the necessity for revealing the substance of the [attorney-client conversation] against the unlikelihood of any cognizable injury to the rights, interests, estate or memory of [the client]." See Cohen, supra, at 464, 357 A.2d, at 693. The American Law Institute, moreover, has recently recommended withholding the privilege when the communication "bears on a litigated issue of pivotal significance" and has suggested that courts "balance the interest in confidentiality against any exceptional need for the communication." Restatement (Third) of the Law Governing Lawyers § 127, at 431, Comment d; see also 2 C.

Mueller & L. Kirkpatrick, Federal Evidence, § 199, p. 380 (2d ed. 1994) ("[I]f a deceased client has confessed to criminal acts that are later charged to another, surely the latter's need for evidence sometimes outweighs the interest in preserving the confidences").

Where the exoneration of an innocent criminal defendant or a compelling law enforcement interest is at stake, the harm of precluding critical evidence that is unavailable by any other means outweighs the potential disincentive to forthright communication. In my view, the cost of silence warrants a narrow exception to the rule that the attorney-client privilege survives the death of the client. Moreover, although I disagree with the Court of Appeals' notion that the context of an initial client interview affects the applicability of the work product doctrine, I do not believe that the doctrine applies where the material concerns a client who is no longer a potential party to adversarial litigation.

Accordingly, I would affirm the judgment of the Court of Appeals. Although the District Court examined the documents in camera, it has not had an opportunity to balance these competing considerations and decide whether the privilege should be trumped in the particular circumstances of this case. Thus, I agree with the Court of Appeals' decision to remand for a determination whether any portion of the notes must be disclosed.

With respect, I dissent.

FURTHER NOTE ON THE ATTORNEY–CLIENT PRIVILEGE

1. Basis for the privilege. The attorney-client privilege was well-established in the United States by the early nineteenth century. In Chirac v. Reinicker, 24 U.S. (11 Wheat.) 280, 294, 6 L.Ed. 474 (1826), the Supreme Court wrote, "The general rule is not disputed, that confidential communications between client and attorney, are not be revealed, at any time. The privilege, indeed, is not that of the attorney, but of the client; and it is indispensable for the purpose of private justice." For history, see Introductory Note on the Attorney–Client Privilege, casebook p. 942.

The core justification for the privilege is obvious. An attorney cannot be expected to give appropriate counsel to a client without fully understanding the facts relevant to the client's problem, and the client cannot be expected to reveal those facts without an assurance that what he says will be held in confidence. (Indeed, many clients are reluctant or unwilling to reveal their secrets even when they know of the privilege.) The cost of the privilege is also obvious: If an attorney can refuse to reveal information provided by the client, important facts will sometimes be kept from a judge or other person who needs them. It is possible to overestimate the extent of that cost, however. In many instances, the attorney knows the facts precisely because of the existence of the privilege. If no such privilege existed, the client would never have confided the information, and the need for the information would have remained equally unsatisfied.

2. Scope of the privilege. The scope of the privilege varies somewhat from jurisdiction to jurisdiction, but Wigmore's classic formulation describes the core privilege:

> Where legal advice of any kind is sought from a professional legal advisor in his capacity as such, the communications relating to that purpose, made in confidence by the client, are at his instance permanently protected from disclosure by himself or by the legal advisor, except the protection be waived.

8 J. Wigmore, Evidence in Trials at Common Law § 2292, p. 554 (4th ed., 1961). The attorney-client privilege is available to an individual or to an organization, including a corporation, a partnership, or a governmental organization. An attorney-client relationship is created when the client reasonably believes that the attorney is providing, or is willing to consider providing, legal services. The privilege extends to communications during discussions about whether the attorney will represent the client, even if the attorney is not, in the end, employed. The privilege also extends to advice given without charge. The privilege can be waived by client, either by voluntarily disclosing the communication or by failing to claim the privilege. See C. Mueller and L. Kirkpatrick, Modern Evidence, Doctrine and Practice § 5.8–5.30 (1995); 24 C. Wright and K. Graham, Federal Practice and Procedure: Evidence §§ 5471–5507 (1986).

3. Compare the work-product doctrine and the attorney-client privilege. Note that the work-product doctrine is different in scope from the attorney-client privilege. The work-product doctrine only protects materials prepared in anticipation of litigation, whereas the attorney-client privilege protects communications made in connection with legal advice of any kind, whether or not related to litigation. On the other hand, the work-product doctrine covers information from other sources than the client, notably witness statements and document compilations. The work-product doctrine can be overcome if the information either cannot be obtained from other sources or can only be obtained with great difficulty, but there is no exception to the attorney-client privilege based on the unavailability of the information from other sources.

4. Exceptions to the attorney-client privilege. Nonetheless, the attorney-client privilege is not absolute. With some variation from one jurisdiction to another, there is no privilege in the following circumstances:

(1) **Furtherance of crime or fraud.** If the services of the lawyer were sought or obtained to enable or aid anyone to commit or plan to commit what the client knew or reasonably should have known to be a crime or fraud;

(2) **Claimants through the same deceased client.** As to a communication relevant to an issue between parties who claim through the same deceased client . . . ;

(3) **Breach of duty by a lawyer or client.** As to a communication relevant to an issue of breach of duty to his client or by the client to his lawyer;

(4) **Document attested by a lawyer.** As to a communication relevant to an issue concerning an attested document to which the lawyer is an attesting witness;

(5) **Joint clients.** As to a communication relevant to a matter of common interest between or among two or more clients if the communication was made by any of them to a lawyer retained or consulted in common, when offered between or among any of the clients or

(6) **Public officer or agency.** As to a communication between a public officer or agency and its lawyers unless the communication concerns a pending investigation, claim, or action and the court determines that disclosure will seriously impair the ability of the public officer or agency to process the claim or conduct a pending investigation, litigation, or proceeding in the public interest.

Revised Uniform Rules of Evidence (1986) 502(d). See also proposed (but ultimately rejected) Fed.R.Evid. 503, 56 F.R.D. 183, 235 (1973)(omitting the exception for public officer of agency); Restatement of the Law Governing Lawyers, Proposed Final Draft No. 1 (1996) §§ 131–134B.

In addition, an attorney's ethical responsibilities may impose obligations permitting, and on occasion requiring, her to reveal client communications. For example, most jurisdictions permit an attorney to reveal client communications if the attorney knows or has reason to believe that the client will commit a crime causing death or injury, or will commit criminal fraud. Some jurisdictions also permit an attorney to reveal such communications in cases of non-criminal fraud. And most jurisdictions require an attorney to reveal to a court the fact that her client has committed perjury, even when the basis for the attorney's knowledge is a client communication. See Rest. (Third) of the Law Governing Lawyers, Proposed Final Draft No. 1 (1996) § 117A, Reporter's Note, pp. 329–333 (containing a table of the rules in all states and the ABA Model Rules and Code).

5. The attorney-client privilege in a corporate setting. As is apparent from *Upjohn*, the operation and justification of the attorney-client privilege is substantially different for an individual client and an organizational client such as a corporation. Prior to the Court's decision in *Upjohn*, some jurisdictions restricted the attorney-client privilege in a corporation to communications between the attorney and the "control group" in the corporation. The consequence of the control-group test was to inhibit the corporation in conducting investigations of legal matters in which low-level employees possessed relevant information. The importance of the issue was shown in the early 1970s, when the proposed (and ultimately rejected) Federal Rules of Evidence were being debated by the Advisory Committee on the Federal Rules. An early version of the proposed rule contained the control group test. But, as recounted by Professors Wright and Graham, attorneys representing corporations lobbied first the Advisory Committee and then Congress, with the result that the rule eventually adopted by Congress simply provided that the privilege "shall be governed by the principles of the common law as they may be interpreted by the courts of the United States in light of reason and experience." Fed.R.Evid. 501. 24 C. Wright and K. Graham, Federal Practice and Procedure: Evidence § 5471, pp. 45–8 (1986). Are you convinced by the Court's opinion in *Upjohn* that the control group test should have been abandoned?

A lurking problem with the attorney-client privilege in the corporate setting is that a corporate employee—particularly a low-level employee outside the "control group"—cannot protect the information he provides to the corporation's attorney because the corporation rather than the employee decides whether to assert the attorney-client privilege. If the employee cannot control whether the information he provides will be revealed by the corporation, does the attorney-client privilege in this setting serve its conventional function of encouraging a person to provide information to the attorney? Or does it serve the somewhat different purpose of encouraging a corporation to conduct internal investigations through its general counsel's office, confident that any information revealed during the course of the investigation will be protected by the privilege? A further problem is that the corporate employee is not providing information to his *own* attorney. Thus, any information revealed by the employee to the corporate counsel may be used by the corporation against the employee, for example, in disciplinary or termination proceedings. The corporate counsel has an obligation to inform the employee of this fact, and possibly to recommend that he retain his own private attorney. ABA Code of Professional Conduct, Rule 1.13(d). In this connection, consider In re: Grand Jury Subpoena Duces Tecum, 112 F.3d 910 (8th Cir.1997), in which the court held that a conversation between First Lady Hillary Clinton and two government lawyers employed at the White House was not covered by the attorney-client privilege. In part, the court rested its decision on the ground that the conversations implicated Mrs. Clinton's interests "in her personal capacity," and the White House lawyers were not representing her in that capacity.

6. Attorney-client privilege after death of the client. The most dramatic example used by those who oppose the assertion of the attorney-client privilege after the client's death is a criminal case in which the accused claims that the real murderer, now deceased, confessed his deed to his attorney before he died. The accused seeks to compel that attorney to testify to prevent the conviction of an innocent man. See State v. Macumber, 112 Ariz. 569, 544 P.2d 1084 (1976)(finding no exception to the privilege), cited by Justice O'Connor in her dissent. Even if there should be an exception in that case, does that mean that there should have been no attorney-client privilege in *Swidler & Berlin*? Is it a small step or an impossible leap from "exonerat[ing] an innocent criminal defendant" (*Macumber*) to requiring the attorney to testify when "a compelling law enforcement interest is at stake" (*Swidler & Berlin*)?

7. Additional reading. See Hazard, "An Historical Perspective on the Attorney–Client Privilege," 66 Calif.L.Rev. 1061 (1978); Alexander, "The Corporate Attorney–Client Privilege: A Study of the Participants," 63 St. John's L.Rev. 191 (1989); Saltzburg, "Corporate and Related Attorney–Client Privilege Claims: A Suggested Approach," 12 Hofstra L.Rev. 279 (1984); Frankel, "The Attorney–Client Privilege After the Death of the Client," 6 Geo.J. of Legal Ethics 45 (1992).

b. EXAMINATIONS AND EXPERTS

p. 969

NOTE ON DISCOVERY OF EXPERT WITNESSES

The standard on appellate review of a decision to admit or exclude expert scientific testimony under *Daubert* is whether the District Court has abused its discretion. General Electric Co. v. Joiner, ___ U.S. ___, 118 S.Ct. 512, 139 L.Ed.2d 508 (1997). On remand in Daubert v. Merrell Dow Pharmaceuticals, Inc., 43 F.3d 1311 (9th Cir.1995), the Court of Appeals held that proffered expert testimony to the effect that Bendectin causes birth defects did not meet the test for admissibility established by the Supreme Court.

California has declined to follow the Supreme Court in *Daubert*. In People v. Leahy, 8 Cal.4th 587, 34 Cal.Rptr.2d 663, 882 P.2d 321 (1994), the California Supreme Court continues to adhere to the old *Kelly/Frye* standard. People v. Kelly, 17 Cal.3d 24, 130 Cal.Rptr. 144, 549 P.2d 1240 (1976); Frye v. United States, 293 Fed. 1013 (D.C.Cir.1923). Under that standard, expert testimony must be based on or deduced from a " 'well-recognized scientific principle or discovery ... sufficiently established to have gained general acceptance in the particular field in which it belongs.' " 8 Cal.4th at 594.

For general discussion of expert testimony and scientific evidence, see Federal Judicial Center, Reference Manual on Scientific Evidence (1994). See also Symposium, "Scientific Evidence After the Death of *Frye*," 15 Cardozo L.Rev. 1745 (1994).

3. OTHER PRIVILEGES

p. 985

FURTHER NOTE ON PRIVILEGED MATTER

1. Other privileges. In Jaffee v. Redmond, 518 U.S. 1, 116 S.Ct. 1923, 135 L.Ed.2d 337 (1996), the Supreme Court held that Fed.R.Evid. 501 provides a psychotherapist-patient privilege, protecting from disclosure notes taken by a licensed clinical social worker during counseling sessions with the defendant. The Court noted that all fifty states and the District of Columbia recognize some form of psychotherapist privilege.

4. DISCOVERY ABUSES

p. 993

NOTE ON ABUSE OF DISCOVERY: SANCTIONS AND CONTROLS

2. Reforming discovery. Professor Mullenix is skeptical about the recent discovery reforms. She writes:

> [T]his article suggests that reform of federal civil discovery may not have been necessary at all: There is no strong evidence documenting the alleged massive discovery abuse in the federal courts. The rulemakers never established the existence of discovery abuse before embarking on

their crusade to revamp discovery. Indeed, existing empirical studies challenged the received notion of pervasive discovery abuse.

* * *

[T]he rulemakers undertook the most massive procedural reform since the original enactment of the Federal Rules, and did so largely because of myth, anecdote, and lawyers' war stories.

Mullenix, "Discovery in Disarray: The Pervasive Myth of Pervasive Discovery Abuse and the Consequences for Unfounded Rulemaking," 46 Stan. L.Rev. 1393, 1396, 1445 (1994). For an entertaining article, see Yablon, "Stupid Lawyer Tricks: An Essay on Discovery Abuse," 96 Colum.L.Rev. 1618 (1996).

Professors Cooter and Rubinfeld analyze discovery abuse using the tools of economics. They define an abusive discovery request as one in which "request and compliance costs exceed the increase in the expected value of the requesting party's claim." Cooter and Rubinfeld, "Reforming the New Discovery Rules," 84 Georgetown L.J. 61, 63 (1995). If a party expects to learn information worth $1,000 but the cost of both requesting the information and complying with the request exceeds $1,000, the request is abusive as they define the term. They suggest a two-part fee-shifting rule under which the requesting party would pay some of the costs of complying with a request. Their aim is to reduce abusive discovery requests by forcing the requesting party to "internalize" more of the discovery costs.

C. THE PRETRIAL CONFERENCE

p. 999

NOTE ON THE PRETRIAL CONFERENCE

2. In Chiropractic Alliance of New Jersey v. Parisi, 164 F.R.D. 618 (D.N.J.1996), the parties agreed between themselves to waive the deadline specified in the pretrial order for filing a summary judgment motion. When the motion was filed later than permitted by the order, the court dismissed it as untimely under Rule 16(f).

p. 1000

NOTE ON THE PRETRIAL CONFERENCE IN FEDERAL COURT: WHO CAN BE COMPELLED TO ATTEND?

The Court of Appeals for the Fifth Circuit agrees with Judge Posner (dissenting in *Heileman Brewing*) on what constitutes a good faith attempt to settle. In Dawson v. United States, 68 F.3d 886 (5th Cir.1995), the District Court sanctioned the United States for refusing to offer anything in settlement of a prisoner's Federal Tort Claims Act suit for damages, in supposed violation of a local court rule requiring "parties in every civil suit [to] make a good faith effort to settle." The Court of Appeals upheld the right of the United States to refuse to offer anything in settlement and instead to insist on going to trial:

> Early settlement of cases is an extremely laudable goal, which federal judges have considerable power to encourage and facilitate.... On the other hand, ... parties may have valid and principled reasons for not wishing to settle particular cases. These reasons may not be based necessarily on the merits of a particular case, or the party's possible exposure in it, but because of the effect that a settlement might have on other pending or threatened litigation.

at 897.

Chapter 8

TRIAL

A. JUDGMENT WITHOUT TRIAL

1. DEVICES TO AVOID PLENARY TRIAL

p. 1014

NOTE ON DEVICES TO AVOID PLENARY TRIAL

3. Voluntary dismissal. Fed.R.Civ.P. 42(a)(2) allows a District Court to dismiss a complaint without prejudice "upon such terms and conditions as the court deems proper." A dismissal under Rule 42(a)(2) may be reversed only for abuse of discretion. Metropolitan Federal Bank of Iowa v. W.R. Grace & Co., 999 F.2d 1257, 1262 (8th Cir.1993). In Grover by Grover v. Eli Lilly and Co., 33 F.3d 716 (6th Cir.1994), Ohio plaintiffs in a diversity suit claimed that they suffered birth defects caused by their maternal grandmothers' having taken DES during pregnancy. The District Court certified to the Ohio Supreme Court the question whether a grandchild could state a cause of action under Ohio law. The Ohio Supreme Court decided, by a vote of 4 to 3, that a claim could only be stated by the woman who took the drug or by her child. The District Court dismissed plaintiffs' complaint without prejudice under Rule 42(a)(2) in order to permit refiling "should the Ohio Legislature or the Ohio Supreme Court, at some point in the future" change the law to allow the cause of action. The Court of Appeals found an abuse of discretion and reversed, holding that defendant was entitled to a dismissal on the merits.

2. DEFAULT JUDGMENTS

p. 1019

NOTE ON DEFAULTS AND DEFAULT JUDGMENTS

As may be seen by the Court of Appeals' second decision in *Cirami*, courts are often reluctant to apply the extreme sanction of a default judgment. But this may be changing. See Pretzel & Stouffer v. Imperial Adjusters, Inc., 28 F.3d 42 (7th Cir.1994), in which defendant answered the first complaint in a timely fashion. Plaintiff filed an amended complaint, and defendant was ordered to answer by a certain date. Nineteen days after that date, defendant missed a status conference and had not yet filed its answer. The District Court entered default. Seven days later, defendant sought vacation of the default and attempted to file an answer. The District Court found that defendant had neither a good excuse for its tardiness nor a valid defense on the merits. At a "prove-up" for damages two weeks later, the District Court entered default judgment. The Court of Appeals affirmed:

> It is not an abuse of ... discretion if the district court finds that docket conditions require a rigorous application of Rule 55. We have long since moved away from the position of disfavoring default judgments, and we are therefore increasingly reluctant to set them aside.

at 47.

3. SETTLEMENT

p. 1029

NOTE ON SETTLEMENT AGREEMENTS

1. Settlements the most common disposition. Professors Gross and Syverud compare cases that settle with those that go to a jury trial:

> The trials we see are the products of a procedural system that is devouring itself. As we have refined and elaborated the rules for jury trials, we have multiplied the costs both to the parties and to the courts. The costs to the parties drive them to skip all these expensive procedures and settle; the costs to the system drive judges and rulemakers to find new ways to encourage them to do so. Increasingly, the cases that litigants insist on trying are not only rare but peculiar. ... Ordinary cases of every sort are compromised and settled, and those that are not settled are unusual even if the context is a garden-variety, two-car crash. Trials are the most visible aspect of our system of adjudication, and they show it as its worst. They are the slowest, most expensive, and most contentious cases, in which compromise has failed, and in which the verdict is most likely to seem arbitrary or extreme.

Gross and Syverud, "Don't Try: Civil Jury Verdicts in a System Geared to Settlement," 44 U.C.L.A.L.Rev. 1, 7–8 (1996).

2. Approval of court. It remains true that most settlements do not require the approval of the court as is required for a settlement of a class action or a suit by a minor or incompetent. But in recent years, there has been a pronounced movement in the federal courts, strongly encouraged by the Civil Justice Reform Act of 1990 and by amendment of Fed.R.Civ.P. 16 in 1993, toward significantly increased involvement by District Judges in encouraging, facilitating, even coercing settlement. Professor Galanter and Ms. Cahill comment on this increasing judicial involvement:

> What do we know of the effects of judicial intervention on the number or quality of settlements? As to number, the available studies provide no basis for thinking judicial promotion leads to a number of settlements that is sufficiently higher than would otherwise occur to compensate for the opportunity costs of the judicial attention diverted from adjudication. ... As to the effects of judicial promotion on the quality of

130   PLEADING AND PROCEDURE   Ch. 8

settlements, we simply do not know. ... Are settlements arranged by judges less variable, more principled, more reflective of the merits? No one knows.

Galanter and Cahill, " 'Most Cases Settle': Judicial Promotion and Regulation of Settlement," 46 Stan.L.Rev.1339, 1388–9 (1994).

5. Offer of settlement rules. Recent articles on the operation of Fed.R.Civ.P. 68 and analogous state rules include Anderson and Rowe, "Empirical Evidence on Settlement Devices: Does Rule 68 Encourage Settlement?," 71 Chicago–Kent L.Rev. 519 (1995); Bonney, Tribek, and Wrona, "Rule 68: Awakening a Sleeping Giant," 65 Geo.Wash.L.Rev. 379 (1997); Cooper, "Rule 68, Fee Shifting, and the Rulemaking Process," in Reforming the Civil Justice System 108 (Kramer, ed., 1996); Sherman, "From 'Loser Pays' to Modified Offer of Judgment Rules: Reconciling Incentives to Settle with Access to Justice," 76 Tex.L.Rev.1863 (1998).

4. SUMMARY JUDGMENT

p. 1060

NOTE ON SUMMARY JUDGMENT

7. Local rules in many District Courts supplement Fed.R.Civ.P. 56(e) by requiring a party opposing a motion for summary judgment to file a brief containing a statement of material facts in dispute, with "appropriate citations" to depositions, affidavits, and other evidence supporting the opposing party's position. Litigants cannot afford to ignore such rules. In Waldridge v. American Hoechst Corp., 24 F.3d 918 (7th Cir.1994), plaintiff, opposing a motion for summary judgment, submitted an affidavit of her expert witness together with a list of deposition excerpts supporting her position and notebooks containing the depositions. However, "she did not make any effort to identify with specificity what factual issues were disputed, let alone supply the requisite citations to the evidentiary record." at 922. The District Judge, acting sua sponte, granted summary judgment against plaintiff for failure to comply with the local rule. The Court of Appeals affirmed:

> Rules like [local rule] 56.1 no doubt benefit the parties themselves by requiring their opponents to clarify exactly what they dispute and on what evidence they rely. ... But they are of significantly greater benefit to the court, which does not have the advantage of the parties' familiarity with the record and often cannot afford to spend the time combing the record to locate the relevant information.

at 923–24.

8. Summary judgments are often much harder to obtain in state than in federal court. For a criticism of Virginia state court practice under which summary judgments are particularly difficult to obtain, see Sinclair and Hanes, "Summary Judgment: A Proposal for Procedural Reform in the Core Motion Context," 36 Wm & Mary L.Rev. 1633 (1995).

B. THE RIGHT TO JURY TRIAL

2. THE SEVENTH AMENDMENT

p. 1067

NOTE ON THE RIGHT TO JURY TRIAL UNDER THE UNITED STATES CONSTITUTION

4. Useful recent additions to the literature include Weinstein, "Protecting A Juror's Right to Privacy: Constitutional Constraints and Policy Options," 70 Temple L.Rev. 1 (1997); Syverud, "ADR and the Decline of the American Civil Jury," 44 U.C.L.A.L.Rev. 1935 (1997); Note, "Developments in the Law: The Civil Jury," 110 Harv.L.Rev. 1408 (1997); Gross and Syverud, "Don't Try: Civil Jury Verdicts in a System Geared to Settlement," 44 U.C.L.A.L.Rev. 1 (1996); Symposium, "Jury Research and Reform," 79 Judicature 214 (1996); Smith, "The Historical and Constitutional Contexts of Jury Reform," 25 Hofstra L.Rev. 377 (1996); Lettow, "New Trial for Verdict Against Law: Judge–Jury Relations in Early Nineteenth–Century America," 71 Notre D.L.Rev. 505 (1996).

p. 1094

NOTES AND QUESTIONS

2. The Supreme Court has again declined to decide whether there is a Seventh Amendment right to jury trial in a suit for back pay under Title VII of the Civil Rights Act of 1964. Landgraf v. USI Film Products, 511 U.S. 244, 252 n. 4, 114 S.Ct. 1483, 128 L.Ed.2d 229 (1994).

In Lebow v. American Trans Air, Inc., 86 F.3d 661 (7th Cir.1996), an employee claimed to have been fired for union organizing in violation of the federal Railway Labor Act, 45 U.S.C. § 151 et seq. He sought, inter alia, reinstatement, back pay, and compensatory and punitive damages. The Court of Appeals found that plaintiff was entitled to a jury trial under the Seventh Amendment.

p. 1117

NOTE ON THE SEVENTH AMENDMENT, ADMINISTRATIVE COURTS, AND OTHER NON–ARTICLE III COURTS

7a. Seventh Amendment right to jury trial in copyright cases. In Feltner v. Columbia Pictures Television, Inc., ___ U.S. ___, 118 S.Ct. 1279, 140 L.Ed.2d 438 (1998), plaintiff sought statutory damages under the federal Copyright Act. There was no dispute about the constitutional right to a jury determination of liability for statutory damages. The only disputed point was whether the jury must also determine the amount. Section 504(c)(1) of the Copyright Act provided for statutory damages as follows: "[T]he copyright owner may elect, at any time before final judgment is rendered, to recover, instead of actual damages and profits, an award of statutory damages for all infringements involved in the action, with respect to any one work, ... in a sum of not less than $500 or more than $20,000, as the court considers just...."

The Supreme Court held that the Seventh Amendment required that the determination of the amount of statutory damages must be made by a jury. It wrote:

> Unlike many of our recent Seventh Amendment cases, which have involved modern statutory rights unknown to 18th-century England, ... in this case there are close analogues to actions seeking statutory damages under § 504(c). Before the adoption of the Seventh Amendment, the common law and statutes in England and this country granted copyright owners causes of action for infringement. More importantly, copyright suits for monetary damages were tried in courts of law, and thus before juries.

at 1285. In response to defendant's argument that statutory damages were "equitable in nature," analogous to the civil penalty in *Tull v. United States* (for which a judge may determine the amount), the Court wrote:

> We are not persuaded. We have recognized the "general rule" that monetary relief is legal, ... and an award of statutory damages may serve purposes traditionally associated with legal relief, such as compensation and punishment. ... Nor, as we have previously stated, is a monetary remedy rendered equitable simply because it is "not fixed or readily calculable from a fixed formula." ... And there is historical evidence that cases involving discretionary monetary relief were tried before juries.

* * *

> In *Tull* ... we were presented with no evidence that juries historically had determined the amount of civil penalties to be paid to the Government. Moreover, the awarding of civil penalties to the Government could be viewed as analogous to sentencing in a criminal proceeding. ... Here, of course, there is no similar analogy, and there is clear and direct historical evidence that juries, both as a general matter and in copyright cases, set the amount of damages awarded to a successful plaintiff.

at 1287–8.

7b. Seventh Amendment right to jury trial in patent cases. It has long been settled that there is a Seventh Amendment right to jury trial in patent cases, but the scope of that right has been disputed. In Markman v. Westview Instruments, Inc., 517 U.S. 370, 116 S.Ct. 1384, 134 L.Ed.2d 577 (1996), the Supreme Court unanimously held that the "construction" of a patent claim is an issue for the judge. Construction determines what a patent claim covers, based on a reading of the patent document. After the Court found historical evidence and its own precedents inconclusive, it considered the "relative interpretive skills of judges and juries": "Where history and precedent provide no clear answers, functional considerations also play their part in the choice between judge and jury to define terms of art." at 1393, 1395.

"Infringement" of a patent determines whether defendant's actions have violated a patent, and is a question for the jury. But whether infringement has occurred depends on the scope of the patent as construed by the judge. A dissenter in the Court of Appeals in *Markman* had emphasized the practical importance of the construction of a patent claim: "[T]his is not just about claim language, it is about ejecting juries from infringement cases. All these pages and all these words cannot camouflage what the court [of appeals] well knows: to decide what the [patent] claims mean is nearly always to decide the case." Markman v. Westview Instruments, 52 F.3d 967, 989 (Fed.Cir.1995).

8. Suits against the federal government not covered by the Seventh Amendment. One Court of Appeals had held that the American Red Cross is not a part of the federal government for purposes of the Seventh Amendment and that litigants against the Red Cross are entitled to a jury. Marcella v. Brandywine Hospital, 47 F.3d 618 (3d Cir.1995). District Courts are split on the issue. Compare, e.g., Doe v. American National Red Cross, 847 F.Supp. 643 (W.D.Wis.1994) (jury trial permitted), with Berman v. American National Red Cross, 834 F.Supp. 286 (N.D.Ind.1993) (contra).

A District Judge may use an "advisory jury" in a suit against the federal government under the Federal Tort Claims Act, pursuant to Rule 39(c). It is entirely within the judge's discretion whether to accept or reject all or part of an advisory verdict. See, e.g., Hamm v. Nasatka Barriers, Inc., 166 F.R.D. 1 (D.D.C.1996).

8a. Suits against foreign sovereigns not covered by the Seventh Amendment. The Courts of Appeal have uniformly held that the Seventh Amendment does not require jury trials in suits against foreign sovereigns under the federal Foreign Sovereign Immunity Act, 28 U.S.C. § 1602 et seq. See, e.g., Universal Consolidated Companies, Inc. v. Bank of China, 35 F.3d 243 (6th Cir.1994); Ruggiero v. Compania Peruana de Vapores, 639 F.2d 872 (2d Cir.1981).

> The circuit courts ... have uniformly found that (1) the most important characteristic of suits under the Act is that they are suits against foreign states, not that they are suits based in tort or contract or asking for damages or injunctive relief; (2) actions against foreign states were not known at common law in 1791 and were not analogous to any actions so known[.]

35 F.3d at 245.

9. Additional reading. For a vigorous argument that the Supreme Court's distinction between private rights and public rights suits is without historical foundation, see Redish and La Fave, "Seventh Amendment Right to Jury Trial in Non–Article III Proceedings: A Study in Dysfunctional Constitutional Theory," 4 Wm & Mary Bill of Rts.J. 407 (1995).

p. 1120

NOTE ON DEMANDING AND WAIVING JURY TRIAL

5. Professor Vidmar argues that juries are neither incompetent nor biased in medical malpractice cases:

> Multiple studies using different methodologies, conducted by different authors, and addressing different facets involved in the debate over the competence of juries to decide liability in medical malpractice cases appear to contradict the claims that juries are biased against doctors and that most cases are too technically complex to be reasonably decided by a group of laypersons. Anecdotes about the widespread malperformance of juries do not stand up to systematic data.

Vidmar, "Are Juries Competent to Decide Liability in Tort Cases Involving Scientific/Medical Issues? Some Data from Medical Malpractice," 43 Emory L.J. 885, 906 (1994).

C. SELECTION OF THE TRIER OF FACT

1. THE JURY

a. THE JURY PANEL

p. 1128

NOTE ON THE JURY PANEL

3. Current practices—voter lists and others. For an empirical study concluding that supplementing voter lists with drivers' license lists does *not* increase minority representation in jury pools, see Note, "Jury Source Lists: Does Supplementation Really Work?" 82 Cornell L.Rev. 390 (1997).

b. VOIR DIRE

p. 1141

NOTE ON VOIR DIRE

1. Challenges for cause and peremptory challenges. In Ross v. Oklahoma, 487 U.S. 81, 108 S.Ct. 2273, 101 L.Ed.2d 80 (1988), a state trial court wrongly refused to grant a challenge for cause, forcing a criminal defendant in a capital case to use a peremptory challenge to strike the potential juror. The defendant used all his peremptory challenges, but did not challenge for cause any of the jurors who comprised the jury that decided the case. The Supreme Court held that the wrongful denial of the challenge for cause did not deny the defendant due process under the Fourteenth Amendment to the Constitution.

Compare *Ross* to Kirk v. Raymark Industries, 61 F.3d 147 (3d Cir.1995), in which the District Court in a civil case wrongly refused to grant two challenges for cause, forcing the defendant to use two of its three peremptory challenges to strike those prospective jurors. (Recall that parties in civil cases in federal court are each entitled to three peremptory challenges. 28 U.S.C. § 1870.) The Court of Appeals held that "the remedy for impairment or denial or the statutory right to exercise peremptory challenges is per se reversal without any requirement of proving prejudice." at 162. Note that defendant's unsuccessful argument in *Ross* was based on a constitutional right to due process; in *Kirk,* by contrast, defendant's successful argument was based on a statutory right under § 1870.

p. 1150

FURTHER NOTE ON VOIR DIRE

1. In Campbell v. Louisiana, ___ U.S. ___, 118 S.Ct. 1419, 140 L.Ed.2d 551 (1998), the Court held that a white criminal defendant has standing to challenge the exclusion of blacks from the grand jury.

2a. In Purkett v. Elem, 514 U.S. 765, 115 S.Ct. 1769, 131 L.Ed.2d 834 (1995)(per curiam), defendant in a state court unarmed robbery case objected to the prosecutor's use of two of his six peremptories to exclude black men. The defendant objected to the exclusions under *Batson*. The prosecutor explained his strikes:

> "I struck [juror] number twenty-two because of his long hair. He had long curly hair. He had the longest hair of anybody on the panel so far. He appeared to not be a good juror for that fact, the fact that he had long hair hanging down shoulder length, curly, unkempt hair. Also he had a mustache and a goatee type beard. And juror number twenty-four also has a mustache and a goatee type beard. Those are the only two people on the jury ... with facial hair.... And I don't like the way they looked, with the way the hair is cut, both of them. And the mustaches and the beards look suspicious to me."

at 766. Further, juror twenty-four had had a shotgun pointed at him in a robbery. The prosecutor stated that he feared that the juror would think that " 'to have a robbery you have to have a gun, and there is no gun in this case.' " Id.

The state trial judge overruled the *Batson* objection without explanation and seated the jury. Defendant's conviction was affirmed on appeal in the state court system. In a federal habeas corpus challenge to the conviction, the Court of Appeals for the Eighth Circuit held that the exclusion of juror twenty-two violated *Batson*:

> [W]here the prosecution strikes a prospective juror who is a member of the defendant's racial group, solely on the basis of factors which are facially irrelevant to the question of whether that person is qualified to serve as a juror in the particular case, the prosecution must at least articulate some plausible race-neutral reason for believing that those factors will somehow affect the person's ability to perform his or her duties as a juror. In the present case, the prosecutor's comments, "I

don't like the way [he] look[s], with the way the hair is cut.... And the mustache[ ] and the beard[ ] look suspicious to me," do not constitute such legitimate race-neutral reasons for striking juror 22.

Elem v. Purkett, 25 F.3d 679, 683 (8th Cir.1994).

The Supreme Court disagreed. It construed *Batson* to mean:

> [O]nce the opponent of a peremptory challenge has made out a prima facie case of racial discrimination (step 1), the burden of production shifts to the proponent of the strike to come forward with a race-neutral explanation (step 2). If a race-neutral explanation is tendered, the trial court must then decide (step 3) whether the opponent of the strike has proved purposeful discrimination. ... The second step of this process does not demand an explanation that is persuasive, or even plausible. ...
>
> ... It is not until the *third* step that the persuasiveness of the justification becomes relevant—the step in which the trial court determines whether the opponent of the strike has carried his burden of proving purposeful discrimination. ... At that stage, implausible or fantastic justifications may (and probably will) be found to be pretexts for purposeful discrimination. But to say that a trial judge *may choose to disbelieve* a silly or superstitious reason at step 3 is quite different from saying that a trial judge *must terminate* the inquiry at step 2 when the race-neutral reason is silly or superstitious.

514 U.S. at 767–68 (emph. in orig.).

Justice Stevens, joined by Justice Breyer, dissented. Justice Stevens read *Batson* as requiring that a plausible explanation be advanced at the second step:

> At the second step of this inquiry, neither a mere denial of improper motive nor an incredible explanation will suffice to rebut the prima facie showing of discriminatory purpose. At a minimum, as the Court held in *Batson*, the prosecutor 'must articulate a neutral explanation related to the particular case to be tried' [quoting *Batson*, 476 U.S. at 98, 106 S.Ct. at 1724]. Today the Court holds that it did not mean what it said in *Batson*.

at 770.

The Court's analysis in *Purkett* has two consequences. First, a prosecutor can satisfy his burden at step two by advancing any reason at all so long as it is race-neutral. Second, a reviewing court—on direct appeal or on habeas corpus—will have to give some kind of deference to the fact-finding of the trial judge at the third step. If the trial judge chooses to believe that a "silly or superstitious" race-neutral explanation is the true explanation, that finding of fact must be "presumed to be correct" by a federal court on habeas corpus. at 769.

Professor Carlson, in an article published before *Purkett* was decided, concludes, "The peremptory challenge as we know it, is dead." Carlson, "*Batson, J.E.B.*, and Beyond: The Paradoxical Quest for Reasoned Peremptory Strikes in the Jury Selection Process," 46 Baylor L.Rev. 947, 1004

(1994). Is the Supreme Court in *Purkett* trying to breath life back into the dead body?

Professor Brand, also in an article published before *Purkett,* doubted whether *Batson* eliminates race in juror selection.

> [T]he search for purpose or intent is difficult to prove in any context, but it is particularly difficult to prove with respect to race. This difficulty, combined with the deference accorded trial court findings of fact, may make identifying racism in the courtroom, to say nothing of eliminating it, an impossible task.

Brand, "The Supreme Court, Equal Protection and Jury Selection: Denying that Race Still Matters," 1994 Wisc.L.Rev. 511, 612.

Professor Melilli conducted an extensive study of *Batson* challenges as reported in appellate opinions. He concluded:

> ... *Batson* has [not] effectively circumscribed race- and gender-based peremptory challenges; toward that end, *Batson* is almost surely a failure. Instead, *Batson* has, almost inadvertently, demonstrated a number of truisms that support the extermination of the peremptory challenge.... [Among other things,] *Batson* as applied in the lower courts has demonstrated the futility of simultaneously attempting to preserve the essential character of the peremptory challenge and to redefine "discrimination" in such a way as to prohibit the exercise of peremptory challenges on the basis of certain group stereotypes.... *Batson* has provided us with the first opportunity to examine the reasons lawyers use peremptory challenges [by requiring them to provide to the court race and gender-neutral justifications].... Stripped of its mystique, the peremptory challenge turns out in large part to have operated as an excuse for the inadequate functioning of the challenge for cause. It has also been revealed to be the refuge for some of the silliest, and sometimes nastiest, stereotypes our society has been able to invent.... It is time for the peremptory challenge to go. It will not be missed.

Melilli, "*Batson* in Practice: What We Have Learned About *Batson* and Peremptory Challenges," 71 Notre Dame L.Rev. 447, 503 (1996). Professor Marder has also argued for the abolition of peremptory challenges. Marder, "Beyond Gender: Peremptory Challenges and the Roles of the Jury," 73 Texas L.Rev. 1041 (1995).

3. In State v. Davis, 504 N.W.2d 767 (Minn.1993), cert. denied 511 U.S. 1115, 114 S.Ct. 2120, 128 L.Ed.2d 679 (1994), the Minnesota Supreme Court upheld a peremptory challenge that had been justified on the ground that the prospective juror was a Jehovah's Witness. Justice Thomas, joined by Justice Scalia, dissented from the Supreme Court's denial of certiorari.

> It is at least not obvious, given the reasoning in *J.E.B.*, why peremptory strikes based on religious affiliation would survive equal protection analysis. ... Once the scope of the logic in *J.E.B.* is honestly acknowledged, it cannot be glibly asserted that the decision has no implications for peremptory strikes based on classifications other than sex[.]

511 U.S. at 117. See also Barton, "Religion-Based Peremptory Challenges after *Batson v. Kentucky* and *J.E.B. v. Alabama*: An Equal Protection and

First Amendment Challenge," 94 Mich.L.Rev. 191 (1995) (arguing that religion-based peremptories are unconstitutional).

United States v. Somerstein, 959 F.Supp. 592 (E.D.N.Y.1997), relied on *Batson* to disallow peremptory challenges to Jews. The court found that such challenges could be considered both racial and religious. It was willing to forbid race-based challenges in all cases, but to forbid faith-based challenges only because of a religious element in the particular suit: "[D]efendants are kosher caterers specializing in making kosher affairs, and they are accused of criminal conduct in connection with an alleged scheme to defraud their employees' benefit funds. [Because], arguably, the religious element is intertwined in the criminal charges, the Court rules that the religion of the jurors would be relevant as a foundation for a Batson challenge."

People of the State of New York v. Rambersed, 170 Misc.2d 923, 649 N.Y.S.2d 640 (1996), relied on *Batson* to disallow peremptory challenges to Italian–Americans.

4. Professor Vikram Amar argues that equal protection and due process arguments do not fully capture what is at stake in the juror selection process. He encourages a greater focus on the analogy between the right to vote and the right to serve as a juror. Amar, "Jury Service as a Political Participation Akin to Voting," 80 Cornell L.Rev. 203 (1995). Professor Alschuler argues that it is both desirable and constitutional in criminal cases with a minority defendant to have some kind of racial quota system to ensure minority representation on the grand jury, and perhaps on the petit jury as well. Alschuler, "Racial Quotas and the Jury," 44 Duke L.J. 704 (1995).

p. 1151

NOTE ON JURY SIZE AND UNANIMITY

2. Size. For a concise recounting of the history of the movement from the 12–person to smaller juries, see Resnik, "Changing Practices, Changing Rules: Judicial and Congressional Rulemaking on Civil Juries, Civil Justice, and Civil Judging," 49 Ala.L.Rev. 133, 136–152 (1997). For an eloquent argument, on historical and modern-day policy grounds, for the retention of the twelve-person civil jury, see Arnold, "Trial by Jury: The Constitutional Right to a Jury of Twelve in Civil Trials," 22 Hofstra L.Rev. 1 (1993).

2. THE JUDGE

p. 1166

NOTE ON THE RECUSAL OF THE JUDGE

3. In El Fenix de Puerto Rico v. The M/Y Johanny, 36 F.3d 136 (1st Cir.1994), a defendant insurance company resisted payment to a boat owner on the ground that the owner had intentionally scuttled the vessel. On the first day of trial, one of plaintiff's witnesses noticed Bob Fisher, a "local yachtsman well versed in maritime matters," sitting in the courtroom as a spectator. According to the witness, Fisher said in casual conversation the next day that the judge had " 'asked him to sit through the trial and listen

to the evidence presented by the parties.'" at 138–39. Nearly three weeks later, after judgment had been entered for the defendant, plaintiff moved for a new trial or an alteration of the judgment; suggested that the judge should be disqualified because of a possible appearance of partiality; and moved to depose Fisher. The judge disqualified himself from further participation in the case and vacated the judgment. In his recusal order, the judge wrote:

> [T]he Court invited both Mr. and Mrs. Bob Fisher, long time personal friends, to attend a public trial. [The invitation] was prompted by the fact that the Fishers are both boat afficionados and Mr. Fisher, who is currently retired, would enjoy the trial. *To conclude from the presence of Mr. and Mrs. Fisher that the Court somehow surreptitiously connived to seek the opinion of a non-witness to make its decision is a strained conclusion to say the least. Plaintiff's argument on this issue has the tenor of a dubious strategy influenced by an unfavorable result.*

at 139 (emph. in orig.). On later reconsideration, the judge vacated his recusal order and reinstated the judgment.

The Court of Appeals held that the judge should not have recused himself:

> "[D]isqualification is appropriate only if the facts provide what an objective, knowledgeable member of the public would find to be a *reasonable basis* for doubting the judge's impartiality. Were less required, a judge could abdicate in difficult cases at the mere sound of controversy, or *a litigant could avoid adverse decisions by alleging the slightest of factual bases for bias.*"

at 141 (emph. in orig.). The Court of Appeals further held that once a judge recused himself, he had no further power over the case either to vacate the judgment or later to reconsider the recusal and reinstate the judgment. The Court of Appeals reinstated the judgment itself and reassigned the case to another District Judge to consider post-judgment motions.

5. What should be done when there is reason to think that a judge may be, or may have been, mentally incompetent? There is no statutory provision for recusal of a federal judge based on mental incompetence. (Grounds for recusal under 28 U.S.C. §§ 144 and 455 include financial conflict, bias, prejudice, and personal knowledge of disputed facts.) Can a judgment be reopened under Rule 60(b)(6) based on an argument that the judge was mentally incompetent at the time of decision? In United States v. State of Washington, 98 F.3d 1159 (9th Cir.1996), three Northwest Indian tribes sought relief from a 1979 judgment in a fishing rights case on the ground that the judge had rendered the decision when he was suffering from the early stages of Alzheimer's disease. In 1992, a newspaper article disclosed that the judge had died of Alzheimer's disease and suggested that he had been suffering from the disease at the time of the decision. The court found that Rule 60(b)(6) could be used in "extraordinary circumstances" warranting relief from an "erroneous judgment," but it concluded that this was not such a case: The judge's son was quoted in the article as saying that he had been mentally competent at the time of the decision; the Indian tribes had specifically requested that the judge rule on the motion in question despite the judge's expressed desire to retire due to physical weakness from surgery; and the Court of Appeals had affirmed the ruling on appeal.

E. THE PROVINCE OF THE JURY

2. PUTTING THE CASE TO THE JURY

p. 1217

NOTE ON INSTRUCTIONS TO THE JURY

Tiersma, "Reforming the Language of Jury Instructions," 22 Hofstra L.Rev. 37 (1993), notes that despite a trend toward more easily understood jury instructions some instructions are still difficult or impossible to understand. Professor Tiersma provides useful examples of changes to approved jury instructions in California.

4. MOTIONS AFTER VERDICT

p. 1237

NOTE ON SETTING ASIDE A VERDICT

After an adverse jury verdict, a party will sometimes move in the alternative either for judgment as a matter of law (notwithstanding the verdict) or for a new trial. Fed.R.Civ.P. 50(c) requires that the District Court rule on both motions at the same time, even if ruling on one motion seems to make ruling on the other unnecessary. In Arenson v. Southern University Law Center, 43 F.3d 194 (5th Cir.1995), plaintiff won a jury verdict, after which defendants moved in the alternative either for judgment as a matter of law or for a new trial. The District Court granted judgment as a matter of law and did not reach the motion for a new trial. The Court of Appeals then reversed the judgment. On remand, the District Court belatedly granted the motion for a new trial. After defendants won the new trial, the Court of Appeals again reversed, holding that because the District Court had not earlier ruled on the motion for a new trial it did not have the power to do so later. *Arenson* provides a cautionary tale: A moving party must insist that the District Court rule at the same time on both motions.

p. 1246

NOTE ON EXCESSIVE OR INADEQUATE VERDICTS

2. Remittitur is allowed in federal courts only on condition that the plaintiff have the choice between either accepting the lower damage amount or being allowed another jury trial. See Hetzel v. Prince William County, ___ U.S. ___, 118 S.Ct. 1210, 140 L.Ed.2d 336 (1998), in which the Supreme Court held that a reduction in damages without offering plaintiff the choice of another jury trial violated the jury trial guarantee of the Seventh Amendment.

Chapter 9
SPECIAL PROBLEMS OF MODERN LITIGATION

C. ARBITRATION

p. 1349

NOTE ON ARBITRATION

Section 4 of the Federal Arbitration Act allows a federal District Court to compel arbitration only in the district or districts specified in a forum selection clause of the arbitration agreement. Merrill Lynch, Pierce, Fenner & Smith, Inc. v. Lauer, 49 F.3d 323 (7th Cir.1995). A United States Magistrate Judge cannot serve as an arbitrator even if the parties so agree. DDI Seamless Cylinder International, Inc. v. General Fire Extinguisher Corp., 14 F.3d 1163 (7th Cir.1994).

For a vigorous criticism of the Supreme Court's recent arbitration decisions, see Carrington and Haagen, "Contract and Jurisdiction," 1996 Sup.Ct.Rev. 331.

Chapter 10

REVIEW OF THE DISPOSITION

INTRODUCTORY NOTE ON APPELLATE REVIEW

p. 1355

6. A lively debate has arisen about whether there is enough appellate capacity in the United States Courts of Appeals. Those on one side would reduce the subject matter jurisdiction of the federal court in order to reduce the number of appellate cases. Those on the other would increase the number of judges. See, e.g., Judges Edith Jones and Stephen Reinhardt, each reviewing T. Baker, Rationing Justice on Appeal: The Problems of the U.S. Courts of Appeal (1994), in "Surveys without Solutions: Another Study of the United States Courts of Appeals," 73 Texas L.Rev. 1485, 1505 (1995). Two articles describe significant problems in the Courts of Appeals stemming from their substantially increased caseload. See Dragich, "Once a Century: Time for a Structural Overhaul of the Federal Courts," 1996 Wisc.L.Rev. 11; Richman and Reynolds, "Elitism, Expediency, and the New Certiorari: Requiem for the Learned Hand Tradition," 81 Cornell L.Rev. 273 (1996).

B. FEDERAL APPELLATE REVIEW

1. REVIEWABILITY OF DECISIONS

p. 1376, after COOPERS & LYBRAND v. LIVESAY

DIGITAL EQUIPMENT CORP. v. DESKTOP DIRECT, INC.

United States Supreme Court, 1994.
511 U.S. 863, 114 S.Ct. 1992, 128 L.Ed.2d 842

JUSTICE SOUTER delivered the opinion of the Court.

Section 1291 of the Judicial Code confines appeals as of right to those from "final decisions of the district courts." 28 U.S.C. § 1291. This case raises the question whether an order vacating a dismissal predicted on the parties' settlement agreement is final as a collateral order even without a district court's resolution of the underlying cause of action. See Cohen v. Beneficial Indus. Loan Corp., 337 U.S. 541, 546, 69 S.Ct. 1221, 1225–1226, 93 L.Ed. 1528 (1949). We hold that an order denying effect to a settlement agreement does not come within the narrow ambit of collateral orders.

I

Respondent, Desktop Direct, Inc. (Desktop) sells computers and like equipment under the trade name "Desktop Direct." Petitioner, Digital Equipment Corporation is engaged in a similar business and in late 1991 began using that trade name to market a new service it called "Desktop Direct from Digital." In response, Desktop filed this action in the United States District Court for the District of Utah, charging Digital with unlawful use of the Desktop Direct name. Desktop sent Digital a copy of the complaint, and negotiations between officers of the two corporations ensued. Under a confidential settlement reached on March 25, 1992, Digital agreed to pay Desktop a sum of money for the right to use the "Desktop Direct" trade name and corresponding trademark, and for waiver of all damages and dismissal of the suit. That same day, Desktop filed a notice of dismissal in the District Court.

Several months later, Desktop moved to vacate the dismissal and rescind the settlement agreement, alleging misrepresentation of material facts during settlement negotiations. The District Court granted the motion, concluding "that a fact finder could determine that [Digital] failed to disclose material facts to [Desktop] during settlement negotiations which would have resulted in rejection of the settlement offer." After the District Court declined to reconsider that ruling or stay its order vacating dismissal, Digital appealed.

The Court of Appeals for the Tenth Circuit dismissed the appeal for lack of jurisdiction, holding that the District Court order was not appealable under § 1291, because it neither "end[ed] the litigation on the merits" nor "[fell] within the long-recognized 'collateral order' exception to the final judgment requirement." 993 F.2d 755, 757 (1993). Applying the three-pronged test for determining when "collateral order" appeal is allowed, see *Cohen*, supra; Coopers & Lybrand v. Livesay, 437 U.S. 463, 98 S.Ct. 2454, 57 L.Ed.2d 351 (1978), the Court of Appeals concluded that any benefits claimed under the settlement agreement were insufficiently "important" to warrant the immediate appeal as of right. Although Digital claimed what it styled a "right not to go to trial," the court reasoned that any such privately negotiated right as Digital sought to vindicate was different in kind from an immunity rooted in an explicit constitutional or statutory provision or "compelling public policy rationale," the denial of which has been held to be immediately appealable. 933 F.2d at 758–760.

* * *

II

A

The collateral order doctrine is best understood not as an exception to the "final decision" rule laid down by Congress in § 1291, but as a "practical construction," of it, *Cohen,* supra, 337 U.S., at 546, 69 S.Ct. at 1225–1226; see, e.g., Coopers & Lybrand v. Livesay, supra, 437 U.S., at 468, 98 S.Ct., at 2457–2458. We have repeatedly held that the statute entitles a party to appeal not only from a district court decision that "ends the litigation on the merits and leaves nothing more for the court to do but execute the judgment," Catlin v. United States, 324 U.S. 229, 233, 65 S.Ct. 631, 633, 89 L.Ed. 911 (1945), but also from a narrow class of decisions that do not terminate the litigation, but must, in the interest of "achieving a healthy legal system," cf. Cobbledick v. United States, 309 U.S. 323, 326, 60 S.Ct. 540, 541, 84 L.Ed. 783 (1940) nonetheless be treated as "final." The latter category comprises only those district court decisions that are conclusive, that resolve important questions completely separate from the merits, and that would render such important questions effectively unreviewable on appeal from final judgment in the underlying action. See generally *Coopers & Lybrand,* supra. Immediate appeals from such orders, we have explained, do not go against the grain of § 1291, with its object of efficient administration of justice in the federal courts, see generally, Richardson-Merrell, Inc. v. Koller, 472 U.S. 424, 105 S.Ct. 2757, 86 L.Ed.2d 340 (1985).

But we have also repeatedly stressed that the "narrow" exception should stay that way and never be allowed to swallow the general rule.

* * *

[W]e conclude, despite Digital's position that it holds a "right not to stand trial" requiring protection by way of immediate appeal, that rights under private settlement agreements can be adequately vindicated on appeal from final judgment.

C

The roots of Digital's argument that the settlement with Desktop gave it a "right not to stand trial altogether" (and that such a right *per se* satisfied the third *Cohen* requirement) are readily traced to Abney v. United States, 431 U.S. 651, 97 S.Ct. 2034, 52 L.Ed.2d 651 (1977), where we held that § 1291 entitles a criminal defendant to appeal an adverse ruling on a double jeopardy claim, without waiting for the conclusion of his trial. After holding the second *Cohen* requirement satisfied by the distinction between the former jeopardy claim and the question of guilt to be resolved at trial, we emphasized that the Fifth Amendment not only secures the right to be free from multiple punishments, but by its very terms embodies the broader principle, " 'deeply ingrained ... in the Anglo–American system of jurisprudence,' " that it is intolerable for " 'the State, with all its resources ... [to] make repeated attempts to convict an individual [defendant], thereby subjecting him to embarrassment, expense and ordeal and compelling him to live in a continuing state of anxiety and insecurity.'" 431 U.S., at 661–662, 97 S.Ct., at 2041 (quoting Green v. United States, 355 U.S. 184, 187–188, 78 S.Ct. 221, 223, 2 L.Ed.2d 199 (1957)). We found that immediate appeal was the only way to give "full protection" to this constitutional right "not to face trial at all." 431 U.S. at 662, and n. 7, 97 S.Ct., at 2041.

* * *

Abney's rationale, was applied in Nixon v. Fitzgerald, 457 U.S. 731, 742, 102 S.Ct. 2690, 2697, 73 L.Ed.2d 349 (1982), where we held to be similarly appealable an order denying the petitioner absolute immunity from suit for civil damages arising from actions taken while petitioner was President of the United States. Seeing this immunity as a "functionally mandated incident of the President's unique office, rooted in the ... separation of powers and supported by our history," id., at 749, 102 S.Ct., at 2701, we stressed that it served "compelling public ends," id., at 758, 102 S.Ct., at 2705, and would be irretrievably lost if the former President were not allowed an immediate appeal to vindicate this right to be free from the rigors of trial, see id., at 752, n. 32, 102 S.Ct., at 2702.

Next, in Mitchell v. Forsyth, 472 U.S. 511, 105 S.Ct. 2806, 86 L.Ed.2d 411 (1985), we held that similar considerations supported appeal under § 1291 from decisions denying government officials qualified immunity from damage suits. An "essential attribute," id. at 525, 105 S.Ct., at 2815, of this freedom from suit for past conduct not violative of clearly established law, we explained, is the "entitlement not to stand trial or face the other burdens of litigation," id., at 562, 105 S.Ct., at 2815, one which would be "effectively lost if a case [were] erroneously permitted to go to trial." Ibid. Echoing the reasoning of *Nixon v. Fitzgerald*, supra (and Harlow v. Fitzgerald, 457 U.S. 800, 102 S.Ct. 2727, 73 L.Ed.2d 396 (1982)), we explained that requiring an official with a colorable immunity claim to defend a suit for damages would be "peculiarly disruptive of effective government," and would work the very "distraction ... from ... dut[y], inhibition of discretionary action, and deterrence of able people from public service" that qualified immunity was meant to avoid.

* * *

Digital ... maintains that it obtained dual rights under the settlement agreement with Desktop, not only a broad defense to liability but the "right not to stand trial," the latter being just like the qualified immunity held immediately appealable in *Mitchell*. As in *Mitchell*, that right must be enforceable on collateral order appeal, Digital asserts, or an adverse trial ruling will destroy it forever.

While Digital's argument may exert some pull on a narrow analysis, it does not hold up under the broad scrutiny to which all claims of immediate appealability under § 1291 must be subjected. To be sure, *Abney* and *Mitchell* are fairly cited for the proposition that orders denying certain immunities are strong candidates for prompt appeal under § 1291. But Digital's larger contention, that a party's ability to characterize a district court's decision as denying an irreparable "right not to stand trial" altogether is sufficient as well as necessary for a collateral order appeal, is neither an accurate distillation of our case law nor an appealing prospect for adding to it.

* * *

Nor does limiting the focus to whether the interest asserted may be called a "right not to stand trial" offer much protection against the urge to push the § 1291 limits. We have after all, acknowledged that virtually every right that could be enforced appropriately by predismissal might loosely be described as conferring a "right not to stand trial," see *e.g.*, *Midland Asphalt* [*Corp. v. United States*, 489 U.S., 794, 109 S.Ct. 1494, 103 L.Ed.2d 879]; *Van Cauwenberghe v. Biard*, 486 U.S. 517, 524, 108 S.Ct. 1945, 1950–1951, 100 L.Ed.2d 517 (1988). Allowing immediate appeals to vindicate every such right would move § 1291 aside for claims that the district court lacks personal jurisdiction, see *Van Cauwenberghe*, that the statute of limitations has run, see 15B C. Wright, A. Miller & E. Cooper, Federal Practice and Procedure § 3918.5, and n. 65, p. 521 (1992), that the movant has been denied his Sixth Amendment right to speedy trial, that an action is barred on claim preclusion principles, that no material fact is in dispute and the moving party is entitled to judgment as a matter of law, or merely that the complaint fails to state a claim. Such motions can be made in virtually every case.

* * *

E

As Digital reads the cases, the only things standing in the way of an appeal to perfect its claimed rights under the settlement agreement are the lone statement in *Midland Asphalt*, to the effect that only explicit statutory and constitutional immunities may be appealed immediately under § 1291, and language (said to be stray) repeated in many of our collateral order decisions, suggesting that the "importance" of right asserted is an independent condition of appealability. The first, Digital explains, cannot be reconciled with *Mitchell*'s holding, that denial of qualified immunity (which we would be hard-pressed to call "explicitly ... guarantee[d]" by a particular constitutional or statutory provision) is a collateral order under § 1291; as between *Mitchell* and the *Midland Asphalt* dictum, Digital says, the dictum must give way. As for the second obstacle, Digital adamantly maintains that "importance" has no place in a doctrine justified as supplying a gloss on Congress's "final decision" language.

1

These arguments miss the mark. First, even if *Mitchell* could not be squared fully with the literal words of the *Midland Asphalt* sentence * * * that would be only because the qualified immunity right is inexplicit, not because it lacks a good pedigree in public law.

* * *

2

The more fundamental response, however, to the claim that an agreement's provision for immunity from trial can distinguish it from other arguable rights to be trial-free is simply that such a right by agreement does not rise to the level of importance needed for recognition under § 1291. This, indeed, is the bone of the fiercest contention in the case. In disparaging any distinction between an order denying a claim grounded on a explicit constitutional guarantee of immunity from trial and an order at odds with an equally explicit right by private agreement of the parties, Digital stresses that the relative "importance" of these rights heavily relied upon by the Court of Appeals, is a rogue factor. No decision of this Court, Digital maintains has held an order unappealable as "unimportant" when it has otherwise met the three *Cohen* requirements, and whether a decided issue is thought "important," it says, should have no bearing on whether it is "final" under § 1291.

* * *

While there is no need to decide here that a privately conferred right could never supply the basis of a collateral order appeal, there are surely sound reasons for treating such rights differently from those originating in the Constitution or statutes. When a policy is embodied in a constitutional or statutory provision entitling a part to immunity from suit (a rare form of protection), there is little room for the judiciary to gainsay its "importance." Including a provision in a private contract, by contrast, is barely a prima facie indication that the right secured is "important" to the benefitted party (contracts being replete with boilerplate), let alone that its value exceeds that of other rights not embodied by agreements (e.g., the right to be free from a second suit based on a claim that has already been litigated), or that it qualifies as "important" in *Cohen*'s sense, as being weightier than the societal interests advanced by the ordinary operation of final judgement principles. * * *

* * *

Nor are we swayed by Digital's last-ditch effort to come within *Cohen*'s sense of "importance" by trying to show that settlement-agreement "immunities" merit first-class treatment for purposes of collateral order appeal, because they advance the policy favoring voluntary resolution of disputes. It defies common sense to maintain that parties' readiness to settle will be significantly dampened (or the corresponding public interest impaired) by a rule that a district court's decision to let allegedly barred litigation go forward may be challenged as a matter of right only on appeal from a judgment for the plaintiff's favor.

* * *

B

In preserving the strict limitations on review as of right under § 1291, our holding should cause no dismay, for the law is not without its safety valve to deal with cases where the contest over a settlement's enforceability raises serious legal questions taking the case out of the ordinary run. While Digital's insistence that the District Court applied a fundamentally wrong legal standard in vacating the dismissal order here may not be considered in deciding appealability under § 1291, it plainly is relevant to the availability of the discretionary interlocutory appeal from particular district court orders "involv[ing] a controlling question of law as to which there is substantial ground for difference of opinion," provided for in § 1292(b) of Title 28. Indeed, because we suppose that a defendant's claimed entitlement to a privately negotiated "immunity from suit" could in some instances raise "a controlling question of law ... [which] ... may materially advance the ultimate termination of the litigation," the discretionary appeal provision (allowing courts to consider the merits of individual claims) would seem a better vehicle for vindicating serious contractual interpretation claims than the blunt, categorical instrument of § 1291 collateral order appeal. See *Van Cauwenberghe*, 486 U.S. at 529–530, 108 S.Ct. at 1953–1954; Coopers & Lybrand, 437 U.S., at 474–475, 98 S.Ct., at 246.[9]

IV

* * * We hold that a refusal to enforce a settlement agreement claimed to shelter a party from suit altogether does not supply the basis for immediate appeal under § 1291. The judgment of the Court of appeals is therefore

Affirmed.

---

9. We recognize that § 1292 is not a panacea, both because it depends to a degree on the indulgence of the court from which review is sought and because the discretion to decline to hear an appeal is broad, see e.g., Cooper & Lybrand, 437 U.S., at 475, 98 S.Ct., at 2461 (serious docket congestion may be adequate reason to support denial of certified appeal). On the other hand, we find nothing in the text or purposes of either statute to justify the concern, expressed here by Digital, that a party's request to appeal under § 1292(b) might operate, practically or legally, to prejudice its claimed right to immediate appeal under § 1291.

p. 1389

NOTE ON APPEALABILITY OF NON–FINAL ORDERS IN FEDERAL COURTS

1. An amendment has been proposed to Fed.R.Civ.P. 23 that would permit interlocutory appeals of class certification decisions by the District Court. Proposed Rule 23(f) provides:

> APPEALS: A court of appeals may in its discretion permit an appeal from an order of a district court granting or denying class action certification under this rule if application is made to it within ten days after entry of the order. An appeal does not stay proceedings in the district court unless the district court of the court of appeals so orders.

66 U.S.L.W. 4323 (April 24, 1998.) If not disapproved by Congress, the amendment will go into effect on December 1, 1998.

1b. In Swint v. Chambers County Commission, 514 U.S. 35, 115 S.Ct. 1203, 131 L.Ed.2d 60 (1995), the Supreme Court addressed questions of (1) summary judgments denying immunity-based defenses and (2) "pendent appellate jurisdiction." *Swint* arose out of warrantless police raids of a nightclub. The owners and two others brought a civil rights suit under 42 U.S.C. § 1983 against three individual police officers and the County Commission. The District Court denied summary judgment to the three police officers who had asserted a qualified immunity from suit. The court also denied summary judgment to the County Commission, which had argued that the police officers were not "policymakers." (The County Commission was liable under § 1983 only for violations of federal law that occurred "pursuant to official governmental policy or custom.")

(1) *Immunity-based defenses.* Under Mitchell v. Forsyth, 472 U.S. 511, 105 S.Ct. 2806, 86 L.Ed.2d 411 (1985), the denial of summary judgment to the three individual officers who had asserted official immunity was clearly an appealable collateral order. The Commission sought to bring itself within the rule in *Mitchell*, arguing that its defense that the police officer was not a policymaker was an immunity defense. The Court disagreed: "The Commission's assertion ... does not rank, under our decisions, as an immunity from suit. Instead, the plea ranks as a 'mere defense to liability.'" at 1208.

(2) *"Pendent appellate jurisdiction."* The Court of Appeals already had jurisdiction to decide the appeals of the three individual police officers. In the interest of judicial economy, the Court of Appeals decided the Commission's appeal under an asserted "pendent appellate jurisdiction." The Supreme Court held that in this case the court should not have decided the Commission's appeal, although it declined to establish a clean rule: "We need not definitively or preemptively settle here whether or when it may be proper for a court of appeals with jurisdiction over one ruling to review, conjunctively, related rulings that are not themselves independently reviewable." at 1212.

E. EXTRAORDINARY RELIEF FROM JUDGMENTS
p. 1407

NOTE ON PROCEDURES FOR RELIEF FROM A JUDGMENT

Fed.R.Civ.P. 60(b) enumerates six grounds for reopening a judgment. The first three are available for one year after the entry of judgment; the last three are not subject to a time limitation. In addition to these six enumerated grounds, the Rule also provides, "This rule does not limit the power of a court to entertain *an independent action* to relieve a party from a judgment, order, or proceeding, or to grant relief to a defendant not actually personally notified as provided in Title 28, U.S.C., § 1655, or to set aside a judgment for fraud upon the court" (emph. added). In United States v. Beggerly, 118 S.Ct. 1862, 1868 (1998), the Court held that an "independent action" is available only to "prevent a grave miscarriage of justice."

In *Beggerly*, the United States had earlier brought a quiet title action (the *Adams* litigation) concerning land on Horn Island in Mississippi. At various times, Horn Island had been controlled by France, Britain and Spain, and it eventually came under the control of the United States in 1803 as part of the Louisiana Purchase. During the *Adams* litigation, United States government officials searched public title records and could find no indication that any part of Horn Island had ever been granted to a private landowner. The *Adams* litigation was settled after the United States agreed to pay a sum of money to those who claimed title to land on the island. After the settlement, a specialist employed by respondents found documents in the National Archives that, according to her, indicated that the island had passed into private hands by a grant from the Spanish government in 1781. If that were true, title to Horn Island would not have passed to the United States in 1803, but rather would have remained in respondents' predecessors in title. Respondents filed a new quiet title action seeking to reopen the judgment entered pursuant to the settlement in the *Adams* litigation twelve years earlier, relying on the provision of Rule 60(b) allowing for an "independent action" relieving a party from an earlier judgment. The Court held that these facts did not amount to a "grave miscarriage of justice" that would bring the case with the "independent action" provision of the Rule.

†